NUMBER 78

Yale French Studies

O1
CW00816189

Yale French Studies

Allan Stoekl, *Special editor for this issue*
Liliane Greene, *Managing editor*
Editorial board: Ora Avni (Chair), Sahar Amer, Peter Brooks,
   Shoshana Felman, Didier Maleuvre, Christopher Miller,
   Kevin Newmark, Eliza Nichols, Charles Porter, Allan
   Stoekl
Staff: Lauren Doyle-McCombs, Kathryn Oliver
Editorial office: 315 William L. Harkness Hall.
Mailing address: 2504A-Yale Station, New Haven,
   Connecticut 06520.
Sales and subscription office:
   Yale University Press, 92A Yale Station
   New Haven, Connecticut 06520
   Published twice annually by Yale University Press.

Designed by James J. Johnson and set in Trump Medieval
Roman by The Composing Room of Michigan, Inc.
Printed in the United States of America by the Vail-
Ballou Press, Binghamton, N.Y.

ISSN 0044–0078
ISBN for this issue 0–300–04843–2

ALLAN STOEKL

Editor's Preface

There seems to be taking place, both in the US and abroad, a considerable revival of interest in the work of Georges Bataille, who died nearly thirty years ago (in 1962). In the last five years, no fewer than five major works have been published in English translation.[1] More are, it appears, on the way. What makes this all the more remarkable is that during his lifetime Bataille was known mainly as the editor of *Critique*, a review that still flourishes, and as an author of "erotic" or "pornographic" novels (two of these, indeed, were among his first publications in English translation: *Madame Edwarda*, in the 1950s, and *Story of the Eye*, in the mid–1970s). He was not at all considered a major "thinker," be it in literary criticism, economics, philosophy, anthropology, sociology, or anything else; while Jean-Paul Sartre's agenda, which included terms such as "freedom," "choice," "responsibility," and "commitment," dominated the postwar intellectual scene, Bataille's concern with "expenditure" was seen (if at all) as only a holdover from the prewar "festivals" of the surrealists (that is how Sartre characterized it in both *What is Literature?* and *Saint Genet, Comedian and Martyr*). Sartre's works were best-sellers and were immediately translated; Bataille's sat in publishers' warehouses

1. See *Inner Experience*, trans. Leslie Ann Boldt (Albany: State University of New York Press, 1987). *Guilty*, trans. Bruce Boone (Venice, California: Lapis Press, 1988), *The Accursed Share*, trans. Robert Hurley (New York: Zone Books, 1988), *Visions of Excess (Selected Writings, 1927–39)*, ed. and trans. Allan Stoekl (Minneapolis: The University of Minnesota Press, 1985), and *The College of Sociology*, ed. Denis Hollier, trans. Betsy Wing (Minneapolis: The University of Minnesota Press, 1988). In addition, the Mary Dalwood translation of *L'Erotisme* (dating from 1962), formerly entitled *Death and Sensuality*, and now *Erotism*, has been republished by City Lights Books in San Francisco.

YFS 78, *On Bataille*, ed. Allan Stoekl, © 1990 by Yale University.

(*La Part Maudite [The Accursed Share]*, the book for which Bataille had the highest hopes, sold about fifty copies on publication in 1949).

So what has happened? Clearly Bataille became better known, in the 1960s and 1970s, due to the influence of writers whose concerns in many ways ran counter to the great existentialist emphasis placed on "Man"; Barthes, Foucault, Derrida, and some of the "Tel Quel" group members "wrote on" Bataille, incorporating or appropriating his work, to the point where one could write only of "Derrida's Bataille," "Foucault's Bataille," if one chose to do so at all. One could see this in commentaries on Derrida (in English), for example, where Derrida's reading of Bataille's Hegel (in the article "From a Restricted to a General Economy: A Hegelianism without Reserve")[2] was often presented as simply Derrida's reading of Hegel—a neat, and characteristic, excision. But today the situation is quite different: Bataille is no longer simply a footnote at best in the works of other writers, but a major theorist in his own right. Why?

Perhaps Bataille, so obviously a "precursor" of much of the major post- or antihumanist work of the sixties, exerts a strong appeal because he nevertheless seems to hold onto the possibility of an ethics. This seems fitting enough in the current era of "glorious" and shameful excess, religious crisis, and paralysis (or end) of history—experiences that Bataille directly or indirectly addresses in his writing. Among the representatives of the later "sixties" generation, language or writing extends its dominion "to infinity," but at the same time it becomes virtually impossible to think of a larger and coherent system of values or truths: in Foucault, Deleuze, and Derrida strategies are enacted—be they political or textual—which are necessarily divorced from a larger, coherent, goal or movement. In Bataille, on the other hand, in works such as *The Accursed Share*, there at least seems to be the promise of a direction for history, as well as of a way of coordinating, in theory, a fundamental and indeed universal economic factor ("expenditure," "*dépense*"), largely ignored by "bourgeois" economists, with social and cultural practices. In other words, Bataille can tell us where we are going (a posthistorical period in which "expenditure" will be, albeit impossibly, "recognized") and

---

2. This essay is contained in Derrida's *Writing and Difference*, trans. Alan Bass (Chicago: The University of Chicago Press, 1977). Michel Foucault's influential early essay on Bataille, "A Preface to Transgression," can be found in the Foucault anthology *Language, Counter-Memory, Practice*, ed. Donald Bouchard, trans. D. Bouchard and S. Simon (Ithaca: Cornell University Press, 1977).

how and why things change (social and cultural mutations are to a great extent nothing more than the various modes of affirming, or refusing, "expenditure"). Most important (and this is the ethical dimension), he shows how the ignoring of "expenditure" is historically regressive and physically dangerous (excess wealth, if spent on armaments, will make the next and final world war inevitable) and how its recognition and correct interpretation is beneficial and life-affirming (the awareness of "expenditure" will result in a regime that allocates surplus resources for peaceful and, it might be hoped, orgiastic purposes).

Of course one finds problems in Bataille's approach, and, one can argue, they arise exactly to the extent that his work repeats—or mimics, parodies—the orientations of an optimistic Hegelian model of historical development. Indeed it becomes as hard for Bataille to arrive at an effective and complete version of social and economic integration as it was, in a different way, for Marx: throughout the three volumes of *The Accursed Share*, we never really get a convincing portrayal of the virtually utopian future that awaits us, when "expenditure" will be taken into account in governmental planning, and the great nation States will be devoted to the same aims as those held for millennia by "primitive" chiefs, lovers, and mystics. Somehow capitalism and narrow bourgeois planning are to be supplanted—but by what? A higher form of State socialism? Indeed how can one even write of a society, well organized or not, that has as its goal, its totem, the "nothing" of sheer squandering and of mystical experience? And how will it be squandering if, in the end, its recognition makes possible the stable and happy endstate of humanity?—It will be a useful "squandering" indeed.

Thus one can see why Derrida (in the article on Bataille mentioned above) characterizes Bataille's chapter on the Marshall Plan in *The Accursed Share* as "muddled"; but, it seems, one gains sophistication only at the cost of losing the acuity of Bataille's critique, grounded as it is in the realm of seemingly tangible things—wars, revolutions, stock-market crashes, orgasms. Derrida shifts from a general *economy* to a general *writing*; the excessiveness is now to be found not in social constructions but in the movement of writing on writing. Harmless enough, some of Derrida's critics (including Foucault) maintain—Bataille's positions, such as they are, gain coherence only by losing any contact with, and effect in, the world.

But are the two positions that different? After all, Bataille's "expenditure," strictly speaking, amounts to *nothing*; it can only be discussed as an oppositional term, an excluded element on which a coherent (intellectual, social) construction or formation nevertheless depends. And even then one is betraying it, because by discussing it one is already giving it the status not of nothing but of a thing, a useful, manipulable or recoverable object. Even if one sees Bataille's "economy" affecting the movement of metaphysics alone, that movement, which both excludes and posits, is necessary to and inseparable from the radicality of a *"non-sens,"* of a recalcitrant or unemployable negativity. The Hegelian dialectic affirmed by Derrida (for example), like Bataille's dead God, will be present in its very dismemberment, in a mimicking which cannot dispense with the coherent double it shadows. In exactly the same way, the "general economy" involves certain coherent devices—such as the Marshall Plan—which lead to, guarantee, expel, end in, are defeated by, are parodied by—a negativity, a "nothing" that cannot be, but must be, written, represented, implemented.

But if such radically opposed versions of Bataille are equally valid (or, in their exclusion of the opposite number, equally invalid), what then is *proper* to Bataille? Strictly speaking, *nothing*. This can be seen clearly in the "Letter to René Char on the Incompatibilities of the Writer," included in this issue of *Yale French Studies.* The literary author for Bataille does not "choose" anything, his or her project must not be confused with the world of labor and sense. There is no project; he or she is not attempting to "do" anything. (The writer might fight for something, but only out of sheer passion, not as a result of calculation or "weighing odds.") The "object" of the writer, if one can call it that, is only the defeat of all accomplishment. But therein lies the problem, because any "saying" or "writing," no matter how disjointed or disseminated, is already the product of a project, of a constructive activity not different in kind from that of the most servile "committed" writer. In this light, "true" literature for Bataille can only be the "nothing" *and* the imposition and betrayal of that "nothing" through the coherent project of writing. Indeed the "nothing" is inseparable from, it "is," betrayal in writing, as writing.

But that betrayal opens, in turn, ever larger vistas of betrayal. Bataille's novels—*Blue of Noon, L'Abbé C.*—themselves often seem to be set in and against a background of political "engagement" and crisis. From a certain angle, they read like parodies of thesis novels. It may be that as soon as one recommences a project, no matter how rigorously devoted it is to a "sheer expenditure," it will always lead back to a social and even moral environment or context, because writing as coherent project (even if its theme is the challenge to all coherency) is itself betrayal. The betrayal of a rigorous writing of "nothing" that excludes all choice, all constructive action, is thus inseparable from a thematics of (the betrayal of) choice and constructive action on all levels, including the political or social.

So perhaps in Bataille there is the necessity of morality and representation, no matter how "accursed," along with its impossibility. There is the rigor of the textual procedure, the repetitious writing and betrayal of the sense of the "nothing" (the "general writing"), elaborated at the expense of the ethical, and there is, in and through that very writing, the impossibility of maintaining its purity, and thus the consequent, incessant, repositing of the ethical, even in the representation of its defeat or sundering (the "general economy").

There is a certain paradox, then, in devoting an issue of *Yale French Studies* to Bataille. Issues of this journal are usually devoted to important literary or critical movements (surrealism, existentialism, structuralism, psychoanalysis), questions (pedagogy, closure), or authors (Mallarmé, Sartre, Simone de Beauvoir, Racine). The problem with Bataille is that one cannot really associate his name with a method (how can a rigorous method be based on "nothing"?), nor is Bataille an "author" in the conventional sense, since the style of his writing is fragmented often to the point of unreadability, his "concerns" run the gamut of literature, sociology, economics, philosophy, esthetics (all the while seeming only to undermine the coherency of each of these disciplines)—and, above all, as we have seen, his real "concern," what we loosely call "expenditure," is nothing but "nothing."

But "nothing" is nothing if it is not already implied in and against a system, a sense, a plan, a history; it is the "heterogeneous" that serves as an excluded term which justifies and defeats. In that way it always again betrays and is betrayed. Bataille's writing can only prolong this betrayal, perhaps more "consciously" than before—but that very consciousness is itself a betrayal. And any writing "on" Bataille that would explicate, debate, or condemn his text can only do so from a "higher" vantage point, one of a greater consciousness, which will only add another stratum of betrayal, inseparable from but against Bataille's own betrayals. We end up performing "on" Bataille the same mutilation that he performs in his rewriting of Nietzsche, "on"

Nietzsche, *Sur Nietzsche.* Thus the articles in this issue of *Yale French Studies* rewrite Bataille's "philosophy," they interrogate his "concepts," "politics," "economics," and "esthetics"; they attempt to revise the past and the future on the basis of his text. It is necessary work, I think, especially given the apparent "end of history" in which we find ourselves; bereft of the complacencies that derive from a closed, coherent, though sometimes "transgressive" or "marginal," but ultimately dialectical, model of history—which in turn guarantees a morality, politics and esthetics—we have *nothing* to turn to.

I especially want to thank Liliane Greene, managing editor of *Yale French Studies,* without whose unflagging effort this issue could not have been completed. This number contains quite a few translations, and Mme Greene carefully reviewed each of them, an enormous task given the difficulty of some of the pieces. Lauren Doyle-McCombs and Kathryn Oliver provided valuable assistance to Mme Greene. And, of course, my gratitude goes to the translators who so generously put much time and effort into their work: Jonathan Strauss, Christopher Carsten, Katherine Lydon, Hilari Allred, Amy Reid, Kathryn Aschheim, Rhonda Garelick, Robert Livingston, and Joaniko Kohchi.

Hors Textes

GEORGES BATAILLE

Hegel, Death and Sacrifice[1]

> The animal dies. But the death of the animal is the becoming of
> consciousness.

I. DEATH

Man's Negativity

In the *Lectures* of 1805–1806, at the moment of his thought's full
maturity, during the period when he was writing *The Phenomenology of Spirit*, Hegel expressed in these terms the black character of
humanity:

"Man is that night, that empty Nothingness, which contains everything in its undivided simplicity: the wealth of an infinite number
of representations, of images, not one of which comes precisely to
mind, or which [moreover], are not [there] insofar as they are really
present. It is the night, the interiority—or—the intimacy of Nature
which exists here: [*the*] pure personal-Ego. In phantasmagorical representations it is night on all sides: here suddenly surges up a blood-
spattered head; there, another, white, apparition; and they disappear
just as abruptly. That is the night that one perceives if one looks a
man in the eyes: then one is delving into a night which becomes
terrible; it is the night of the world which then presents itself to us."[2]

1. Excerpt from a study on the—fundamentally Hegelian—thought of Alexander
Kojève. This thought seeks, so far as possible, to be Hegel's thought, such a contemporary spirit, knowing what Hegel did not know (knowing, for example, the events that
have occurred since 1917 and, as well, the philosophy of Heidegger), could grasp it and
develop it. Alexander Kojève's originality and courage, it must be said, is to have
perceived the impossibility of going any further, the necessity, consequently,
of renouncing the creation of an original philosophy and, thereby, the interminable
starting-over which is the avowal of the vanity of thought. This essay was first published in *Deucalion* 5 (1955). With permission of Editions Gallimard © 1988.
2. G. W. F. Hegel, *Jenenser Philosophie des Geistes* in *Sämtliche Werke*, ed.
Johannes Hoffmeister, (Leipzig: Felix Meiner, 1931), vol. 20 180–81. Cited by Kojève in

YFS 78, *On Bataille*, ed. Allan Stoekl, © 1990 by Yale University.

Of course, this "beautiful text," where Hegel's Romanticism finds expression, is not to be understood loosely. If Hegel was a romantic, it was perhaps in a *fundamental* manner (he was at any rate a romantic at the beginning—in his youth—, when he was a commonplace revolutionary), but he did not see in Romanticism the method by which a proud spirit deems itself capable of subordinating the real world to the arbitrariness of its own dreams. Alexander Kojève, in citing them, says of these lines that they express "the central and final idea of Hegelian philosophy," which is "the idea that the foundation and the source of human objective reality (*Wirklichkeit*) and empirical existence (*Dasein*) are the Nothingness which manifests itself as negative or creative Action, free and self-conscious."

To permit access to Hegel's disconcerting world, I have felt obliged to mark, by a careful examination, both its violent contrasts and its ultimate unity.

For Kojève, "the 'dialectical' or anthropological philosophy of Hegel is in the final analysis a *philosophy of death* (or, which is the same thing, of atheism)" (K, 537; TEL, 539).

But if man is "death living a human life" (K, 548; TEL, 550), man's negativity, given in death by virtue of the fact that man's death is essentially voluntary (resulting from risks assumed without necessity, without biological reasons), is nevertheless the principle of action. Indeed, for Hegel, Action is Negativity, and Negativity Action. On the one hand, the man who negates Nature—by introducing into it, like a flip-side, the anomaly of a "pure, personal ego"—is present within that Nature's heart like a night within light, like an intimacy within the exteriority of those things which are *in themselves*—like a phantasmagoria in which nothing takes shape but to evanesce, nothing appears but to disappear, where nothing exists except absorbed without respite in the *annihilation* of time, from which it draws the beauty of a dream. But there is a complementary aspect: this negation of Nature is not merely given in consciousness—where that which exists *in itself* appears (but only to disappear)—; this negation is exteriorized, and in being exteriorized, really (*in itself*) changes the reality of Nature. Man works and fights; he transforms the given; he transforms Nature and in destroying it he creates a

Introduction to the Reading of Hegel, (Paris: Gallimard, 1947), 573. (TEL edition [Paris: Gallimard, 1980], 575.) Henceforth cited in the text, as K; TEL).

world, a world which was not. On the one hand there is poetry, the destruction that has surged up and diluted itself, a *blood-spattered head*; on the other hand there is Action, work, struggle. On the one hand, "pure Nothingness," where man "differs from Nothingness only *for a certain time*" (K, 573; TEL, 575). On the other, a historical World, where man's Negativity, that Nothingness that gnaws him from within, creates the whole of concrete reality (at once object and subject, real world changed or unchanged, man who thinks and changes the world).

Hegel's Philosophy is a Philosophy of Death—or of Atheism[3]

The essential—and the original—characteristic of Hegelian philosophy is to describe the totality of what is; and, consequently, at the same time that it accounts for everything which appears before our eyes, to give an integrated account of the thought and language which express—and reveal—that appearance.

"In my opinion," says Hegel, "Everything depends on one's expressing and understanding Truth not (only) as substance, but also as subject."[4]

---

3. In this paragraph, and the following, I repeat in a different form what has been said by Alexander Kojève. But not only in a different form; essentially I have to develop the second part of that sentence, which is, at first glance, difficult to comprehend in its concrete aspect: "The being or the annihilation of the 'Subject' is the temporalizing annihilation of Being, which must be *before* the annihilated being: the being of the 'Subject' necessarily has, therefore, a beginning. And being the (temporal) annihilation of the nothingness in Being, being nothingness which nihilates (insofar as Time), the "Subject" is essentially negation of itself: therefore it has an end." In particular, I have followed for this (as I have already done in the preceding paragraph) the part of *Introduction to the Reading of Hegel* which concerns parts 2 and 3 of the present study, i.e., Appendix II, "The Idea of Death in the Philosophy of Hegel," Kojève, 527–73. (TEL, 529–75.) [Translator's note: This appendix, from which all of Bataille's references to Kojève are taken, remains untranslated in English; it is not included in Allan Bloom's reedition (and abridgment) of Kojève's *Introduction to the Reading of Hegel* (New York: Basic Books, 1969).]

4. Cf., G. W. F. Hegel, *The Phenomenology of Spirit*, trans. A. V. Miller (Oxford: Oxford University Press, 1977), 9–10. In his footnotes, Bataille attributes the French versions he uses of Hegel to Jean Hyppolite's translation of *The Phenomenology of Spirit* and often also cites the pages from *Introduction à la lecture de Hegel* where Alexandre Kojève quotes the same passages. However, Kojève's version differs from that of Hyppolite and Bataille's from both. It is the latter that I have translated. Page references will hereafter be given to the English translation by A. V. Miller, which is often at significant variance with the quotations as I have rendered them. [Translator's note.]

In other words, natural knowledge is incomplete, it does not and cannot envisage any but abstract entities, isolated from a whole, from an indissoluble totality, which alone is concrete. Knowledge must at the same time be anthropological: "in addition to the ontological bases of natural reality," Kojève writes, "[knowledge] must find those of human reality, which alone is capable of being revealed through Discourse" (K, 528; TEL, 530). Of course, this anthropology does not envisage Man as do the modern sciences but as a movement impossible to isolate from the heart of the totality. In a sense, it is actually a theology, where man has taken the place of God.

But for Hegel, the human reality which he places at the heart, and center, of the totality is very different from that of Greek philosophy. His anthropology is that of the Judeo-Christian tradition, which emphasizes Man's *liberty, historicity,* and *individuality.* Like Judeo-Christian man, the Hegelian man is a spiritual (i.e., "dialectical") being. Yet, for the Judeo-Christian world, "spirituality" is fully realized and manifest only in the hereafter, and Spirit properly speaking, truly "objectively real" Spirit, is God: "an infinite and eternal being." According to Hegel, the "spiritual" or "dialectical" being is "necessarily *temporal* and finite." This means that death alone assures the existence of a "spiritual" or "dialectical" being, in the Hegelian sense. If the animal which constitutes man's natural being did not die, and—what is more—if death did not dwell in him as the source of his anguish—and all the more so in that he seeks it out, desires it and sometimes freely chooses it—there would be no man or liberty, no history or individual. In other words, if he revels in what nonetheless frightens him, if he is the being, identical with himself, who risks (identical) being itself, then man is truly a Man: he separates himself from the animal. Henceforth he is no longer, like a stone, an immutable given, he bears within him *Negativity;* and the force, the violence of negativity cast him into the incessant movement of history, which changes him and which alone realizes the totality of the concrete real through time. Only history has the power to finish what is, to finish it in the passage of time. And so the idea of an eternal and immutable God is in this perspective merely a provisional end, which survives while awaiting something better. Only completed history and the spirit of the Sage (of Hegel)—in whom history revealed, then revealed in full, the development of being and the totality of its becoming— occupy a sovereign position, which God only provisionally occupies, as a regent.

The Tragi-Comic Aspect of Man's Divinity

This way of seeing things can with justice be considered comic. Besides, Hegel never expressed it explicitly. The texts where it is *implicitly* affirmed are ambiguous, and their extreme difficulty ultimately kept them from full consideration. Kojève himself is circumspect. He does not dwell on them and avoids drawing precise conclusions. In order to express appropriately the situation Hegel got himself into, no doubt involuntarily, one would need the tone, or at least, in a restrained form, the horror of tragedy. But things would quickly take on a comic appearance.

Be that as it may, to pass through death is so absent from the divine figure that a myth situated in the tradition associated death, and the agony of death, with the eternal and unique God of the Judeo-Christian sphere. The death of Jesus partakes of comedy to the extent that one cannot unarbitrarily introduce the forgetting of his eternal divinity—which is his—into the consciousness of an omnipotent and infinite God. Before Hegel's "absolute knowledge," the Christian myth was already based precisely on the fact that nothing divine is possible (in the pre-Christian sense of *sacred*) which is finite. But the vague consciousness in which the (Christian) myth of the death of God took form differed, nonetheless, from that of Hegel: in order to misrepresent a figure of God that limited the infinite as the totality, it was possible to add on, in contradiction with its basis, a movement toward the finite.

Hegel was able—and it was necessary for him—to add up the sum (the Totality) of the movements which were produced in history. But humor, it seems, is incompatible with work and its necessary assiduity. I shall return to this subject; I have merely, for the moment, shuffled cards. . . . It is difficult to pass from a humanity humiliated by divine grandeur to that . . . of the apotheosized and sovereign Sage, his pride swollen with human vanity.

A Fundamental Text

In what I have written up to this point, only one necessity emerges in a precise fashion: there can be authentic Wisdom (absolute Wisdom, or in general anything approaching it) only if the Sage raises himself, if I can put it this way, to the height of death, at whatever anguish to him.

A passage from the preface to the *Phenomenology of Spirit*[5] force-fully expresses the necessity of such an attitude. There is no doubt from the start of the "capital importance" of this admirable text, not only for an understanding of Hegel, but in all regards.

"Death," writes Hegel, "—if we wish so to name that unreality—is the most terrible thing there is and to uphold the work of death is the task which demands the greatest strength. Impotent beauty hates this awareness, because understanding makes this demand of beauty, a requirement which beauty cannot fulfill. Now, the life of Spirit is not that life which is frightened of death, and spares itself destruction, but that life which assumes death and lives with it. Spirit attains its truth only by finding itself in absolute dismemberment. It is not that (prodigious) power by being the Positive that turns away from the Negative, as when we say of something: this is nothing or (this is) false and, having (thus) disposed of it, pass from there to something else; no, Spirit is that power only to the degree in which it contemplates the Negative face to face (and) dwells with it. This prolonged sojourn is the magical force which transposes the negative into given-Being."

The Human Negation of Nature and of the Natural Being of Man

In principle, I ought to have started the passage just cited at an earlier point. I did not want to weigh this text down by giving the "enigmatic" lines which precede it. But I shall sketch out the sense of the omitted lines by restating Kojève's interpretation, without which the consequences, in spite of an appearance of relative clarity, would remain closed to us.

For Hegel, it is both fundamental and altogether worthy of astonishment that human understanding (that is, language, discourse) should have had the force (an incomparable force) to separate its constitutive elements from the Totality. These elements (this tree,

5. Cf., Hegel, *The Phenomenology of Spirit*, trans. A. V. Miller, 19. Cited by Kojève, 538–39. (TEL, 540–41.) Kojève, Hyppolite, and Bataille all translate the German "Zerrissenheit" by "déchirement," which I in turn have given as "dismemberment," the same word which appears in Miller's translation of Hegel. It is important to note that the word "déchirement" has the meanings of "shredding" and "tearing" and, unlike "dismemberment," does not imply a disarticulation into predetermined units. In *L'Expérience intérieure*, for example, Bataille speaks of himself as left in "lambeaux" (shreds, as of cloth or paper) which his "inability to respond *achevait de . . . déchirer*," (Paris: Gallimard, 1954), 19). [Translator's note.]

this bird, this stone) are in fact inseparable from the whole. They are "bound together by spatial and temporal, indeed material, bonds which are indissoluble." Their separation implies the human Negativity toward Nature of which I spoke, without pointing out its decisive consequences. For the man who negates nature could not in any way live outside of it. He is not merely a man who negates Nature, he is first of all an animal, that is to say the very thing he negates: he cannot therefore negate Nature without negating himself. The intrinsic totality of man is reflected in Kojève's bizarre expression, that totality is first of all Nature (natural being), it is "the anthropomorphic animal" (Nature, the animal indissolubly linked to the whole of Nature, and which supports Man). Thus human Negativity, Man's effective desire to negate Nature in destroying it—in reducing it to his own ends, as when, for example, he makes a tool of it (and the tool will be the model of an object isolated from Nature)—cannot stop at Man himself; insofar as he is Nature, Man is exposed to his own Negativity. To negate Nature is to negate the animal which props up Man's Negativity. It is undoubtedly not the understanding, breaker of Nature's unity, which seeks man's death, and yet the separating Action of the understanding implies the monstrous energy of thought, of the "pure abstract I," which is essentially opposed to fusion, to the inseparable character of the elements—constitutive of the whole—which firmly upholds their separation.

It is the very separation of Man's being, it is his isolation from Nature, and, consequently, his isolation in the midst of his own kind, which condemn him to disappear definitively. The animal, negating nothing, lost in a global animality to which it offers no opposition—just as that animality is itself lost in Nature (and in the totality of all that is)—does not truly disappear. . . . No doubt the individual fly dies, but today's flies are the same as those of last year. Last year's have died? . . . Perhaps, but *nothing* has disappeared. The flies remain, equal to themselves like the waves of the sea. This seems contrived: a biologist can separate a fly from the swarm, all it takes is a brushstroke. But he separates it *for himself*, he does not separate it for the flies. To separate itself from the others a fly would need the monstrous force of the understanding; then it would name itself and do what the understanding normally effects by means of language, which alone founds the separation of elements and by founding it founds itself on it, within a world formed of separated and denominated entities. But in this game the human animal finds death; it finds precisely human death, the only one which frightens, which freezes—but which only frightens and transfixes the man who is absorbed in his future disappearance, to the extent that he is a separated and irreplaceable being. The only true death supposes separation and, through the discourse which separates, the consciousness of being separated.

"Impotent Beauty Hates the Understanding"

Up to this point, Hegel's text presents a *simple* and *common* truth, but one enunciated in a philosophical manner which is, properly speaking, sibylline. In the passage from the Preface cited above, Hegel, on the contrary, affirms and describes a *personal* moment of violence—Hegel, in other words the Sage, to whom an absolute Knowledge has conferred definitive satisfaction. This is not an unbridled violence. What Hegel unleashes here is not the violence of Nature, it is the energy, or the violence, of the Understanding—the Negativity of the Understanding—opposing itself to the pure beauty of the dream, which cannot act, which is impotent.

Indeed, the beauty of the dream is on that side of the world where nothing is yet separated from what surrounds it, where each element, in contrast to the abstract objects of the Understanding, is given concretely, in space and time. But beauty cannot *act*. It can only be and preserve itself. Through action it would no longer exist, since action would first destroy what beauty is: beauty, which seeks nothing, which is, which refuses to move itself but which is disturbed by the force of the Understanding. Moreover, beauty does not have the power to respond to the request of the Understanding, which asks it to uphold and preserve the work of *human* death. Beauty is incapable of it, in the sense that to uphold that work, it would be engaged in Action. Beauty is sovereign, it is an end, or it is not: that is why it is not susceptible to acting, why it is, even in principle, powerless and why it cannot yield to the active negation of the Understanding, which changes the world and itself becomes other than it is.[6]

6. Here my interpretation differs slightly from Kojève's (146 [TEL, 148]). [Translator's note: this passage too is missing from Bloom's abridgment of Kojève, which starts only with the lectures given in 1937–38. (The passage in question is from the 1936–37 lectures.)] Kojève simply states that "impotent beauty is incapable of bending to the requirements of the Understanding. The esthete, the romantic, the mystic, flee the idea of death and speak of Nothingness itself as something which *is.*" In particular, he admirably describes the mystic in this way. But the same ambiguity is found in

This beauty without consciousness of itself *cannot therefore* really—but not for the same reason as life, which "recoils in horror from death and wants to save itself from annihilation"—bear death and preserve itself in it. This impotent beauty at least suffers from feeling the breakup of the profoundly indissoluble Totality of what is (of the concrete-real). Beauty would like to remain the sign of an accord of the real with itself. It cannot become conscious Negativity, awakened in dismemberment, and the lucid gaze, absorbed in the Negative. This latter attitude presupposes the violent and laborious struggle of Man against Nature and is its end. That is the historic struggle where Man constitutes himself as "Subject" or as "abstract I" of the "Understanding," as a separated and named being.

"That is to say," Kojève clarifies, "that thought and the discourse which reveals the real are born of the negative Action which actualizes Nothingness by annihilating Being: the given being of Man (in the Struggle) and the given being of Nature (through Work—which results, moreover, from the real contact with death in the Struggle.) That is to say, therefore, that the human being himself is none other than that Action: he is death which lives a human life" (K, 548; TEL, 550).

I want to insist on the continual connection between an abyssal aspect and a tough, down-to-earth aspect in this philosophy, the only one having the ambition to be complete. The divergent possibilities of opposed human figures confront each other and assemble in it: the figure of the dying man and of the proud one, who turns from death, the figure of the master and that of the man pinned to his work, the figure of the revolutionary and that of the skeptic, whose egotistical interest limits desire. This philosophy is not only a philosophy of death. It is also one of class struggle and work.

But within the limits of this study I do not intend to envisage this other side. I would like to compare that Hegelian doctrine of death with what we know about "sacrifice."

---

philosophers (in Hegel, in Heidegger), at least ultimately. In truth, Kojève seems to me wrong not to have envisaged, beyond classical mysticism, a "conscious mysticism," conscious of making a Being from Nothingness, and, in addition, defining that impasse as a Negativity which would no longer have a field of action (at the end of history). The atheistic mystic, *self-conscious*, conscious of having to die and to disappear, would live, as Hegel *obviously said concerning himself*, "in absolute dismemberment"; but, for him, it is only the matter of a certain period: unlike Hegel, he would never come out of it, "contemplating the Negative right in the face," but never being able to transpose it into Being, refusing to do it and maintaining himself in ambiguity.

II. SACRIFICE

*Sacrifice, on the one hand, and on the other, the Gaze of Hegel
Absorbed in Death and Sacrifice*

I shall not speak of the interpretation of sacrifice which Hegel gives in
the chapter of the *Phenomenology* devoted to Religion.[7] It no doubt
makes sense in the development of the chapter, but it strays from the
essential and, from the point of view of the theory of sacrifice, it is, in
my opinion, of less interest than the implicit representation which is
given in the text of the Preface and which I shall continue to analyze.

Concerning sacrifice, I can essentially say that, on the level of
Hegel's philosophy, Man has, in a sense, revealed and founded human
truth by sacrificing; in sacrifice he destroyed the animal[8] in himself,
allowing himself and the animal to survive only as that noncorporeal
truth which Hegel describes and which makes of man—in Heidegger's words—a being unto death (*Sein zum Tode*), or—in the words of
Kojève himself—"death which lives a human life."

Actually, the problem of Hegel is given in the action of sacrifice. In
sacrifice, death, on the one hand, essentially strikes the corporeal
being; and on the other hand, it is precisely in sacrifice that "death
lives a *human* life." It should even be said that sacrifice is the precise
response to Hegel's requirement, the original formulation of which I
repeat:

"Spirit attains its truth only by finding itself in absolute dismemberment. It does not attain that (prodigious) power by being the
Positive that turns away from the Negative . . . no, Spirit is that
power only in the degree to which it contemplates the Negative face
to face [and] dwells with it . . ."

If one takes into account the fact that the institution of sacrifice is
practically universal, it is clear that Negativity, incarnated in Man's
death, not only is the arbitrary construction of Hegel, but also that it
has played a role in the spirit of the simplest men, without any com-

7. *The Phenomenology of Spirit*, chapter 8: Religion, B.: Religion in the form of
Art, a) The abstract work of art (434–35). In these two pages, Hegel dwells on the
disappearance of *objective essence*, but without developing its consequences. On
the second page Hegel limits himself to considerations proper to "aesthetic religion"
(the religion of the Greeks).

8. Still, although animal sacrifice seems to predate human sacrifice, there is nothing to prove that the choice of an animal signifies the unconscious desire to oppose the
animal as such; man is only opposed to corporeal being, the being that is given. He is,
furthermore, just as opposed to the plant.

mon grounds comparable to those which are regulated once and for all by the ceremonies of a Church—but nonetheless in a univocal manner. It is striking to see that across the world a communal *Negativity* has maintained a strict parallelism in the development of rather stable institutions, which have the same form and the same effects.

Whether He Lives or Dies, Man Cannot Immediately Know Death

I shall speak later of the profound differences between the man of sacrifice, acting in ignorance (unconscious) of the full scope of what he is doing, and the Sage (Hegel) surrendering to the implications of a Knowledge which, in his own eyes, is absolute.

Despite these differences, the question of manifesting the Negative still remains (and still under a concrete form, i.e., at the heart of the Totality, whose constitutive elements are inseparable). The privileged manifestation of Negativity is death, but death, in fact, reveals nothing. In theory, it is his natural, animal being whose death reveals Man to himself, but the revelation never takes place. For when the animal being supporting him dies, the human being himself ceases to be. In order for Man to reveal himself ultimately to himself, he would have to die, but he would have to do it while living—watching himself ceasing to be. In other words, death itself would have to become (self-) consciousness at the very moment that it annihilates the conscious being. In a sense, this is what takes place (what at least is on the point of taking place, or which takes place in a fugitive, ungraspable manner) by means of a subterfuge. In the sacrifice, the sacrificer identifies himself with the animal that is struck down dead. And so he dies in seeing himself die, and even, in a certain way, by his own will, one in spirit with the sacrificial weapon. But it is a comedy!

At least it would be a comedy if some other method existed which could reveal to the living the invasion of death: that finishing off of the finite being, which *his* Negativity—which kills him, *ends* him and definitively suppresses him—accomplishes alone and which it alone can accomplish. For Hegel, *satisfaction* can only take place, desire can be appeased only in the consciousness of death. If it were based on the exclusion of death, satisfaction would contradict that which death designates, if the satisfied being who is not conscious, not utterly conscious, of what in a constitutive manner he is, i.e., mortal, were eventually to be driven from satisfaction by death. That is why the consciousness that he has *of himself* must reflect (must mirror) the movement of negativity which creates him, which makes a man of him for the very reason that it will one day kill him.

He will be killed by his own negativity, but for him, thereafter, there will be nothing left; his is a creative death, but if the consciousness of death—of the marvelous magic of death—does not touch him before he dies, during his life it will seem that death is not destined to reach him, and so the death awaiting him will not give him a *human* character. Thus, at all costs, man must live at the moment that he really dies, or he must live with the impression of really dying.

Knowledge of Death Cannot Do Without a Subterfuge: Spectacle

This difficulty proclaims the necessity of *spectacle,* or of *representation* in general, without the practice of which it would be possible for us to remain alien and ignorant in respect to death, just as beasts apparently are. Indeed, nothing is less animal than fiction, which is more or less separated from the real, from death.

Man does not live by bread alone, but also by the comedies with which he willingly deceives himself. In Man it is the animal, it is the natural being, which eats. But Man takes part in rites and performances. Or else he can read: to the extent that it is sovereign—authentic—, literature prolongs in him the haunting magic of performances, tragic or comic.

In tragedy,[9] at least, it is a question of our identifying with some character who dies, and of believing that we die, although we are alive. Furthermore, pure and simple imagination suffices, but it has the same meaning as the classic subterfuges, performances, or books, to which the masses have recourse.

Agreement and Disagreement between Naive Behaviors and Hegel's Lucid Reaction

By associating it with sacrifice and, thereby, with the primary theme of *representation* (in art, in festivals, in performances), I have sought to demonstrate that Hegel's reaction is fundamental human behavior. It is not a fantasy or a strange attitude, it is *par excellence* the

9. I discuss comedy further on.

expression endlessly repeated by tradition. It is not Hegel alone, it is all of humanity which everywhere always sought, obliquely, to seize what death both gave and took away from humanity.

Between Hegel and the man of sacrifice there nevertheless remains a profound difference. Hegel was *conscious* of his representation of the Negative: he situated it, lucidly, in a definite point of the "coherent discourse" which revealed him to himself. That Totality included the discourse which reveals it. The man of sacrifice, who lacked a discursive consciousness of what he did, had only a "sensual" awareness, i.e., an obscure one, reduced to an unintelligible emotion. It is true that Hegel himself, beyond discourse, and in spite of himself (in an "absolute dismemberment,") received the shock of death even more violently. More violently, above all, for the primary reason that the broad movement of discourse extended its reach beyond limits, i.e., within the framework of the Totality of the real. Beyond the slightest doubt, for Hegel, the fact that he was still alive was simply an aggravation. The man of sacrifice, on the other hand, maintains his life essentially. He maintains it not only in the sense that life is necessary for the representation of death, but [also in the sense that] he seeks to *enrich* it. But from an external perspective, the palpable and *intentional* excitement of sacrifice was of greater interest than the *involuntary* sensitivity of Hegel. The excitement of which I speak is well-known, is definable; it is *sacred* horror: the richest and the most agonizing experience, which does not limit itself to dismemberment but which, on the contrary, opens itself, like a theatre curtain, onto a realm beyond this world, where the rising light of day transfigures all things and destroys their limited meaning.

Indeed, if Hegel's attitude opposes learned consciousness and the limitless organization of a discursive thinking to the naiveté of sacrifice, still that consciousness and that organization remain unclear on one point; one cannot say that Hegel was unaware of the "moment" of sacrifice; this "moment" is included, implicated in the whole movement of the *Phenomenology*—where it is the Negativity of death, insofar as it is assumed, which makes a man of the human animal. But because he did not see that sacrifice in itself bore witness to the *entire* movement of death,[10] the final experience—the one

10. Perhaps for lack of a Catholic religious experience. I imagine Catholicism closer to pagan experience; I mean to a universal religious experience from which the Reformation distanced itself. Perhaps a profound Catholic piety could alone have introduced the inward sense without which the phenomenology of sacrifice would be im-

peculiar to the Sage—described in the Preface to the *Phenomenology* was at first *initial* and *universal*—he did not know to what extent he was right—with what precision he described the intimate movement of Negativity; he did not clearly separate death from the feeling of sadness to which naive experience opposes a sort of shunting yard of the emotions.

Pleasure and the Sadness of Death

It was precisely the univocal character of death for Hegel that inspired the following commentary from Kojève, which applies, again, to the passage from the Preface: (K, 549; TEL, 551). "Certainly, the idea of death does not heighten the *well-being* of Man; it does not make him *happy* nor does it give him any pleasure." Kojève wondered in what way satisfaction results from a familiarity with the Negative, from a *tête-à-tête* with death. He believed it his duty, out of decency, to reject vulgar satisfaction. The fact that Hegel himself said, in this respect, that Spirit "only attains it truth by finding itself in absolute dismemberment" goes together, in principle, with Kojève's Negation. Consequently, it would even be superfluous to insist. . . . Kojève simply states that the idea of death "is alone capable if satisfying man's pride." . . . Indeed, the desire to be "recognized," which Hegel places at the origin of historical struggles, could be expressed in an intrepid attitude, of the sort that shows a character to its best advantage. "It is only," says Kojève, "in being or in becoming aware of one's mortality or finitude, in existing and in feeling one's existence in a universe without a beyond or without a God, that Man can affirm his liberty, his historicity and his individuality—'unique in all the world'—and

---

possible. Modern knowledge, much more extensive than that of Hegel's time, has assuredly contributed to the solution of that fundamental enigma (why, without any plausible reason, *has humanity in general* "sacrificed"?), but I seriously believe that a correct phenomenological description could only be based on at least a Catholic *period.*

    —But at any rate, Hegel, hostile to *being* which does nothing,—to what simply *is,* and is not *Action,*—was more interested in military death; it is through such death that he perceived the theme of sacrifice (but he himself uses the word in a moral sense): "The state-of-the-soldier," he states in his *Lectures* of 1805–06, "and war are the objectively real sacrifice of the personal-I, the danger of death for the particular,—that contemplation of his abstract immediate Negativity . . ." (in Hegel, *Sämtliche Werke,* vol. 20, 261–62. Cited by Kojève in *Introduction to the Reading of Hegel,* 558 [TEL, 560]). Nonetheless, religious sacrifice has, even from Hegel's point of view, an essential signification.

have them be recognized. (Ibid.). But if Kojève sets aside vulgar satis-faction—happiness—he now also sets aside Hegel's "absolute dis-memberment": indeed, such dismemberment is not easily reconciled with the desire for recognition.

Satisfaction and dismemberment coincide, however, in one point, but here they harmonize with *pleasure*. This coincidence takes place in "sacrifice"; it is generally understood as the *naive form of life,* as every existence in present time, which manifests what Man *is:* the novelty which he signifies in the world after he has become *Man,* on the condition that he has satisfied his *"animal"* needs.

At any rate, *pleasure,* or at least sensual pleasure, is such that in respect to it Kojève's affirmation would be difficult to uphold: the idea of death helps, in a certain manner and in certain cases, to multiply the pleasures of the senses. I go so far as to believe that, under the form of defilement, the world (or rather the general imagery) of death is at the base of erotism. The feeling of sin is connected in lucid consciousness to the idea of death, and *in the same manner* the feeling of sin is connected with pleasure.[11] There is in fact no *human* pleasure without some irregularity in its circumstances, without the breaking of an interdiction—the simplest, and the most powerful of which, is currently that of nudity.

Moreover, possession was associated in its time with the image of sacrifice; it was a sacrifice in which woman was the victim. . . . That association from ancient poetry is very meaningful; it refers back to a precise state of sensibility in which the sacrificial element, the feel-ing of sacred horror itself, joined, in a weakened state, to a tempered pleasure; in which, too, the taste for sacrifice and the emotion which it released seemed in no way contrary to the ultimate uses of pleasure.

It must be said too that sacrifice, like tragedy, was an element of a celebration; it bespoke a blind, pernicious joy and all the danger of that joy, and yet this is precisely the principle of *human joy;* it wears out and threatens with death all who get caught up in its movement.

Gay Anguish, Anguished Gaiety

To the association of death and pleasure, which is not a given, at least is not an immediate given in consciousness, is obviously opposed the

11. This is at least possible and, if it is a matter of the most common interdictions, banal.

sadness of death, always in the background of consciousness. In principle, *consciously,* humanity "recoils in horror before death." In principle, the destructive effects of Negativity have Nature as their object. But for Man's Negativity to drive him into a confrontation with danger, for him to make of himself, or at least of the animal, of the natural being that he is, the object of his destructive negation, the banal prerequisite is his unconsciousness of the cause and the effects of his actions. Now, it was essential for Hegel to *gain consciousness* of Negativity as such, to capture its horror—here the horror of death—by upholding and by looking the work of death right in the face.

Hegel, in this way, is less opposed to those who "recoil" than to those who say: "it is nothing." He seems to distance himself most from those who react with gaiety.

I want to emphasize, as clearly as possible, after their similarity, the opposition between the naive attitude and that of the—*absolute*—Wisdom of Hegel. I am not sure, in fact, that of the two attitudes the more naive is the less *absolute.*

I shall cite a paradoxical example of a gay reaction in the face of the work of death.

The Irish and Welsh custom of the "wake" is little known but was still practiced at the end of the last century. It is the subject of Joyce's last work,[12] *Finnegans Wake*—the deathwatch of Finnegan (however, the reading of this famous novel is difficult at best). In Wales, the coffin was placed *open,* standing at the place of honor of the house. The dead man would be dressed in his finest suit and top hat. His family would invite all of his friends, who honored the departed all the more the longer they danced and the deeper they drank to his health. It is the death of an *other,* but in such instances, the death of the other is always the image of one's own death. Only under one condition could anyone so rejoice; with the presumed agreement of the dead man—who is an other—, the dead man that the drinker in his turn will become shall have no other meaning than his predecessor.

This paradoxical reaction could be considered a response to the desire to deny *the existence of death.* A logical desire? Not in the least, I think. In Mexico today, death is commonly envisaged on the same level as the amusements that can be found at festivals:

12. On the subject of this obscure book, *vide* E. Jolas, "Elucidation du monomythe de James Joyce" in *Critique* (July 1948): 579–95.

skeleton puppets, skeleton candies, skeleton merry-go-rounds—but this custom is associated with an intense cult of the dead, a visible obsession with death.[13]

If I envisage death gaily, it is not that I too say, in turning away from what is frightening: "it is nothing" or "it is false." On the contrary, gaiety, connected with the work of death, causes me anguish, is accentuated by my anguish, and in return exacerbates that anguish: ultimately, gay anguish, anguished gaiety cause me, in a feverish chill,[14] "absolute dismemberment," where it is my joy that finally tears me apart, but where dejection would follow joy were I not torn all the way to the end, immeasurably.

There is one precise opposition that I would like to bring out fully: on the one hand Hegel's attitude is less whole than that of naive humanity, but this is meaningless unless, reciprocally, one sees that the naive attitude is powerless to maintain itself without subterfuge.

Discourse Gives Useful Ends to Sacrifice "Afterwards."

I have linked the meaning of sacrifice to Man's behavior once his animal needs have been satisfied: Man differs from the natural being which he also is; the sacrificial gesture is what he humanly is, and the spectacle of sacrifice then makes his humanity manifest. Freed from animal need, man is sovereign: he does what he pleases—his pleasure. Under these conditions he is finally able to make a rigorously autonomous gesture. So long as he needed to satisfy animal needs, he had to act with an end in view (he had to secure food, protect himself from the cold). This supposes a servitude, a series of acts subordinated to a final result: the natural, animal satisfaction without which Man properly speaking, sovereign Man, could not subsist. But Man's intelligence, his *discursive thought*, developed as functions of servile labor. Only sacred, poetic words, limited to the level of impotent beauty, have retained the power to manifest full sovereignty. Sacrifice, consequently, is a *sovereign, autonomous* manner of being only to the extent that it is uninformed by *meaningful* discourse. To the extent that discourse informs it, what is *sovereign* is given in terms of

13. This came out in the documentary which Eisenstein drew from his work for a long film: ¡*Viva Mexico!* The crux of this film dealt with the bizarre practices which I have discussed.

14. Reading "chaud et froid" for "chaud-froid," which means a dish prepared hot but served cold.

servitude. Indeed by definition what is *sovereign* does not *serve.* But simple discourse must respond to the question that discursive thought asks concerning the meaning that each thing must have on the level of utility. In principle, each thing is there to *serve* some purpose or other. Thus the simple manifestation of Man's link to annihilation, the pure revelation of Man to himself (at the moment when death transfixes his attention) passes from sovereignty to the primacy of servile ends. Myth, associated with ritual, had at first the impotent beauty of poetry, but discourse concerning sacrifice slipped into vulgar, self-serving interpretation. Starting with effects naively imagined on the level of poetry, such as the appeasing of a god or the purity of beings, the end of meaningful discourse became the abundance of rain or the city's well-being. The substantial work of Frazer, who recalls those forms of sovereignty that were the most *impotent* and, apparently, the least propitious for happiness, generally tends to reduce the meaning of the ritual act to the same purposes as labor in the fields, and to make of sacrifice an agrarian rite. Today that thesis of the *Golden Bough* is discredited, but it seemed reasonable insofar as the same people who sacrificed inscribed sovereign sacrifice within the frame of a language of plowmen. It is true that in a very arbitrary manner, which never merited the credence of rigorous reason, these people attempted, and must have labored to submit sacrifice to the laws of action, laws to which they themselves were submitted, or labored to submit themselves.

Impotence of the Sage to Attain Sovereignty on the Basis of Discourse

Thus, the sovereignty of sacrifice is not absolute either. It is not absolute to the extent that the institution maintains within the world of efficacious activity a form whose meaning is, on the contrary, sovereign. A slippage cannot fail to occur, to the benefit of servitude.

If the attitude of the Sage (Hegel) is not, for its part, sovereign, at least things function in the opposite direction; Hegel did not distance himself and if he was unable to find authentic sovereignty, he came as near to it as he could. What separated him from it would even be imperceptible were we not able to glimpse a richer image through these alterations of meaning, which touch on sacrifice and which have reduced it from an *end* to a simple *means.* The key to a lesser rigorousness on the part of the Sage is the fact, not that discourse engages his sovereignty within a frame that cannot suit him and which atrophies it, but precisely the opposite: sovereignty in Hegel's attitude proceeds from a movement which *discourse* reveals and which, in the Sage's spirit, is never separated from its revelation. It can never, therefore, be fully *sovereign;* the Sage, in fact, cannot fail to subordinate it to the goal of a Wisdom which supposes the completion of discourse. Wisdom alone *will be* full autonomy, the sovereignty of being. . . . At least it *would be* if we could find sovereignty by searching for it: and, in fact, if I search for it, I am undertaking the project of being-sovereignly: but the *project* of being-sovereignly presupposes a servile being! What nonetheless assures the sovereignty of the moment described is the "absolute dismemberment" of which Hegel speaks, the rupture, for a time, of discourse. But that rupture itself is not sovereign. In a sense it is an accident in the ascent. Although the two sovereignties, the naive and the sage ones, are both sovereignties of death, beyond the difference between a decline at birth (between a gradual alteration and an imperfect manifestation), they differ on yet another precise point: on Hegel's part, it is precisely a question of an accident. It is not a stroke of fate, a piece of bad luck, which would be forever deprived of sense. Dismemberment is, on the contrary, full of meaning. (*"Spirit only attains its truth,"* writes Hegel (but it is my emphasis), "by finding itself in absolute dismemberment.") But this meaning is unfortunate. It is what limited and impoverished the revelation which the Sage drew from lingering in the regions where death reigns. He welcomed sovereignty as a weight, which he let go . . .

Do I intend to minimize Hegel's attitude? But the contrary is true! I want to show the incomparable scope of his approach. To that end I cannot veil the very minimal (and even inevitable) part of failure.

To my mind, it is rather the exceptional certainty of that approach which is brought out in my associations. If he failed, one cannot say that it was the result of an error. The meaning of the failure itself differs from that of the failure which caused it: the error alone is perhaps fortuitous. In general, it is as an authentic movement, weighty with sense, that one must speak of the "failure" of Hegel.

Indeed, man is always in pursuit of an authentic sovereignty. That sovereignty, apparently, was, in a certain sense, originally his, but doubtless that could not then have been in a *conscious* manner, and so in a sense it was not his, it escaped him. We shall see that in a number of ways he continued to pursue what forever eluded him. The essential thing is that one cannot attain it consciously and seek it, because seeking distances it. And yet I can believe that nothing is given us that is not given in that equivocal manner.

Translated by Jonathan Strauss

GEORGES BATAILLE

Open Letter from René Char

We are informing you about a subject that the convulsions of our epoch bring to the fore:

Are there incompatibilities?

Though today it would seem futile to ask such a question, the resources of dialectics, if one judges from known results, permit a favorable response to *everything*. Favorable, however, does not mean *truthful*, and we propose that the modern question of incompatibilities be examined carefully, *modern* because it effects the conditions of existence of our Time which, one will agree, is both dubious and effervescent. It is affirmed that certain functions of the human consciousness, certain contradictory activities, may be associated and maintained by a single individual without disturbing that practical and healthy truth which human collectivities strive to attain. This may be the case, but it is not certain. Politics, economics, social matters, and what moral standards?

In view of the fact that complaints and legitimate claims are raised, that struggles are undertaken and remedies drawn up, do you not think that if the present world is to rediscover a very relative harmony, its burning diversity, it will in part owe this to the fact that the problem of incompatibilities (a rather pressing problem, a fundamental one even, though willfully conjured away) will have been resolved, or at least seriously posed.

To be sure, in every being there are two-parts Ariel, one-part Caliban, prone to and, in addition, a parcel of an amorphous unknown,

YFS 78, *On Bataille,* ed. Allan Stoekl, © 1990 by Yale University.

become diamond if Ariel perseveres. If Ariel resigns, a sickness of flies.

To those who wish to answer us, we leave the care of specifying our question's solid grounding or lack thereof, and its viewpoint indicator.

An awkward and unclear questionnaire, one will object. But it is from you, adversaries or sympathisers, that the questionnaire and responses await a beam of light or, at the very least, of candor.

Empédocle, 1950

GEORGES BATAILLE

Letter to René Char on the Incompatibilities of the Writer*

My dear friend,

The question that you have asked, "Are there any incompatibilities?" has taken on for me the meaning of a long-awaited summons. It is a summons I was losing hope of ever receiving. I perceive more clearly each day how the world in which we live limits its desires to the needs of sleep. But one *word* summons at the right time a kind of recueil, of renewed energy.

It happens frequently enough these days that the end seems near. At this time the need to forget, to cease to react, prevails over the desire to continue living. . . . To reflect about the inevitable, or to try to sleep no longer. . . . Sleep seems preferable. We have witnessed the submission of those overwhelmed by too weighty a situation. Were those who cried out, however, any more awake? What is coming is so strange, so vast, so little commensurate with expectations. . . . At a time when the destiny which leads men is taking on a human shape, the majority is giving itself over to absence. Those who seem resolute or menacing, whose every word is but a mask, have volontarily lost themselves in a night of the intellect. Yet the night in which the rest of the earth now sleeps is pitch-black: the dogmatic slumber of some contrasts with the bloodless confusion of others—a chaos of innumerable grey voices that are wearing themselves out before their drowsy listeners.

Perhaps my vain irony is itself a way to sleep more soundly. . . . Yet I write, I speak, and can only rejoice in the opportunity to *respond*

*This letter to René Char appeared in *Botthege Oscure*, May 1950, and can now be found in vol. 12 of *OC*. Reprinted with permission of the Beinecke Rare Book and Library, Yale University, and of Editions Gallimard © 1988.

YFS 78, *On Bataille,* ed. Allan Stoekl, © 1990 by Yale University.

to you, and even together with you, to *desire* the moment of wakefulness when this universal confusion will, at last, no longer be acceptable; a confusion which now makes of thought a forgetting, a foolishness, the barking of a dog in church.

Moreover, in responding to the question that you have set forth, I feel as though I have finally reached the adversary—an adversary which assuredly is not someone or other, but is existence itself in its entirety, engulfing, lulling, and drowning *desire,*—and that I have attained it finally in the right place. You invite, you provoke one to emerge from the confusion. . . . Perhaps it is an excess which announces that the time has come. How, in the end, is it possible to endure *actions,* that *in such unfortunate guises,* succeed in "effacing" life? Yes, perhaps the time has now come to denounce subordination, that servile attitude with which human life is incompatible—an attitude accepted since time immemorial, but whose excess today obliges us to detach ourselves lucidly. Lucidly! It is, of course, without the least hope.

In fact, to speak in this manner is surely to risk misunderstanding. You, however, know me to be as far from dejection as from hope. I have chosen simply to *live.* I am always astonished by men who, fired-up and eager to act, look down upon the pleasure of living. These men obviously confuse action with life without ever seeing that, while action is the necessary means for the maintenance of life, the only admissible act is the act that effaces itself (or in extreme circumstances prepares to efface itself) before the "burning diversity" of which you speak, and which cannot and never can be reduced to what is useful.

The difficulty of subordinating action to its end stems from the fact that the only admissible action is the most efficacious. Hence, the initial advantage of immoderately giving oneself over to it, of lying and of unrestrained conduct. If all men permitted themselves to act only to the extent that necessity dictates to their total being, falsehood and brutality would be superfluous. It is the overflowing propensity to action and the ensuing rivalries, which increase the efficacy of liars and of the blind. Moreover, given the circumstances, we can do nothing to extricate ourselves—to remedy the evil of excessive action, one has to, or would have, to act! We do nothing more than verbally and vainly condemn those who betray and blind their own kind. Everything, in all this vanity, takes a turn for the worse. No one can condemn action except through silence,—or through poetry, which opens, as it were, its window onto silence. To denounce, to protest, is also to act, and at the same time, it is to shy away from the exigencies of action!

It seems to me that we shall never sufficiently indicate a basic incompatibility of this *life without measure,* a life which alone counts, which alone is the meaning of all humanity, and consequently, of *measureless action* itself. I am speaking by and large of what, beyond productive activity, and, in our disorder, is the analogue of holiness. Action can obviously have value only *in so far* as it has humanity as its "raison d'être." It rarely, however, accepts this measure for, of all the opiums, action brings the heaviest sleep. The place action occupies makes one think of those trees that hide the forest, that profess to be the forest itself.

For this reason, it seems fitting for us to oppose equivocation, and, *being unable to act truly,* for us to slip away without further ado. I say *we,* but I am thinking of you, of myself, of those who resemble us. Leave the dead to the dead (barring the impossible), and action (if it is possible) to those who passionately confuse it with life.

By this I do not mean that all action ought to be relinquished regardless of what may happen. For undoubtedly we should never fail to oppose criminal or unreasonable actions, but we must clearly recognize the following: because rational and admissible action (from the general standpoint of humanity) becomes, as we might have foreseen, the lot of those who act *without measure,* and which therefore runs the risk, a rational one at first, of being changed dialectically into its opposite, we can only hope to oppose it on the condition that we substitute ourselves, or rather, that we have the heart and the strength to substitute ourselves, for those whose methods we do not fancy.

Blake says somewhere that "to speak without acting is to breed pestilence."

The incompatibility of a life without measure and immoderate action is, in my eyes, decisive. We are touching upon that problem whose "conjuring away" contributes without a doubt to the present blind advance of all humanity. Though at first it might seem peculiar, I believe that this conjuring away was the inevitable consequence of the weakening of religion. Religion formulated this particular problem of incompatibility which, moreover, was its unique problem. Little by little, however, it was abandoned to secular thought which *did not yet know how to formulate it.* We cannot regret this, for religion, having posed the problem from a position of authority, posed it badly. Above all, it did so ambiguously—in the beyond. The principle of action remained bound to *this* world. . . . All of action's true aims remained celestial. It is for us, finally, to formulate the problem in its rigorous dimensions.

Your question then, after my too general affirmation, compels me to specify the present facts and scope of the incompatibility which seems fundamental to me.

Although the debate concerning literature and "engagement" appears to have subsided, its decisive nature has not yet been clearly perceived. All the more reason then not to leave it at that. First of all, it is important to define just what propels the phenomenon of literature which cannot be made to serve a master. NON SERVIAM is said to be the devil's motto. If this is so, then literature is diabolical.

At this point I would like to set aside all reserve and allow passion to speak. This is not an easy task, for it implies a resignation to the impotence of desires that are too intense. Insofar as my discourse is due to passion itself, I would like to avoid any recourse to reason's tired means of expression. Be that as it may, *you* will be able to perceive how vain and even impossible this resolution seems to me. Would it be too vague if I said that at the thought of speaking sagaciously about these matters, I experience a great discomfort? Nevertheless, I am writing to you, you who will see through the weakness of these reasonable words to what reason can grasp only in an illusory way.

First of all, let me affirm that I honestly know nothing about what I am, or what my fellow men are, or what the world in which we live might be—impenetrable appearance, paltry light vacillating in a night without conceivable bounds that surrounds us in every direction. I am clinging in my astonished helplessness to a cord. I do not know if I love the night. Perhaps I do, for fragile human beauty moves me in that disquieting way only when I understand that the night from whence it comes, and into which it goes, is unfathomable. How I *love* the distant outline that men have ceaselessly left of themselves in this darkness! That far-off image delights me. I love it, and I often feel the pain from loving it too much. Humanity, sordid or tender, and always *astray*, even in its miseries, its stupidity, and crimes, presents an intoxicating defiance. It isn't Shakespeare who suffered those heartrending cries, it is HUMANITY. Little matter if HUMANITY endlessly betrays itself, and in so doing, betrays what is greater than itself. HUMANITY is most touching in its inanity when night grows filthier, when the horror of night turns its creatures into a vast heap of rubbish.

One speaks about the "unbearable" universe that I portray in my books, as though I were displaying my open wounds the way the wretched do. It is true that, on the surface, I like to deny, or at least to neglect or discount, the multiple recourses which help us to *endure*. I scorn them less perhaps than it would appear, but I most certainly hasten to *give back* my own small portion of life to that which *divinely* slips away before us, and which slips away from the will to reduce the world to the efficacy of reason. I have nothing against reason and rational order, for in the numerous cases where it is clearly opportune, like everyone else, I am in favor of them both. Nevertheless, I do not know whether anything in this world has ever appeared *adorable* which did not exceed the functions of utility, did not wreak havoc upon and benumb as it charmed, and, in short, was not at the extreme limit of endurance. I, who know myself to be clearly limited to atheism, am perhaps wrong for never having demanded less from this world than the Christians did from God. Did not the idea of God itself, while having as its logical outcome a reasonable account of the world, also have the means to chill (the blood)? Was it not itself "unbearable"? All the more unbearable then is *that which is*, of which we know nothing (except in detached bits), about which nothing can give an explanation, and whose fullest expression is to be found only in man's powerlessness and death. I do not doubt that by withdrawing from what is reassuring, we draw near to ourselves, to that divine moment that is dying within us, that already has the strangeness of laughter, the beauty of an agonizing silence. We have known for a long time that nothing can be found in God that we cannot find in ourselves. In so far as useful action has not neutralized man, he himself is God, destined for the continual rapture of an "unbearable" joy. Neutralized man no longer bears this agonizing dignity. Today it is art alone which inherits, before our very eyes, the *delirious* role and character of religions. Today it is art which gnaws at and transfigures us, which expresses with its so-called falsehoods a truth that is empty at last of precise meaning.

I am not unaware that human *thought* turns entirely away from the object about which I am speaking, and which is *what we supremely are*. Thought does this infallibly. With no less necessity do our eyes turn away from the dazzling sun.

For those who wish to limit their perceptions to the vision of the disinherited, these notions are but the delirium of a writer. . . . I am wary of protesting. But at your invitation, I am writing to you and to those who resemble us, and you apprehend my subject matter better than I, for you have the advantage of never *spinning it into essays.* Do you believe that such a subject does not require a choice from those who assume it? A book that is often despised, but which nonetheless bears witness to one of those extreme moments where human destiny seeks itself, recounts that no one can serve two masters. I myself would say that, however much one might desire it, no one can serve *one master* (whoever it may be) without denying the sovereignty of life within himself. In spite of the useful character of judge and benefactor attributed to God, the incompatibility formulated by the Gospel is nonetheless, at the outset, the very incompatibility between practical activity and the subject of my discourse.

By definition, one cannot do without useful activity. It is one thing to respond to the sad dictates of necessity, to allow it to take the lead when we form those judgments which determine our conduct. It is something very different to make of the sorrows of man the supreme judge and ultimate value, and to accept only the object of my discourse as *sovereign.* On the one hand, one receives life in an attitude of submission as a burden and a source of obligation. In this way, a *negative* morality matches the servile need of a constraint which no one, without committing a crime, may contest. On the other hand, life is the desire for what can be loved limitlessly, and morality here is *positive.* This morality gives value exclusively to desire and to its object. It is commonly maintained that an incompatibility exists between literature and puerile morality (it has been said that one does not make fine literature with fine sentiments). In order to make our position clear, should we not in return indicate that literature, like *dreaming,* is the expression of desire—of the object of desire—and, consequently, of the absence of constraint and of nimble disobedience?

"Literature and the right to death" denies the seriousness of the question: "What is literature?" which "has received only insignificant answers." "Literature . . . seems to be that vacant element . . . to which reflection, following its own gravity, cannot return without losing its seriousness." But can we not say that this element is precisely the absolutely sovereign object about which I am speaking, and which, manifesting only itself through language, is nevertheless but a void at the heart of language? For language "signifies," and literature deprives phrases of the power to designate anything other than my object. The reason it is so difficult to speak about this object, is that it never appears, not even from the instant I speak of it; for language, it would seem, "is a specific moment of action, and cannot be understood apart from action" (Sartre).

Under these circumstances, the poverty of literature is great; it is a confusion resulting from the powerlessness of language to designate the useless and the superfluous, namely, that human attitude which transcends useful activity (or activity seen in the light of its usefulness). For us, for whom in fact literature was the privileged concern, nothing counts more than books,—books that we read or that we write,—except perhaps what they foster; and we take this inevitable poverty upon ourselves.

To be a writer is nothing less than the possession of the inner ability to add another line to the drawing of that disconcerting vision which fills us with wonder while it terrifies,—it is man's incessant vision of himself. We who write are well aware that humanity could easily do without the images that we create. Even supposing that (one's) literary pastime be diminished to a subservience to action, the wonder of it nevertheless remains! The immediate ineffectiveness of oppression and falsehood is even greater than the inadequacy of authentic literature—there is merely a widening of silence and darkness.

This silence and darkness, however, prepare the muffled crack and tremulous glimmering of fresh thunderstorms; they prepare *the return* of a sovereign conduct that cannot be harnessed to the downward pull of self-interest. It is the writer's task to have silence as his only choice, silence or a threatening sovereignty. Aside from his other major cares, he can only form those fascinating images—innumerable and false—dissipated by recourse to the "signification" of language, but where lost humanity rediscovers itself. The writer does not abolish mankind's need to maintain its existence or the allocation of sustenance among men, nor can he refuse part of his free time for these ends. Nevertheless, he sets the limits of his submission which itself is limited and ineluctable. It is in him and through him that man learns how he himself remains forever elusive, being essentially unpredictable, and how knowledge must finally be resolved into the simplicity of emotion. It is in and through the writer that existence, in a general way, is what a girl is to the man who desires her, whether she love or spurn him, bring him pleasure or despair. The incompatibility of literature and "engagement," which is compulsory, is precisely therefore one of opposites. Never did an *"homme engagé"* ever write anything which wasn't untruth, and which did not go beyond commitment (engagement). If it appears to be otherwise, it is because the commitment in question is not the result of a choice corresponding to a feeling of responsibility or obligation, but is the effect of a passion, of an insurmountable desire which *never left one free to choose.* On the contrary, the commitment whose meaning and binding strength derive from the fear of hunger, enslavement, or the death of others, leads away from literature (petty, at the very least) to a search for the constraints of an unquestionably pressing action; to action to which it would be cowardly or futile not to dedicate oneself entirely. If there is some reason to act, it should be expressed in terms as unliterary as can be.

It is clear that the authentic writer who does not write for paltry reasons or for reasons too shameful to mention, cannot, without uttering platitudes, form his work so as to contribute to the designs of social utility. Insofar as his writing is useful, it will not partake of sovereign truth. Rather, it would drift toward a resigned submission where not only the life of one, but the lives of many men, would remain untouched, and what is humanly sovereign unattained.

Even if the incompatibility between literature and "engagement", were fundamental, it cannot always contradict the facts. The demands of useful action sometimes involve the entirety of one's life. In danger, urgency, or humiliation, there is no more room for the superfluous. From that moment on, *there are no further choices.* One has justly put forward the case of Richard Wright: a black man from the American South who was unable to free himself from the constraints that weighed upon his fellow-men, and who wrote within this framework. These circumstances came to him from the outside; he had thus not *chosen* to be commited. On this subject, Jean-Paul Sartre remarked that "Wright, writing for a tragically divided readership, was able simultaneously to preserve this tear and go beyond it; he made it the pretext for the work of art." It is not essentially unusual for a theoretician of literary "engagement" to situate the work of art—which, indeed, uselessly exceeds the given circumstances—beyond commitment, nor for a theoretician of choice to stress the fact that Wright was unable to choose, and to do so without drawing the conclusions. What is hard to bear is the freedom of preference which precedes the demands made by the external world, and where the author chooses out of conviction to proselytize. He thus intentionally denies the meaning and the occurence of that margin of "useless passion," of vain and sovereign existence, which is generally the privilege of humanity. There is then less chance, in spite of him, that this margin emerge in the guise of an authentic work of art, as in the case of Wright for whom, in the end, preaching is only a pretext. If the urgency is genuine, if a choice is no longer offered, it will always be possible to reserve, perhaps tacitly, the return of the moment when urgency will have ceased. Choice alone, if it is freely made, *subordinates* to commitment what, being sovereign, can only exist with sovereign power.

It may seem vain to linger for so long over a doctrine which probably only reached the minds of the anguished—those troubled by a freedom whose nature was both too great and too vague. Moreover, the least one can say is that this doctrine was unable to establish a precise and strict requirement. In practice, everything had to remain vague, and with the help of natural inconsistency. . . . Furthermore, the author himself has implicitly recognized the contradiction he has come up against: his moral philosophy, an entirely personal one, is based on freedom directed towards choice, but the object of choice is always . . . a sign of traditional morality. These two moral doctrines are autonomous, and, to this day, one has not found the means of moving from one to the other. This problem is not superficial. Sartre himself admits that the edifice of the old moral philosophy is wormeaten, and that his thought has succeeded in undermining what remains . . .

If by following these paths I arrive at the most general of propositions, it appears in the first place that commitment's simplistic blunder brings to light the contrary of what it was looking for. (I have affirmed the exact opposite of what Sartre says about literature.) These viewpoints immediately and gracefully combine. In the second place, it seems to me opportune not to take into account the received opinions concerning the *minor* significance of literature.

Though the problems I have dealt with have other consequences, allow me to present them in a form that henceforth will permit us to intensify an incompatibility, whose misapprehension debased at once life and action, action itself, and literature and politics.

If we give first priority to literature, we must at the same time admit *how little the increase of society's resources concerns us.*

Whoever is in charge of useful activity,—in the sense of a general increase of strength,—assumes interests opposed to the interests of literature. In the traditional family, the poet squanders the patrimony and is cursed; if it strictly obeyed the principle of utility, society would consider the writer to be a waster of resources who does not serve the principle of the society that nourishes him. I personally understand the "good man" who deems it a good thing to do away with or subjugate the writer. This shows that he takes seriously the urgency of the situation. It is perhaps simply the proof of this urgency.

Without renouncing his function, the writer may find himself in agreement with a rational political action aimed at increasing the strength of society. He may even support it in his writings if such action is a negation of the existing state of affairs. If his partisans are in power, he may choose not to combat their measures, choose not to remain silent. Only by denying himself, however, does he lend his support. If he does this, he may confer the authority of his name to his allegiance. The spirit, on the other hand, that gives meaning to this name, cannot follow this example. Whether the writer wants it or not, the spirit of literature always sides with squandering, with the absence of definite goals, and with passion whose only purpose is to eat away at itself, to play the part of gnawing remorse. Literature, when it is not indulgently considered to be a minor distraction, always takes a direction opposite the path of utility along which every society must be directed.

You will forgive me if I conclude with some considerations that are no doubt painfully theoretical, but which will clarify what I am trying to say.

It is no longer relevant to say that the writer is right, and that society that rules is wrong. Both have always been right *and* wrong. Only with calm can one see where the matter stands: two incompatible currents stimulate economic society which will always pit the *ruled* against the *rulers*. The rulers try to produce as much as possible and to reduce consumption. This division can moreover be found in each one of us. Those who are ruled want to consume as much as possible, and to work as little as they can. Now literature itself is consumption and on the whole, the literati are by nature in agreement with those inclined to squander.

What has always prevented one from reaching a decision about this opposition and these fundamental affinities, is that ordinarily, on the side of the consumers, everybody is tugging every which way. Furthermore, the strongest in society, in trying to outdo each other, granted themselves a power over and above the direction of the economy. In fact, the king and the nobility, leaving production management in the hands of the bourgeoisie, did their best to levy a great quantity of consumable products. The Church which took upon itself, in agreement with the nobility, the responsibility of raising sovereign figures above the people, used their immense prestige in the levying of yet another portion. The government of the regime which preceded democracy—royal, feudal, ecclesiastical—had a good sense of the compromise by which the sovereignty, divided superficially enough into opposite domains, *the spiritual and the temporal,* was unduly made to serve both the public good and the special interests of those in power. Indeed, an absolute sovereign attitude would be akin to sacrifice, and not to power or to the appropriation of wealth. Power and the abuse of power by a seventeenth-century sovereign subordinated the sovereign attitude to something other than itself. That attitude is nothing other than the authenticity of man; otherwise, it does not exist. If it serves ends other than itself, it is obviously no longer authentic (in short, to be sovereign is to serve no ends other than the ends of sovereignty). The moment of sovereignty's appearance must decisively prevail over the "political" and financial consequences of its manifestation. It goes without saying that this appearance does not come about by an act of authority, but through a pact with limitless desire. It seems that in the distant past, both gods and kings were slain or paralyzed by sovereignty. Royal sovereignty whose prestige has been or is being ruined, is a degraded sovereignty that, for a long time, has compromised with military power, a power residing with the commander-in-chief of the army. Nothing is farther from the holiness and violence of an authentic moment.

When it was simply the discreet auxiliary to religious or princely prestige, literature, along with art, clearly had no autonomy—it long answered to commands or expectations which revealed its inferiority. Yet from the outset, as soon as literature, avoiding authorial vanity, lays claim to vanity's opposite, sovereignty itself,—at large in the active and irreconcilable world,—it shows itself to be what it always was in spite of its many compromises: a movement irreducible to the aims of social utility. This movement is often taken into account in the basest calculations, but its essence is never debased in spite of its manifestation in particular cases. The truth is that its debasement is only a semblance. Bestsellers and the most servile of poems leave the freedom of poetry or of the novel intact, a freedom which the purest among us may still attain. Legal authority, on the other hand, through irremediable confusion, has ruined the sovereignty of princes and of priests.

By inheriting the divine prestige of these priests and princes, the modern writer most certainly receives at once the richest and the most formidable of inheritances. With good reason is "cursed" the epithet given to their heir's novel dignity. This "curse" may in fact be fortunate (aleatory though it be). What the prince welcomed as the most legitimate and enviable of blessings, the writer receives as a sad accession. His lot consists above all of his guilty conscience, an awareness of the impotence of words, and . . . the hope of never being understood! His "holiness" and his "royalty," perhaps his "divinity," appear at best to humiliate him. Far from being authentically sovereign and divine, what ruins him is the despair, or deeper down, the remorse that he is not God. . . . For he does not authentically possess a divine nature; and, nevertheless, he is not free not to be God!

Born from the decline of a sacred world that died from splendors both deceitful and colorless, *modern* literature at its birth seems more akin to death than does its fallen predecessor. This kinship is misleading. It nevertheless is charged with those disarming conditions that make one feel oneself alone to be "the salt of the earth." The *modern* writer can maintain a relation with productive society only by requiring from that society a protected reserve where, in place of the principle of utility, there reigns openly the denial of "signification," the non-meaning of what is first given to the mind as a finished coherence, an appeal to sensibility without discernable content, to emotion so vivid that it leaves to explication only a contemptible share. Without self-denial, however, or better yet, without lassitude, no one may have recourse to this explosion of untruths that compensate for those of royalty and the Church, and which differ only on one point: they, unlike those of the Church and of royalty, profess themselves to be untruths. The religious and royal hereditary myths were taken to be true. However, the non-meaning of modern literature is more profound than that of stones, for being non-meaning itself, it is the only conceivable meaning that man can still give to the imaginary object of his desire. Such perfect abnegation requires indifference, or rather, the maturity of a dead man. If literature is the silence of significations, it is in truth the prison whose every occupant wishes to escape.

The modern writer though, in compensation for these woes, wins a major privilege over those "kings" whom he succeeds; by renouncing the power which was the minor privilege of "kings," he acquires the major privilege of being able to do *nothing* and to limit himself within an *active* society to the paralysis of death before the fact.

It is too late today to look for an expedient! If the *modern* writer does not yet know what is incumbent upon him,—and the honesty, the rigor, and the lucid humility which this requires,—it matters little. From that moment on, he renounces a sovereign character, incompatible with error. Sovereignty, he should have known, did not bring him aid, but destruction. What he could have asked of sovereignty was to make of him a living corpse, a gay one perhaps, but one gnawed from within by death.

You know that this letter in its entirety is the only true expression I can give to my friendship for you.

Translated by Christopher Carsten

I. Detours of Rewriting

JEAN-LUC NANCY

Exscription

Of the two texts united here, the second alone will account for their
common title. Eleven years separate these two texts, and the reader
will sense this distance.[1] The writing of the second brought me back
however, in an unexpected way, to the first. A continuity seemed
inescapable, of a community with Bataille which goes beyond and
can go without theoretical discussion (which I can suppose lives on,
or at least endures with what can be called the tragic religion of
Bataille). This community therefore also goes beyond commentary,
exegesis, or interpretation of Bataille. It is not without distance or
reservations, but these are precisely theoretical. It is a community in
that Bataille immediately communicates to me that pain and that
pleasure which result from the impossibility of communicating anything at all without touching the limit where all meaning spills out of
itself like a simple ink stain on a word, on the word "meaning."[2] This
spilling and this ink are the ruin of theories of "communication,"
conventional chatter which promotes reasonable exchange and does
nothing but obscure violence, treachery and lies, while leaving the
power of unreason with no chance of being measured. But the reality
of community where nothing is shared without *also* being removed
from that kind of "communication," this reality has always already
revealed the vanity of such speeches. They communicate only the
postulation of the communication of a meaning, and of the meaning
of "communication." As for Bataille, beyond what he says and some-

1. The first, in a slightly different version, was published in the anthology *Misère
de la littérature* (Paris: Bourgois, collection "Première livraison," 1977).

2. See my *La Communauté désoeuvrée* (Minneapolis: The University of Minnesota Press, forthcoming), translated by Peter Connor and Christopher Fynsk.

YFS 78, *On Bataille,* ed. Allan Stoekl, © 1990 by Yale University.

times apart from what he says, he communicates community itself. That is, naked existence, naked writing, and how one silently, hauntingly refers us to the other, making us share meaning's nakedness: neither gods nor thoughts but that *us* imperceptibly and insuperably *exscribed*. Today there is a kind of necessity of saying this, of saying it again: we exist, we write, only "for" this staggering spillage of meaning. More than just a few years are repeated here; our whole tradition must re-appropriate its experience for itself. "Je ferai un vers de vrai rien . . . J'ai fait le vers, ne sais sur quoi" [I will make a verse from nothing at all . . . I made the verse, about what I know not], writes Guillaume de Poitiers around the year 1100.[3]

I. REASONS TO WRITE

Writing, on the Book

In a certain sense—very certain, in fact—it is no doubt nearly impossible today to "rien écrire" [write anything] on the book. This peculiar French usage of the word "rien" obliges one to understand at the same time both: it's no longer possible to write anything on the subject of the book, and it is no longer possible to get out of writing on the book.

It is no longer possible to write anything whatever about the book: if indeed "the question of the book" must be the issue, to borrow the expression from one of the texts which mark the horizon of this impossibility ("Edmond Jabès et la question du livre," by Jacques Derrida), we must at once postulate that as of now this question has been fully treated (although it has not been nor can it ever be the object of any treatise). A wish to posit, to invent anything about it today can only spring from ignorance or naïveté, whether real or feigned. Something definitive is as of now accomplished regarding this question, by a group, a network or whatever one wants to call it, of texts that can't be avoided, named Mallarmé, Proust, Joyce, Kafka, Bataille, Borgès, Blanchot, Laporte, Derrida. An incomplete list no doubt, an unjust one perhaps—it is nonetheless certain that we must not simply pass through them on the way, but *stay there*. Which is not at all fetishistic, idolatrous, or conservative—quite the contrary, as should be clear. It is time to affirm that the question of the book is

3. All citations from the many authors are woven into this text and will not be footnoted out of respect for the spirit of the article.

already *here*. Reactionary pietism consists in the exact opposite, in indefinitely soliciting these same texts so as to extract from them, and start up again in a thousand more or less declared ways, by gloss, imitation or exploitation, a question of the book in the form of speculation, *mise en abyme,* staging, fragmentation, denunciation or enunciation of the book, stretching as far as the eye can read.

I myself should have liked to content myself with patiently recopying these texts here. Nothing can assure me that I should not have done so.

But—at the same time, by the same categorical imperative—it's no longer possible to get out of writing on the book.

For this question is not a question, it is not a subject which can be considered as completely or incompletely explored—still less as exhausted. Exhaustion—an undefined exhaustion—forms rather the subject which must be tackled, here as elsewhere.

As for the book (Mallarmé's title and program), the loose ends of something in our history have now been tied up. The power of this knot does not come from the "genius" of these "authors" but signals the historical, more than historical, power and necessity which must have caused the writing of books to get all knotted up in itself. Since the West—what Heidegger made us think of as the West—decided as far back as human memory goes, to consign to books the knowledge of a truth deciphered in a Book—of the World, of God, indeed of the Id—which was nonetheless impossible to read or write, the West is knotted up with writer's cramp. This is in brief the well-known main reason for what we have continually to go and read again in these texts.

And of what we have to write again—on condition that we not, following the fashion which forgets the implacable lesson of Pierre Ménard, allow the concept of "writing again" to tumble down to the level of the "rewrite."

According to a law which all these texts contain, and articulate, and whose rigor needs no demonstration, this history stricken by writer's cramp can only end by repeating itself. Never fully dealt with, the question of the book marks the resurgence of repetition. Not of sa *propre* [its *own*] repetition because it is, inasmuch as it is, the question of what remains without property (property and literary communism, that is the question). Repetition is the form, the substance of what does not have its identity printed once and for all (nor more than once) in the untranscribable Book. For whoever happens to be deprived of this identity—for everyone in the West—repetition forms the question of the book, the question which must be written in order to dissolve in its writing—what?

In order—but the gesture of writing is never satisfied with a teleology—to dissolve—but in a dissolution itself dissociated from the values of solution conferred on it by metaphysics—not merely the ideal identity inscribed in the blinding whiteness of the Book.

(for in the depth of eternal light, everything which is scattered in the universe is reunited as if bound by love into a single book. Dante.)

but to dissolve this identity to the point of a loss, a privation which is also a privatization, to dissolve even the Book itself to the point of loss, privation, privatization. The Book is there—in every book the virgin refolding of the book takes place (Mallarmé)—we must *write on it*, make it a palimpsest, overload it, muddy its pages with added lines to the point of utmost confusion of signs and of writings: we must in short fulfill its original unreadability, clutching it in the shapeless exhausted hand of the cramp.

What for? we must indeed take the risk: we must write on the book *for a deliverance.* Which would scarcely have to do with Freedom (I mean with that subjective, subject, subjugated Freedom which God or the Spirit of metaphysics automatically confer upon themselves). Writing ought to slip into the interstice of the strange homonym *liber/liber,* into the everyday ambiguity of *livraison* [delivery].

Writing? tormenting yourself, quite vainly hoping for the moment of deliverance? (Bataille)

—and the sentence which follows in the same story, *Histoire de rats:*

My reason for writing is to reach B.

B. is the woman in the story, but her initial and the sentence itself have us read woman, this woman, a woman and a man and B.; Bataille himself, and a place and a book and a thought and deliverance "itself," in person without any allegorism.

Such is repetition: renewal, rewriting of the petition, of the effort to reach and join, of the request, of the demand, of the plea, of the claim, of the supplication. Rewriting on the book is the renewed clamor or murmur of a demand, of a pressing call. If the texts which I have mentioned do *remain* henceforth in our history, it's because they have not dealt with any question but have knotted this call into a lump in one or more throats of writing: a grand glottal spasm.

They have knotted the ethical and more than ethical call for a

deliverance, onto a deliverance. It is imperative not to answer it . . .
the neutral, writes Blanchot, denominating as neutral the literary act
which bringing an *unanswerable problem* to the closure of an *aliquid*
to which the question wouldn't correspond—or rather it would be
indispensable to distinguish with all possible care two incommensurable concepts: the answer to a question and the answer to a call.

It may be that one can answer a call only be repeating it—like
night watchmen. It may be that it is not the response which is imperative, but only the *obligation* of responding, which is called responsibility. How, in the book, can the issue be responsibility? Eluding it is
no longer possible any more than avoiding this: how, in writing where
the Voice is absent (a voice without writing is at once absolutely alive
and absolutely dead. Derrida), is a call to be heard, how can it be a
question of vocation, invocation or advocation? How in general can
the book's full otherness be delivered?

All these texts have exhausted the theme, the theory, the practice,
the metamorphosis, the future, the fugue, or the cut of the book for no
other reason than to repeat this call.

I myself had something else to write, longer and for more than one
person. Long in the writing. It would be a book as long as the Thousand and One Nights, perhaps, but quite different (Proust).

Repetitions

All the same, it is probably better to dot the *i's* of repetition, at the
risk of repeating myself somewhat.

The reduplication of the book at its own heart, the self-representation of literature, each book's story of its own birth—of its own deliv-
ery—its self-analysis, or perhaps the involution of its message in the
display of its code, or the figuration of its procedures in the narrative
or demonstrative process of the formation of its figures or the putting
into play of its rules by the game's rules themselves, all that in a word
I will call autobibliography, all this dates from the invention of the
book. Everything on the strength of which our modernity gained
entire libraries—it had to be, it was necessary by that very necessity
of the book which no written text escapes (the useless prolix epistle
which I am writing already exists in one of the thirty volumes on the
five bookshelves in one of the innumerable hexagons—and so does its
refutation.—*The library of Babel*—, all this makes up the self-repeti-
tion which unavoidably constitutes the book from birth. The reason I

write is to reach B.: Babel, Bible, bibliology, bibliomancy, biblio-
mania, bibliophilia, *bibliothèque* [library].

This is what the book has more accurately ended up reciting and
harking back to, in the age of its material invention: in the age of
printing, age of the true book, age of the fully developed subject and of
communication. Printing has satisfied the need to relate to each
other in an ideal mode (Hegel). Since then everything has happened as
if all the ideal content of communication consisted in autobibliography. All books display the being or the law of the book: from the
beginning it has no object but itself, and this satisfaction. I am writing
to you, daughter, with pleasure, even though I have no news for you
(Mme de Sévigné).

Everything has been said, and we come too late, in the more than
seven thousand years that there have been thinking men: so it is that
the first chapter on books must be begun, in a book entitled *Characters*. The exhaustion of material prescribes the infinite number of
possible ways to form the signs of it. It's the history of the world
which we are now visiting, the goddess tells him: it's the book of its
destinies. Move into another room and there is another world, another book—somewhere in it you will find the *Essays* concerned
with theodicy where it's all written, and you'll read there that all
Borgès ever wrote was but a thought of Leibnitz's which Lichtenberg
had already recopied: the libraries will be cities. No place will be free
of books, even if there should happen to be a lack. You are quite right,
sir, there is a whole chapter missing here, leaving a hole of at least ten
pages in the book, writes Tristram, the author who also recounts his
own birth. Nor will any book be free of books, for, not content to
inscribe our name on anonymous thoughts by a single author, we
appropriate those of thousands of individuals, epochs, and entire libraries, and we steal even from plagiarists, writes Jean Paul plagiariz-
ing himself one more time. The textual anthology—choosing flowers
from books, choosing books so as to arrange in each book the bouquet
of its literariness—continues unabated all the way down to us.

All this repetition *en abyme* of the book constitutes its redundancy, both native to it and more naïve than is usually thought. Redundancy is the overflow of the undulating wave, its excess: the Book has
always been thought of as the endlessly spouting spray of an inex-
haustible ocean—wouldn't a jet of grandeur, of thought, or of considerable emotion, a sentence pursued in large type spaced out to one line
a page, keep the reader in good condition for the length of the book

(Mallarmé). The wave repeats itself and falls back again. This repetition is perhaps properly called composition: to compose is to gather back together, to put back in, to bring back home, and to reduce. Every book brings back the redundancy of the Book to the space delimited by an inscription. In each of its temples, autobibliography is worshiped.

—on condition that it know nothing of the other repetition for which in fact it is only the exchange of the remuneration. The age of printing is indeed the age of the subject—there is no book that is not the book of an 'I,' and 'I' repeats itself, that is how it can be recognized.

I have no more made my book than my book has made me—a book consubstantial with its author. The subject sets itself up as a Book, and only this self-erection has ever secured the substance of a subject—whose frank dissimulation allows desire to be read like an open book: thus, reader, I am myself the matter of my book; you would be unreasonable to spend your leisure on so frivolous and vain a subject. I am not building here a statue to erect at the town crossroads, this is for a nook in a library, and to amuse a neighbor. Others form man; I tell of him, and portray a particular one, very ill-formed. I want people to see my natural and ordinary pace, however off the track it is. My reason for writing is to reach B.—to reach myself, to reach in her my society, her solitude, to reach him, her who says 'I,' not natural, not ordinary.

'I' repeats its desire to itself—but can that desire be anything but off the track? That the I display itself is not enough to make it visible. Someone gets lost irremediably in the matter of his book—someone who will not stop repeating to himself: "the matter of my experience, which will be the matter of my book" and this time it's Proust. Lost in every book, someone—who is and isn't the one who says I—repeats himself. Through the *abyme* of autobibliography and in spite of this *abyme*, an autograph walks into the abyss. Its errant movement begins at the same crossroads as its self-erection.

This is the autograph which takes its singular leave at the very opening of its book. So farewell. Montaigne, this first day of March, fifteen hundred and eighty. Signature of place, signature of name, signature of farewell, it enters it own book as if it were a tomb. It is sameness which, in altering its identity and its singularity, divides their seal (Derrida).

Literal and literary repetition belongs to him who goes astray in his own marks—in the speeches of his own wake, like Finnegan's, signs are on of a mere by token that wills still to be becoming upon this there once a here was: an exodus has begun again, here, and someone has entered into the history of his diaspora. The repeated call comes from him. It's the call of a solitude which preexists any isolation, the invocation of a community which neither contains nor precedes any society. How to deliver the full otherness common to all books? someone asks, some writer or other, an 'I' who is called.

> *bent over the book open to the same*
> *page*
> *what he hears are the songs from*
> *the other side where the others are (Jacqueline Risset)*

The Story he Writes himself about the Book

is a story which conforms with his desire and his exodus. Writing, he says, marks everywhere the end of communism. That is, of what he has never known, because he was born with writing.

But he writes in his books—and in all his books—what communism was, the book's absence. The book never pretends to anything less than retracing what exceeds it. The question of the book's origin will never belong to any book (Derrida)—and yet, O memory! you who have written what I have seen, here will be seen your nobility (Dante). So he writes the world of the bard, the storyteller, the sacred reciter. The first poet, who took this step so as to free himself through the crowd's imagination, knows how to return through it to real life. For he goes off right and left to tell the crowd the exploits which his imagination attributes to the hero. This hero is, fundamentally, no one but himself. But the poet's listeners, who understand him, know how to identify themselves with the hero (Freud). This pure self-poïesis in pure community continually haunts all of literature: and it's a man of the here, a man of the now, who is his own narrator, in the end (Robbe-Grillet).

It was, he says, the world of a mime who had no models and no imitators, the world of the brilliant improviser, of the dancer drunk on god, of the drumbeats, the blows, the whistling of an unwritten music, the world of prayers, supplications, invocations. It's the tribe with its words and recitations, the chanting cry of the primitive commune around its hearth—silent writing of a fire so bright that it tears without leaving a trace (Laporte).

Which is followed, in the story we tell ourselves, by the society of that writing which is not the book but the engraving of sacred characters, the inscription of the Laws on tablets of stone or metal, on columns, pilasters, pediments, and mouldings, hard writing and everywhere the erection of steles setting forth the Order and the Arrangement, the Structure and the Model, for no one and thus for all: this was monumental communism, architectural writing and hieroglyphic monarchy. All the words must have a characteristic aspect of depth or prominence, engraving or sculpture, the writer of maxims (Joubert) says of sacred writing. And every book tends uncontrollably toward the maxim: *maxima sententia*, the greatest thought . . .

Last comes—from nowhere and everywhere, from Egypt, Ionia, Canaan—the book; last comes *ta biblia*, the irremediably plural Bible, the Law, the Prophets, the Scripture, as it divides itself, lays itself out, puts itself *en abyme*, and disseminates itself. It is and is not the Book of only one—author or people.

Last comes the very belated, very old religion of books, and all the exodi begin. Egypt, Ionia, Canaan move, constantly scattering communes crossing the desert.

The history of books begins by losing itself in the book of history. There nothing tells us who if anyone wrote the very first pact which is nonetheless called the Book of the Alliance (*Exodus*, 27:7). It's the history of the pact—a pact of deliverance—broken, kept, betrayed, still offered—and of the renewed call to sign it once again. Scarcely graven before they were broken, the Tablets are never set up, they wander in the Ark with the wandering tribes. The Scrolls unroll and the volume of history swells until it reaches us; the book is inseparable from the story, the history of the novel: the age of the book is romanticism. In our writings thought seems to proceed with the movement of a man who walks straight ahead. In the writings of the ancients, on the contrary, it seems to proceed by the movement of a bird which soars and whirls as it goes forward (Joubert).

Who does not see that I have taken a road along which I shall go, without stopping and without effort, as long as there is ink and paper in the world?

Books begin with their repetition: two stories of genesis mingle, overlap, repeat and contradict themselves. Books are copied, reproduced, *published* because they are not in themselves public as either a song or an obelisk; we transmit them, translate them—

seventy-two Jews, six from each tribe in seventy-two days on the island of Pharos, made the Bible Greek—, we betray them, counterfeit them, imitate them, recopy, recite, and cite them. Whoever says 'I' mixes up books and signatures in his book: In the reasonings and inventions that I transplant into my soil and confound with my own, I have sometimes deliberately not indicated the author, in order to hold in check the temerity of those hasty condemnations that are tossed at all sorts of writings. Here the repeated repetition begins again.

Books are a corruptible matter. Books are made of wood: *biblos, liber, codex, Buch,* it's always bark or tree. It burns, it rots, it decomposes, it can be erased, it falls to the gnawing criticism of mice. Bibliophilia is, just as much as philosophy, an impossible love, its objects discolored, faded, worn-out, cut-up, full of holes. Books are miserable, hateful. Descartes hates the job of making books. There is nothing for the Subject—the other, the same; who says 'I' (think)—in the tomes, nothing but loss of time, a life uselessly consumed in reading the scraps of knowledge that I myself can found. There should be some legal restraint aimed against inept and useless writers, as there is against vagabonds and idlers. Both I and a hundred others would be banished from the hands of our people. This is no jest. Scribbling seems to be a sort of symptom of an unruly age. When did we write so much as since our dissensions began? since our writing has been troubled.

For he who says 'I' *must* nonetheless write, the demonstration is inexorable: thinking through the problem of the ego and the alter ego, of the originary coupling and the human community, Husserl writes: In all this there are essential laws or an essential style the root of which lies first in the transcendental ego, and in the transcendental intersubjectivity which the ego discovers in it, and consequently in the essential structures of transcendental motivation and constitution. Success in elucidating them would in itself give this aprioristic style a supremely honorable rational explanation: final transcendental intelligibility. Husserl writes what he doesn't want—to write. He writes that the originating alteration of the ego, the community of men, forms or deforms style, writing, even intelligibility, the ultimate success of which it deciphers.

Thus supplication through the book began at the same time as the persecution of books. Writing is tied to a cruel simulacrum of torture (Laporte). And now, through the glass everyone can see the inscription being etched on the body of the prisoner. Obviously a simple writing can't be used, it mustn't kill on the spot, but within twelve hours on the average (Kafka, "The Penal Colony").

The officer in charge of the machine executes himself, at the end of the story, by engraving on his own body the law which he has violated: *Be Just!* But only the mad machine is left to apply the law savagely—communism and capitalism writing machines. Yet it is the same appeal: How to deliver the book's full otherness?

Apocalypse

And what if books always announced, always provoked, the resumption in this story of what has no place there, does not happen there? And what if we understood why, today, speaking, writing, we must always speak *several times at the same time*, speaking according to the logic of discourse and thus under the nostalgia of the theological logos, speaking too to make possible a communication of speech which can only be decided on the basis of a communism of relations of exchange and thus of production—but also not speaking, writing in a break with any language of speech and writing (Blanchot)?

At the end of books, there is the *Apocalypse*. This is the kind of prophecy—call, that is—which is actually written. It is the book of the end of the world, the book of the new beginning. Its writer says and I say his name—John—and he names his place of exile—the island of Patmos. This book is a letter to the scattered churches, to the secret community bereft of its communion. In this letter a letter is addressed to each one of the churches, to each one of the assemblies. The letter is repeated, divided, transformed: To the Angel of the Church of Ephesus, write: Thus speaks he who holds the seven stars (John). To them in Ysat Loka. Hearing. The urb it orbs. Then's now with now's then in tense continuant. Heard. Who having has he shall have had. Hear! (Joyce).

John writes in this book the visions which it is given to him to see: but he only writes because the visions command him to write. The Angel speaks to him holding the Book but John does not recopy it: he writes what the Angel dictates to him. What is revealed is not the Angel nor the Book: it is man's writing. He who is announced through revelation, who says in his turn who he is, is he who says—of whom John writes that he says he is the alpha and omega. He is the Book, of course, but also: nothing but the final count of the characters of writing—that is all that is revealed of the seven broken seals of the book of the slaughtered Lamb. It's the end of religion.

John writes all his visions of writings. But in the middle, he is forbidden to write the words of the seven thunderclaps. No book delivers the unheard, inaudible, deafening speech—the primitive tumult the sound of which would have given rise to the exaltation of the mystical community. But the book knows of the scattering of the communion—it is the inscription of it and it communicates its call: Let the hearer say "Come!" *Come!* punctuates the Apocalypse and our books on books. Come, and restore to us the conventions of what disappears, the movement of a heart (Blanchot quoted by Derrida). It's up to you to take the step of meaning. There is no chance of deciding, no future in deciding, in whatever language, what comes in "Come" (Derrida).

It is not a call to communication, but the propagation of the repetition of the appeal, or the order and of the demand which bear, produce, convey, teach nothing, *rien—viens*, —which do not call for a response but for the simple obligation to respond, the responsibility to write again with the twenty-five letters which contain no revelation but only their own exhaustion.

Here the exhaustion is initial: the reason I write is to reach B.—to go from the first to the second letter, to trace letters tied one to the other, which calls writing, which calls a woman, a man, a book, a story and always like B. in the story an impossible unsustainable nudity.

Far beyond and far short of what any speech can unveil of the real—far beyond and far short of any One Book, apocalypse is still to be discovered, the discovery which shakes all books: that the book and the communion are stripped, dis-covered, in all books. The book's absence is the absence of Communion—our communion or a share of one to all and of all to one (Mallarmé). But also the presence— always instantly swallowed up—of the book. John must swallow a little book. I took the little book and swallowed it; in my mouth it had the sweetness of honey, but when I had eaten it, it filled my guts with bitterness.

What communicates, what is taken in communion is nothing, is not nothing, nothing but bitterness, but a call; another communism, in the future but not the close of history, a communism of exodus and repetition, would mean nothing (but, as Blanchot says, *in addition to* what they mean, what do words want: relations of exchange, thus of production?), but this communism would write the deliverance of books, in books. Vain so long as it is bookish (it's Montaigne who made up the word)—and how could it not be, starting right here?—, but no doubt also bookish so long as it is vain, so long as writing, still and once again, is not openly at risk in it.

I repeat: The reasons for writing a book can be reduced to the desire to modify the relations existing between a man and his fellows. These relations are judged unacceptable and are perceived as a dreadful misery (Bataille).

Far calls. Coming, far. End here. Us then (Joyce).

(April 1977)

II. REASONS TO READ

It is becoming urgent to stop commenting on Bataille (even though the commentary on him is still quite sparse). We ought to know it, Blanchot hinted at it, appropriately, refusing to comment on this rejection of commentary. Therefore I have no intention of commenting on him in Blanchot's stead. (But Blanchot so often does nothing but "comment on" Bataille: thinking with him, conversing with him to infinity. Thus he writes: "How had he ended up wishing for the interruption of discourse? And not the legitimate pause which permits the give-and-take of conversations . . . What he had wanted was something quite different, to stop it cold, to break into the circle. And at once it had happened: the heart ceasing to beat, the eternal talking drive stopping.")[4]

Moreover there can be no question of "refusing." There has never been and will never be anything simply reprehensible or simply false in commenting on what, by venturing into writing, has already presented itself for commentary, and in reality has already begun to comment on itself.

But such is the ambiguity of Bataille: he has become involved in discourse, and in writing, deeply enough to expose himself to the full necessity of commentary. And thus to its servility. He has advanced his thought far enough for its seriousness to deprive him of the divine capricious evanescent sovereignty which was however his sole "object." (That limit, heart-rending and sorrowful, joyous and relieved,

4. Maurice Blanchot, *L'Entretien infini* (Paris: Gallimard, 1970), 26.

that deliverance from thought, which does not abdicate—quite the
contrary—but which no longer has reason to be, or has not yet reason
to be. That freedom predating all thought, which there can never be
any question of making into either object or subject.)

But when he eluded the gesture, the proposition and the position
of a thinker, a philosopher, a writer (and he ceaselessly eludes, not
finishing his texts, still less the "sum" or the "system" of his thought,
leaving even his sentences unfinished on occasion, or else relent-
lessly withdrawing by an eccentric, lopsided syntax what the progression of a line of thought was laying down as a logic or a *topic*)—
when he stole away, he also stole from us access to what he was
communicating to us.

"Ambiguity": is that the word? Perhaps, if it's a matter of acting, of
a simulacrum—which we mustn't hesitate to impute to him *also*.
Bataille always *played* at being unable to finish, put on an act of
excess, stretching writing to its bursting point, the excess of what
makes writing: that is to say what simultaneously inscribes and ex-
scribes it. It was a game and an act, for he wrote ceaselessly, writing
everywhere, always, the exhaustion of his writing. He both said and
wrote this game, this act. He wrote that he was guilty of talking about
the glass of alcohol instead of drinking it and getting drunk. Drunk on
words and pages to express and at the same time drown the immense
futile guilt of the game. Saving himself that way, too, as it were, and
always oversure of finding salvation in the game itself. Thus not
detaching himself from too visibly a Christian theater of confession,
absolution and relapse into sin, and of dependence on forgiveness all
over again. (Christianity as theater: the repair of the irreparable.
Bataille himself knew how much theater there was in sacrifice. But
the question is not of opposing to this the abyss of a "purely irreparable." What must rid us of the spirit of catastrophe which dominates
us is a higher freedom, more terrible perhaps but in quite another way.

That theater too is ours: a sacrifice of writing by writing, which
writing redeems. There is no doubt that some have hammed it up
compared with what were, in spite of everything, Bataille's restraint
and sobriety. No doubt that too much has been made of the writer's
nails being torn out, of suffocation in underground vaults of literature
and philosophy. Unless sequences of thought have been hastily reconstructed, gaps filled in with ideas. (A commentary in both cases.)
This does not urge on any critic commentaries on Bataille (and if that
were necessarily the case I would be implicated). There are powerful

and important commentaries, without which we could not even pose the question of his commentary.

But after all Bataille wrote "I want to arouse the greatest mistrust. I only speak of lived experiences; I do not confine myself to imaginary actions" (6, 261).[5]

How can we not be affected by this mistrust? How can we simply go on with reading, then close the book, or make notes in its margins? If I underline just this passage and quote it as I have just done, I betray it already, I reduce it to a "state of intellection" (as Bataille says elsewhere). Yet it had already been reduced to something in which intellection certainly doesn't exhaust everything, but nonetheless oversees the stage. Elsewhere still Bataille writes that writing is the "mask" of a cry and a non-knowledge. What then does that writing do which writes that very thing? How could it not mask what at one moment it unveils? And how could it not mask, in the end, the very mask which it says it is and which it says it is applying to a "screaming silence"? The blow cannot be parried, the mechanism or machination of discourse is implacable. Far from rising to deafen us, the cry (or the silence) has been spirited away by being named or indicated, under a mask which is all the harder to locate for having been supposedly shown, named in its turn, in order to be denounced.

Ambiguity is therefore inevitable, insurmountable. It is nothing other than the ambiguity of *meaning* itself. Meaning should signify, but what makes meaning, or the meaning of meaning as it were, is in truth nothing other than "this empty freedom, this infinite transparence of what finally doesn't have the burden of having a meaning" (6, 76). Bataille never ceased to fight this burden, he wrote only to free himself from it—to reach liberty, to let it reach him—, but writing, speaking, he could only make himself once again responsible for some signification. "Dedicating oneself out of principle to this silence, philosophizing, speaking, is always a murky business: the sliding without which the exercise could not be then becomes the movement of thought itself" (11, 286). The ambiguity lies in emptying experience of thought, through thought; this is philosophy, this is literature. And yet emptied experience is not stupidity—even if there is stupor in it.

Any commentary on Bataille involves him in a direction of mean-

5. All references to Bataille are taken from the *Oeuvres complètes* (Paris, Gallimard, 1970), and will appear in the text as vol., p.

ing, toward something univocal. Therefore Bataille himself, when he wanted to write *on* the thought with which he had most in common, wrote *Sur Nietzsche* in a move essentially intent on *not commenting on* Nietzsche, on not writing *on* him. "Nietzsche wrote with his blood—whoever criticizes him or, better, puts him to the text can do it only if he himself is bleeding." "Let no one doubt it for an instant: you can't understand a word of Nietzsche's work before experiencing that dazzling dissolution in its totality" (6, 15, 22).

But the same goes for all commentary, of whatever author, of whatever text it may be. In a writer's text, and also in a commentator's text (which every writer's text is in its turn) what matters, what thinks (at the very limit of thought if necessary) is what does not lend itself wholly to a univocal meaning but which stumbles under the load of meaning and throws it off balance. Bataille never stops exposing this. Alongside all the themes he deals with, through all the questions he debates, "Bataille" is *nothing but* a protest against the signification of his own discourse. If he is to be read, if reading rebels straight away against the commentary which it is, and against the understanding which it ought to be, we have to read in every line the work or the play of writing *against* meaning.

This has nothing to do with nonsense, nor with the absurd, nor with a mystical, philosophical, or poetic esotericism. Paradoxically, it's straight from the sentence—straight from the words and syntax, a way, often clumsy or lopsided, removed in any case as much as possible from the operation of a "style" ("in the acoustico-decorative sense of the term" as Borgès says) of weighing on meaning itself, given and recognizable, a way of interfering with or impeding the communication of this meaning, not first to us, but to this meaning itself. And reading must remain in its turn unwieldy, awkward and, without ceasing to decode, beyond decoding. This reading remains caught in the strange materiality of language, it conforms with the singular communication which is carried on not only by meaning but by language itself or rather, which is nothing more than the communication of language with itself without making out meaning, in a suspension of meaning, fragile, repeated. Real reading goes forward unknowing, it always opens a book like an unjustifiable cut in the supposed *continuum* of meaning. It must go astray at this break.

This reading—which is first of all reading itself, all reading, inevitably given over to the sudden, flashing, sliding movement of a writing which precedes it and which it will rejoin only by reinscribing it elsewhere and otherwise, in ex-scribing it outside itself—this reading still does not comment (this is a *beginning* reading, an *incipit* which is always begun again), it is neither equal to nor in a position for interpreting, for causing meaning. It is rather a surrender to that abandon to language where the writer has exposed himself. "There is no pure and simple communication; what is communicated has a direction [*sens*] and a color" (2, 315), (and *sens* here means movement, advance). It does not know where it is going, and doesn't have to. No other reading is possible without it, and every "reading" (in the sense of commentary, exegesis, interpretation) must come back to it.

But in this way Bataille and his reader are already displaced with respect to ambiguity. There is not on the one hand the ambiguity of meaning—of all possible meanings, the ambiguity of univocal meanings multiplied by all "acts of intellection"—and on the other hand the "ambiguity" of the meaning which unburdens itself of all possible meaning. Something quite different is finally in question, which Bataille knew: it is perhaps the very thing that he "knew" above all, *"knowing nothing."* It's not a question of that necessary, ridiculous machination of meaning which puts itself forward as it withdraws, or which puts on a mask as it signifies itself. To leave it at that condemns writing without appeal (certainly this condemnation haunted Bataille) and also condemns to being ridiculous or intolerable the wish to affirm a writing removed from intellection and identical to life ("I have always put into my writings my whole life and my whole self, I know nothing about what might be purely intellectual problems" [6, 261]). For this is still, always, a discourse full of meaning and which steals the "life" *of which it speaks.*

There is something else, and without the "knowledge" of it Bataille would not have written anymore than anyone else: in truth "ambiguity" does not exist, or it exists only as long as thought considers meaning. But there is no more ambiguity once it is clear (and it necessarily is before any consideration of meaning) that writing *ex-scribes* meaning just as much as it inscribes significations. It ex-scribes meaning, that is it shows that what it's about, the thing itself, Bataille's "life" or "cry," and finally the existence of everything which is "in question" in the text (including most singularly writing's own existence) that all these are outside the text, take place outside writing.

At the same time this "outside" is not that of a referent to which signification would refer (thus the "real" life of Bataille, signified by the words "my life") the referent does not present itself as such except by signification. But this "outside"—entirely exscribed into the text—is the infinite retreat of meaning by which each existence exists. Not the brute datum, material, concrete, reputed to be outside meaning and which meaning represents but the "empty freedom" through which the living being comes to presence—and absence. This freedom is not empty in the sense of being vain. No doubt it is not directed toward a project, a meaning or a work. But it uses the work of meaning to expose, to lay bare the unusable, unexploitable, unintelligible and unfoundable *being* of being-in-the-world. *That there is* being, or some being or even beings, and in particular that there is *us*, our community (of writing-reading): that is what instigates all possible meanings, that is what is the very place of meaning, but which has no meaning.

Writing, and reading, is to be exposed, to expose oneself to this not-having (to this not-knowing) and thus to "exscription." The exscribed is exscribed from the first word, not as an "unsayable" or as an "uninscribable" but on the contrary as that opening into itself of writing to itself, to its own inscription as the infinite discharge of meaning—in all the senses one should give the expression. Writing, reading, I exscribe the thing itself, "existence," the "real"—which *is* only exscribed and whose *being* alone is what's at stake in inscription. In inscribing significations, we exscribe the presence of what withdraws from all signification, being itself (life, passion, substance. . .) .

The being of existence can be presented: it presents itself when exscribed. Bataille's cry is neither masked nor stifled; it makes itself heard as *the cry that is not heard*. In writing the real does not represent itself, it presents the unheard-of-violence and restraint, the surprise and freedom of being in exscription where writing at every moment discharges itself, unburdens itself, empties itself, of itself.

But "exscripted" is not a word in the language nor can one fabricate it as I do here without being mangled by one's own barbarism. The word "exscripted" exscribes nothing and writes nothing, it makes clumsy gestures to indicate what must write itself alone, straight out of the always uncertain thought of language. "The nudity of the word 'write' remains," writes Blanchot,[6] who compares it to the nudity of Madame Edwarda.

There remains Bataille's nakedness, his naked writing, exposing

6. Blanchot, *Après-coup* (Paris, Minuit, 1983), 91.

the nakedness of all writing. Obscure and clear like a skin, like a pleasure, like a fear. But comparisons are not enough. The nakedness of writing *is* the nakedness of existence. Writing is naked because it "exscripts," existence is naked because it is "exscripted."

From one to the other passes the light and violent tension of that suspension of meaning which comprises all "meaning"; that *jouissance* so absolute that it accedes to its own joy only by losing itself in it, by spilling itself into it, and it appears as the absent heart (absence which beats like a heart) of presence. It is the heart of things which is exscripted.

In a sense Bataille must be present to us with that presence which distances signification and which itself would be communication. Not a united body of work made communicable, interpretable ("Collected Works," so precious and necessary, still cause unease; they communicate as complete what was only written in pieces and by chance) but the dawdling, now over, of an exscription of finitude. Released in it are an infinite *jouissance,* a pain and a pleasure so real that touching them (reading exscripted) convinces us at once of the absolute meaning of their nonsignification.

In yet another sense, it is Bataille himself, dead. That is, the exasperation of every moment of reading in the certitude that the man who wrote what is being read existed and the confounding evidence that the meaning of his work and the meaning of his life are the same nakedness, the same denuding of meaning which distances them from each other as well—by the full distance of an in(x)scription.

The dead Bataille and his books offered as his writing leaves them: they're the same thing, the same ban on comment and comprehension (the same ban on killing). It's the implacable and joyous counterblow one must strike against all hermeneutics so that literature (and) existence can once again expose themselves; in the singularity, in the reality, in the freedom of "the common destiny of man" (11, 311).

Speaking of Bataille's death, Blanchot wrote: "the reading of books must open us to the necessity of that disappearance in which they withdraw. Books themselves refer us to an existence."[7]

(August 1988)

Translated by Katherine Lydon

7. Blanchot, *L'Amitié* (Paris, Gallimard, 1973), 327.

REBECCA COMAY

Gifts without Presents: Economies of "Experience" in Bataille and Heidegger*

What would it take (and what would it give) to think the logic of the gift in its most rigorous form? To think a giving so "pure" it would tolerate no return—no payment, no feedback, no profit, however secret—a giving which would exceed every circuit of compensation and challenge every measure of exchange? A gift so generous it would shatter the circle of adequation on which reason itself depends?

Hegel, Nietzsche, Marx had all insisted, in this regard, on a certain modicum of suspicion. The kickbacks could be subtle, no less potent for being, at times, "symbolic," no less real for being deferred. Hegel had demonstrated zealously, in the *Phenomenology*, how very easily the most innocent seeming gesture of renunciation slides into grandiosity and self-reward. Did not almost every finite shape of consciousness—the unhappy consciousness, the obsequious nobleman,

*I would like to thank Julian Patrick for his careful reading of an earlier version, and Hélène Comay for her generous help with some difficult translations.

All references to Bataille's text, except where indicated, are noted in the text by volume and page of the *Oeuvres Complètes*, 12 volumes (Paris: Gallimard, 1970–89).

The following abbreviations to the texts of Heidegger will be used:

EM: *Einführung in die Metaphysik* (Tübingen: Meyer, 1966).
  G: *Gelassenheit* (Pfullingen: Neske, 1959).
  N: *Nietzsche*, 2 volumes (Pfullingen: Neske, 1961).
  SZ: *Sein und Zeit* (Tübingen: Niemeyer, 1979).
  SU: *Die Selbstbehauptung der deutschen Universität* (Frankfurt: Klostermann, 1983).
  US: *Unterwegs zur Sprache* (Pfullingen: Neske, 1959).
WHD: *Was Heisst Denken?* (Tübingen: Niemeyer, 1954).
ZSD: *Zur Sache des Denkens* (Tübingen: Niemeyer, 1969).
And for Sartre, the following abbreviation:
  NM: "Un nouveau mystique," *Situations* 1 (Paris: Gallimard, 1947).

YFS 78, *On Bataille*, ed. Allan Stoekl, © 1990 by Yale University.

the superstitious sacrificer, the beautiful soul (to name only the most glaring examples)—expose its own immaturity precisely by its inability to let go? Did it not stealthily aggrandize itself with every loss, snatch a victory from every fall? Was it not the very fate of an immature consciousness to remain attached to the calculus of equivalence—ultimately the shopkeeper's scales of justice—the binary logic of *Verstand?* In the *Genealogy,* Nietzsche had linked such a recuperative logic to the resentful phantasms of the servile consciousness. Avaricious, anal, unable to "be done" with things, it was the slave who quietly stockpiled his disadvantages to secure compensation in a future heaven. He took secret payoffs for his petty sacrifices, surreptitiously profited from every pain. Unlike the noble consciousness—wasteful, extravagant, Zarathustra's "squanderer with a thousand hands"—the slave waited, counted, plotted the advantage in every setback, took the measure of every loss. Abstract thinking was the method; constipation, the price; Christianity, the result.

Capitalism, the final product. Marx was to inscribe this entire structure of restitution within the political economy of the day. If every class society is marked by the private accumulation of surplus value, capitalism distinguishes itself by its official ideology of just exchange. For if capitalist accumulation requires every surplus to be reinvested in the system as the investment of a surplus value, it would simultaneously cover the fact by insisting on the appearance of a free exchange.

Adorno once remarked that it is a symptom of class society (and in particular our own society, the society of surplus which creates the very possibility of surplus "theory") that the ability to give has been eroded. Gift-giving—what had been the paradigm of "every undistorted relationship,"[1] the promise of the conciliation of and with nature itself—becomes constricted into the contractual exchange between partners. What such a society cannot think (the logic of identity excludes it) is the possibility of an encounter that would upset the regulated equilibrium of accounts. For the gift would mark a point of incommensurability which would challenge the ideology of adequation and reciprocity on which capitalism must depend. It would upset the homeostatic order of restitution and exchange, introducing a measure beyond calculation, exposing the prevailing ide-

1. Theodor Adorno, *Minima Moralia, Gesammelte Schriften* 4 (Frankfurt: Suhrkamp, 1980), 46ff.

ology of just exchange between equals as just the mask worn by the system to cover up the real inequities of the day.

It is at this point that Bataille and Heidegger—separately and together, at the point of their most unspoken and profound entanglement—may offer food for thought.

I.

I have only a breathless interest for the philosophies of time . . .
—Bataille, *L'Expérience intérieure*

So I would like to argue for a certain "communication" between Heidegger and Bataille. This communication is seemingly awkward for the fact that it never, as such, took place, and it is striking for the great distances which will have to be traversed. For the exchange will span more than the geo-cultural abyss which separates the lecture halls of Freiburg from the literary haunts of wartime Paris. It will span more than the various institutional abysses which separate the philosophical explication of Being from the after-hours researches of an archivist at the Bibliothèque Nationale. While Heidegger was studying the history of Western metaphysics, Bataille, in his spare time, conducted anthropological investigations into human sacrifice, inspected the colorful anuses of orangutans, engaged in stormy, short-lived collaborations with the surrealists, founded alternative cultural journals, suffered rapturously from tuberculosis, joined leftist *groupuscules* in the heady days of the Popular Front, set up (and dissolved) secret societies and a "strange and famous" college, offered "mystical" meditations on the death of God, expounded Weberian-styled analyses of the rise of Protestant industry, ventured ecological speculations on new laws of thermodynamics, analysed Soviet and American economic policies in the early days of the Cold War, commented energetically on modern literature—and was inspired to write many a "dirty" novel and to raise many a disapproving eyebrow. The exchange will span more, too, than the apparent political abyss which separates, in the 1930s, the notorious Rector of Freiburg University from the antifascist activist of the Parisian Left. And it will span more than the genealogical abyss which separates Heidegger and Bataille as, respectively, gravedigger and heir apparent of Nietzsche/Dionysos.

The exchange will also have to straddle a certain conceptual abyss. For if Bataille and Heidegger at times seem close in their descriptions of Enlightenment modernity—the abstract rule of reason, the congealing of subjectivity, the technical exploitation of the earth—their diagnoses of the source of the "problem" diverge sharply, as do their prognoses regarding the direction of a possible cure.

Heidegger and Bataille sketch parallel accounts of the development of modernity as the progressive technologization of experience. Both present a kind of counterhistory to the Hegelian narrative of emancipation. For both thinkers—as for Horkheimer and Adorno, in the twisted wake of Marx, Nietzsche and Weber—the progress of enlightenment brings new and seemingly irreversible forms of domination: the reification of experience and the introduction of the abstract measure of utility; the reduction of qualitative difference to the quantifiable identities of the market; the increasing centrality of productive labor as the determinant of thought and action; the expulsion of the mundane sacred and its replacement by an otherworldly deity; and, last but not least, the (Newtonian) determination of time as an inert continuum of exchangeable now-points (what Benjamin, in 1940, called "homogeneous, empty time," and likened to the numbing "rosary" of sequential history). For both thinkers, the process will culminate in the technological vicissitudes of the present—the reduction of the earth to a standing "stockpile" of resources, the reduction of time to an accumulation of empty instants, the reduction of experience to the private self-possession of a transparent subject. By the 1950s, for better or worse, Bataille and Heidegger (along with so many others) will have come to equate "Russia" and "America" as the complementary flipsides of an apparatus of pure accumulation—maximizing its efficiency, reinvesting all its surpluses to feed the expanding means of production, capturing all existence within the circle of instrumentality and exchange.

But while the two stories may in broad outline coincide, the respective etiologies would seem to differ. Heidegger will attribute this tendency to the "mounting forgetfulness" of a hidden Being: the ontological reduction of Being to another entity (however supreme) to be grasped and plundered, the temporal reduction of an elusive "presence" to a manageable "present" to be trucked and traded. Bataille, on the other hand, will attribute the process to man's violent expulsion of heterogeneous "matter": the defensive splitting of an "original" ambivalence (malefic *and* beneficent, attraction *and* repulsion, sacred *and* mundane) into the more efficient conceptual bifurcations of morality and reason (good *or* bad, heaven *or* earth, desire *or* repulsion). Heidegger's account is ontological, Bataille's seemingly anthropological. Heidegger will ground the process of rationalization in the self-occluding structure of Being, Bataille in the functional exigencies of human self-preservation. For Heidegger, it is the essence of Being to dissemble itself in the various guises of Western metaphysics—*eidos, ousia, substantia, actualitas, perceptio, Geist,* Will to Power—a series of hypostatizations and reductions by which man comes to take, and thus become, the measure of all existence in his obfuscation of Being's unmasterable temporality. For Bataille it is the human need to work which creates the limited or "restricted" economy of instrumentality and exchange: anthropocentric avarice replaces the cosmic prodigality of a solar economy freely expending its resources without return.

For Heidegger, Nietzsche stands at the apex of the metaphysical system of retention. The Will to Power displays precisely the avaricious structure of the classical subject: recursive, self-aggrandizing, constantly (like capital) needing to expand, to become "more" than itself in order to stay the "same" as itself, securing its environment as a constant reserve of stable values, efficiently returning to itself in the static recurrence of the same. Did Nietzsche himself not explicitly determine "life" as the hyperretentive movement of self-production, underwritten by that most "subterranean" of all values, the *Erhaltungswerte?* "To have and to want to have more—growth, in one word—that is life itself" (*Will to Power* §125). Leading Heidegger to ask, without asking, whether the overman would not indeed be closer to his human, all-too human counterpart—the slavish hoarder of the *Genealogy*—than his extravagant gestures would suggest. Bataille, conversely (reading Nietzsche against the fascists, against Heidegger, and at times against Nietzsche himself), will read Nietzsche as fellow profligate and ecstatic. The avaricious "more" of metaphysical accumulation and control (still present, according to Bataille, in 1929, in that telltale little prefix of idealization, *sur-homme* [2, 93–112]) gives way, for the sur-Nietzsche of *Sur Nietzsche,* to the excessive expenditure of a "hyper-will" committed no longer to the ruses of accumulative power but to the abyssal lures of chance.

Heidegger will offer as a countermemory to the tradition a repetition of the Greek "experience" of Being as (absent) presence. Having exhausted itself in the spiral of unleashed technology, metaphysics exposes a secret opening to its other in those momentary glimmers of an experience beyond the reach of calculation. Such an experience recapitulates without restoring the early Greek reflection on Being as the withdrawing gift of a time beyond the cumulative flow of indifferent now-points. Bataille proposes as countermovements to the avaricious grip of reason the unaccountable "experiences" of laughter, tears, dreams, games, art, "perverse sexual activity" (1, 305), "meditation" and the dazzling thrust of "joy in the face of death." For Heidegger, the homogenizing thrust of metaphysics is subverted when "difference" reveals itself as the finite transcendence of Being in its distinction from present beings. For Bataille, "heterogeneity" appears in the ecstatic gestures of human self-abandon. For Heidegger, apparently, Being disposes. For Bataille, apparently, man proposes.

It is, then, an unlikely enough exchange. The two participants themselves did little to facilitate it—the one, typically, not reading, the other, more or less, misreading—a curious scene of misprision and denial whose "economic" implications deserve some scrutiny. Heidegger, in his usual fashion, remained stubbornly immured from the "bohemian" scene of prewar Paris, while Bataille's appreciation of the Freiburg philosopher remained severely limited by local restrictions on foreign currency. Heidegger seems not to have read Bataille. Bataille read Heidegger fitfully, and, by his own account, only in translation (4, 365). By 1937, the only French translation of Heidegger's work was the little anthology by Henri Corbin—a fateful, at times fatal, translation which was to set the mood and tenor of French "existentialism" for a good decade still to come.

Bataille was reluctant to perceive in Heidegger a fellow traveller. His most explicit remarks (though they are rare) typically peg Heidegger as one more "philosopher": snug in his academic commitments, wedded to the values of work and science, sober in the production of discourse. "Not a life dominated by an unjustifiable passion" (11, 285). Fundamental ontology subordinates "experience" to the lures of "knowledge" (5, 19). If Heidegger himself may have had an inkling of "inner experience," he manhandles it in his haste to master it; he cannot communicate it without betrayal. "Contestation" in his hands becomes conformism, another job for the professoriate. The "scientific community" invoked in *Was ist Metaphysik*" is the servile workers' commune: hunched, dwarfish, bent by the spirit of gravity: "a rather nasty, deformed gnome—too polished to be a monster, embarrassed, if not ashamed of being so" (5, 431). If Heidegger perceives the abyssal *glissement* of existents towards the "nothingness" of the unknown, his reaction remains forlorn and defensive. He would retain his grip on certainty. He cannot handle loss. Why the fear and trembling? (Philosophers do not laugh. "I am not a philosopher but a saint, maybe a madman" [5, 218].) Heideggerean "*angoisse*" is still cringing, avaricious, clinging to what escapes it. (Anguish, explains Bataille elsewhere, is still wedded to "the fear of losing" (5, 169); it is caught in the circle of self-preservation (7, 311), marked by the "greedy" concern with consequences (5, 321): it is individuated, reactive, an evasion of chance as such.) The melancholia of "existentialist" *Angst* should yield, thus, to the incandescent "ecstasy" of abandon (11, 304). Laughter, drunkenness, the tug of erotic effervescence—conspicuously missing in Heidegger—would supply the missing affirmation.

> I start from laughter, not, as did Heidegger in *Was ist Metaphysik?*, from *angoisse* . . . (*angoisse* is a sovereign moment, but still in flight from itself, still negative); his published work, as far as I can see, is more a manufactured article than a glass of alcohol. . . . It is a professorial work, its method remains glued [*collée*] to results: what counts for me, rather, is the moment of unglueing [*décollement*], what I teach . . . is a kind of drunkenness, not a philosophy . . . [5, 217ff.]

By Bataille's own estimate, a general economics would begin precisely where fundamental ontology leaves off—at the frayed edges of Heidegger's system, in the silences of his thought. "Even more than the text of Volume 1 of *Sein und Zeit* . . . it is Heidegger's inability to write Volume 2 which brings me close to Heidegger. . . . What I finally manage to say is represented, in Heidegger, only by a silence . . ." (5, 217n and 474).

With these last words, Bataille speaks perhaps more truthfully than he could have known.

II.

—He did not know to what extent he was right—
—Bataille on Hegel, quoted by Derrida

Bataille could not have known the extent to which he was right. Restricted by that rather "determined unknowledge"[2] which was the state of Heidegger studies in France during the war years, Bataille no doubt had a limited perspective on the matter. The few Heidegger texts at his disposal (though he shows signs of having looked only at *What is Metaphysics?*) are marked by the general presuppositions of fundamental ontology—assumptions (to simplify quickly) regarding the integrity and self-consistency of a solitary Dasein projecting itself resolutely into the abyss of its own or "proper" possibilities; assumptions regarding the privilege of work and "equipmentality" as the central category of human existence; assumptions, too (Husserlian ones), regarding the necessity and possibility of "securing" the new *Wissenschaft vom Sein* with all the moorings of a rigorous science— presuppositions which could arguably appear, on balance, to mobilize the most classical terms of metaphysics, bringing "existential" Dasein far closer, for all its abyssal tendencies, to the *fundamentum inconcussum* of the traditional subject than Heidegger's averrals would have it. For if it is true that Heidegger, in *Being and Time*, will attempt to wrest Dasein from the snares of substance-ontology (Dasein is not a *subjectum*, the "ekstatic" exteriority of *Ek-sistenz* replaces the buttressing stability of *Sub-stanz*, etc.), it remains equally true that the "position" of Dasein remains resolutely erect and vertical throughout Heidegger's early writings. As does the position (for these are no doubt inseparable) of the investigating scientific subject. With all the *Mündigkeit* of the "enlightened" agent, authentic Dasein picks up its losses and stands up straight. Phenomenology, meanwhile, establishes its own credentials as the philosophical project of self-recovery. Far from the vertiginous horizontality of the acephalic victim. Far from the abandoned freefall of an unconditional *dépense*.

In *Sein und Zeit* it is only *das Man*—the dizzy and distracted nonself of inauthentic existence—which seems prone to loss. *Selbstverlorenheit*, self-loss, is the essential mark of an evasive immaturity (though admittedly Heidegger would refrain from moralizing [*SZ*, 167, 176]) by which Dasein misses its station and plunges onto the slippery slope of the everyday. *Das man* has the drunken lurch of one who cannot stand up straight. It skids with every step—the move-

2. Jacques Derrida, "De l'économie restreinte à l'économie générale: un hégélianisme sans réserve," in *L'Écriture et la différence* (Paris: Seuil, 1967), 405r..

ment is described, variously, as a whirling, a groundlessness, an uprootedness, an entanglement, a falling, a distraction, a floating, a plunging—and lacks entirely the steadfastness, *Selbständigkeit* to stand on its own two feet. Its failure to stand by itself (*Unselbständigkeit*) is really just its pathological adherence to the nonself (*Unselbst-ständigkeit*) (*SZ*, 117, 322). Even its death is not its own: it would refer that "ownmost possibility" to another—vicariously "experiencing" death as something for "them" to go through, relinquishing phenomenological propriety in favor of the *Ersatzthema* of "the other's death" (*SZ*, 237–41).

Authentic Dasein—immured against this wobbly state of affairs by no more than a "thin wall" (*SZ*, 278) and for no more than a "moment"—pulls itself together from this scattered confusion and reclaims its "own" self in the firm grip [*Ergreifen*] of resolution (*SZ*, 278). Self-possessed, steadfast, "finding" itself in the fundamental "mood" of anxiety, authentic Dasein faces its own death as the "mineness" [*Jemeinigkeit*] of pure possibility, recovering its self as the property lost in the dispersals of *Verlassenheit*. If only for a moment, it stands like a man.

As will science, art, and the nation state in the years immediately to follow. The phallic Dasein of *Being and Time* translates easily, in *What is Metaphysics?* (1929), into the erect "station" of authentic research: metaphysical questioning is to reverse the disciplinary dispersal of the uprooted regional sciences (the institutional version of *das Man*), re-collecting itself from its distracted "lostness" in the ontic through a return to the founding ground. In the *Origin of the Artwork* (1935/36), it is the artwork which adopts the upright posture. Self-subsistent [*Insichstehen*] and autonomous, the artwork (still a *work*) carves out a vertical place of disclosure: "setting up" the world, "setting forth" the earth, allowing the entity to come to "stand" [*zum Stehen*] in the "steadiness" [*Ständige*] of its shining. Art's features here are resolutely Apollinian. For all Heidegger's nods to chthonic hiddenness, it is a classical solar topography which dominates: Heidegger gazes at a Greek temple, while Bataille burrows in the caves of Aurignac; Heidegger turns Van Gogh's shoes into sturdy walking boots,[3] while Bataille contemplates the painter's scorched sunflowers and his mutilated ear.

3. On some of the repercussions of this restitution to the upright posture, see Derrida, "Restitutions: de la vérité en pointure," in *La Vérité en peinture* (Paris: Flammarion, 1978).

And in 1933, it was the German nation that took the stand. If, for reasons of his own, Bataille will assiduously refrain from echoing the political charges that were being levelled against Heidegger by the war's end, he could not have been oblivious to the essential facts at hand. It was more than a "pardonnable error" (11, 573n) that led Heidegger to the Rector's podium. By 1933, fundamental ontology had unmistakably politicized itself according to the ideology of the day: authentic Dasein was to collect itself from its dispersal into the unified order of state "service" [*Dienst*] (distributed Platonically along the triple axes of science, labour, military); *Mitsein*, under-determined in *Being and Time*, had become overdetermined as the *völkisch* collectivity of the German nation; and authenticity had become the hypercephalic movement of self-assertion or, literally, self-(be)heading [*Selbst-be-hauptung*]—affirming one's hegemony through an attachment to a head or *Führer*, combatting acephalic anarchy through the centralizing sway of the state. (It is a question, indeed, of "whether we *stand* in history of simply stagger" (*EM*, 154).) The state erects itself firmly as the standing order of the day. "Alles Grosse steht im Sturm . . ." (*SU*, 19).

III.

> Here again, a German word would render Bataille's thought better. This is *Unselbständigkeit*."
> —Sartre, "Un nouveau mystique"

No doubt there is much in "inner experience" that Heidegger might have been tempted to label "inauthentic." Sartre goes through the curious mental exercise of translating *L'Expérience intérieure* into German in order to make sense of it, and ends up, in effect, suggesting that this "bonne petite extase panthéistique" (*NM*, 184) could be better understood as the puerile fallout of a phenomenological misadventure. That is to say, as a kind of falling. Translated back into the native tongue of philosophy, the whole thing, by Sartre's implication, appears to be a kind of inverted Heideggereanism—Bataille positing self-loss where Heidegger speaks of self-possession, endorsing slipping where Heidegger speaks of standing, looking ("scientistically") to "the others" where Heidegger looks to the solitude of the "own-most" self, living death vicariously through the "imposture" of the others where Heidegger would protect the irreplaceable uniqueness of one's "proper" death, wallowing in the "instant" where Heidegger surges forward to a future "project"—an evasion, in short, of the demands of "existential" authenticity and thus a revision to the moils of the "they." Observe Sartre's translation/gloss: when Bataille stigmatizes "projet," he is speaking of the Heideggerean *Entwurf;* when he challenges the finality of "ipséité," it is really Corbin's trans-lation of *Selbstheit* he has in mind; when he champions "insuffi-sance," it is the evasive state of *Unselbständigkeit* which is meant. And when he promotes "communication," he is only vulgarizing the sense of *Mitsein.*[4] But (since "hell is others") such a febrile collec-tivity could only be a spurious one: the interiority of experience has already been "infected" (*NM,* 161) through the objectivistic gaze of the Others. "Communication" would reduce the autonomous sub-ject to the exteriority of the "social fact"—à la Durkheim, Lévy-Bruhl, and all Bataille's cronies at that "strange and famous college" (*NM,* 165ff.)—and the once steady-footed Dasein would go sliding, fool-like, into the giddy laughter of the crowd. (A laughter whose sincerity Sartre will, in any case, cast some doubts on, finding the whole scene less than funny—the "fall" simply a bad case of slapstick—and the hilarity somewhat forced. "He does not make us laugh . . ." [*NM,* 170].) In short: the whole thing reeks of inauthen-ticity—"une mauvaise foi passionnelle" (*NM,* 187). Sartre recom-mends that Bataille go see a good psychoanalyst (*Daseinsanalyse* presumably not yet having been imported) (*NM,* 188).

At which point Bataille will protest his probity with a flurry of indignation—I have no debts, I never touched Corbin, I wrote mine first, I got it from the man on the street, I got it from the dictionary, I'm the one who introduced Heidegger to France anyway[5]—a verita-

4. "'Projet': another existentialist word. It's the standard translation of one of Heidegger's terms" (*NM,* 168). "The word *ipséité* is a neologism which he has borrowed from Corbin, Heidegger's translator. M. Corbin uses it to render the German term 'Selbstheit,' which signifies the existential return-to-self on the basis of a project" (*NM,* 159). "Once more, a German word would render Bataille's thought better. This is 'Unselbständigkeit'" (*NM,* 171n). "This 'communication'—does it not make one think of the Heideggerean 'Mitsein'?" (*NM,* 164).

5. "When I write *projet,* I'm just thinking of a given project or plan (not Heidegger's *Entwurf*)—for example, my plan to write or to go hunting. The vocabulary of the

ble Freudian "kettle logic" of an argument which would surely obscure all the deepest issues. For if Sartre's complaint is somewhat peevish, his basic point deserves some thought. Sartre knew well that the issue is not dependency, not the give and take of influence. It involves the very logic of inversion. For what the charge of bad faith amounts to is just that self-abandon may be hollow where it remains reactive: underlying the disintegrative posturing may be just the old longing for the One. Hence Sartre's ultimate charge of usury: self-loss is just the prelude to a higher recuperation—wanting to have one's cake and eat it—the less-is-more complacency, the mystic's *qui perd gagne.*

Is *expérience,* then, only an easy inversion of the Heideggerean *Eigentlichkeit*—the sheer negative to phenomenological self-(dis)closure—substituting for the stable order of authenticity only the indifferent anarchy of *das Man?* Mere inversion (as Heidegger himself was later to insist on) could only reinforce what it would surmount. If fundamental ontology can (and must) be inscribed within the circuit of reproductive consumption—the recovery of meaning which is philosophy's founding gesture—it would be no alternative to simply privilege what it excludes. For the dispersal of *das Man* would be only a form of abstract negation, a determinate waste within the system—a "levelling" and "indifference" (to use Heidegger's language)—ultimately a relapse to a precritical form of immediacy. Property relations would not be thereby overcome. Dasein's "falling" would bring only an undifferentiated state of fusion, a fluidity and indifference: self-loss would become naturalized and sterilized as the philosopheme of pure identity.

---

professor gives the word more significance than it has at face value. (I have written *ipséité* in the sense provided in Lalande's dictionary) . . ." (Notes to *Méthode de méditation,* 5, 473ff.). Similarly, in the notes to *La Souveraineté,* Bataille writes: "I am using the word [*projet*] here, as I have always done, in the ordinary sense of the word. Sartre, discussing a book in which I stress this idea (*L'Expérience intérieure*), has seen this as a translation of *Entwurf,* in the sense that Heidegger gave this German word. I am similarly supposed to have borrowed the word *ipséité* from a translation by Henri Corbin, but this translation (whose manuscript I never laid eyes on) came out after the publication, in a review (*Recherches philosophiques,* 1936), of the text in which this word appears. But Sartre is right to emphasize my interest in contemporary German philosophy. It's at my instigation that in 1929 Henri Corbin proposed to my friend Jean Paulhan the publication of *Was ist Metaphysik?* in the NRF" (8, 666).

IV.

> Only in the German language will the book's title take on its full
> significance: *Das innere Erlebnis.* The French word *expérience*
> betrays our author's intention.
> —Sartre, "Un Nouveau mystique"

"In Hegel's mind, what is immediate is bad, and Hegel surely would
have identified what I am calling experience with the immediate"
(10, 249). Surely. Clearly there is much in this "new mysticism"[6] that
begs for demystification. Certainly Bataille's rhetoric can be a little
steamy.

It is the "nostalgia" for "primal continuity" (10, 21), of course,
which cries out most sharply for interpretation—a "nostalgia" which
would seem to oppose to the coils of instrumental reason a purer
substratum of lived experience: an "intimacy lost" with the expulsion of the sacred (7, 62); a "plenitude of total existence" shattered by
the division of labor (1, 530); a "participation" sundered by the rise of
industry (9, 196); a "fusion" ruptured by the gaze of reason (5, 21).
Zarathustra's wish—"be that ocean" (5, 40)—would seem to become
Betaille's command: "life" itself would be that ocean.

> Life . . . passes rapidly from one point to another . . . like a current or
> a sort of streaming of electricity. . . . If a group of people laughs . . . a
> current of intense communication passes through them. . . . The con-
> tagion of a wave, rippling onwards, for those who laugh become united
> like the waves of the sea: there is no longer any partition between
> them . . . they are no more separate than two waves. . . [5, 111–13]

And so on. Risky rhetoric, to say the least. Such language would not
only seem sharply at odds with the appeals to heterogeneity. It seems
almost calculated to provoke suspicion, indeed of the most aching
sort. For the language reeks of the vitalism of the day, and was being
used in another context to promote quite a different political effect.

---

6. Sartre's label. Bataille himself will use, then erase, the term. "Can't we detach
the possibility of mystical experience from its religious antecedents (a possibility
which remains open, however it appears, to the nonbeliever)? Free it from the asceticism of dogma and from the atmosphere of religions? Free it, in a word, from
mysticism—to the point of linking it to the nudity of ignorance?" (5, 422, notes to
L'Expérience intérieure).

Le Bon and Freud had already shown, in theory, how the "crowd" in its porosity gravitates inexorably towards a leader: the centrifugal movement of "contagion" condenses under the gravitational force of a "head" or center. Nietzsche had already exposed the lures of empathy (*Mitleid*) as being the ideology of all conformism, the collusive identification with the environment which marks every accommodation to the status quo. Adorno and Benjamin were meanwhile demonstrating, in practice, the high political cost of every merger. *Einfühlung* would be the mass hysteria induced by a society which had collapsed the social space of politics. It would be the false collectivity which masks the real antagonisms of the day—the "semblance of the masses" occluding the "reality of classes": Benjamin was to see in fascism as such the living embodiment of such a mask.[7]

How to deal with such language? Is it enough to point to the fissures? To insist that the "continuum" is already, profoundly, disrupted? That the immediacy is already a shattered one, and "communication" only the opening of an infinite wound?

> Everything real fractures, cracks. . . . The wound of incompleteness opens individual beings. Through what could be called incompleteness, or animal nakedness, or the wound, diverse separate beings *communicate*. [5, 262ff.]

"Ecstasy is communication. Now communication is not completion" (5, 445). Thus "community" is far from the consensual transparency of a coordinated collectivity: it has the "spaced," self-distanced quality of an encounter already lacerated from the start. Communication is then the "sharing" which is the "shearing" of a split connection—like the cracked, repellent joining which Heidegger (but I anticipate) calls *Riss* or *Trennung*. It is what Nancy calls *partage*.[8] Communication thus presupposes the very isolation which will undermine it. Continuity would be the disrupted place where nothing stable could endure.

> . . . Being isolated, communication, are one reality alone. Nowhere do there exist "isolated beings" which do not communicate, nor "communication" independent of points of isolation. If we are careful

---

7. Walter Benjamin, *Das Passagen-Werk, Gesammelte Schriften* (Frankfurt: Suhrkamp, 1983), vol. 5, 469.

8. Jean-Luc Nancy, *Le Partage des voix* (Paris: Galilée, 1982) and *La Communauté désoeuvrée* (Paris: Bourgois, 1986).

to steer clear of these two illformed concepts (hangovers from infan-
tile beliefs) the most badly knotted problem will be solved. [7, 553]

"Intimacy" would involve, then, not the transparency of identity, but
rather the opaque intransigence of what connects at the point of
greatest secrecy. "Normal" communication (in the "profane" sense of
correspondence and consensus) cannot be more fragile, therefore,
than when "sovereign communication" silently rules. The darkness
of "common subjectivity" (to use Bataille's language) would thus be
prior to the communal mergers of intersubjectivity, at least as clas-
sically conceived.

> Communication, in my sense, is in fact never stronger than when
> communication, in the weak sense, in the sense of profane language
> (. . . which makes us—and the world—penetrable) proves useless,
> and becomes the equivalent of darkness. We speak in various ways to
> convince others and to seek agreement. . . . This incessant effort . . .
> would be apparently impossible if we were not *first* bound to one
> another by the feeling of *common subjectivity,* impenetrable to itself,
> and for which the world of distinct objects is impenetrable. [9, 311]

And is it enough to point out that Bataille's "nostalgia" is at best an
"uneasy" one (5, 155), opposed to every form of pastoralism and every
form of naive escape? This "unease" is, indeed, at the root of Bataille's
confrontation with Breton,[9] with Bäumler (1, 447–65), with Romanticism (9, 206), with Hemingway (8, 230–33), with (at times) Proust (5,
156–75), with naturalism ("the poetic fallacy of animality" [7, 293]),
with sexual liberationism,[10] with "Orientalism" (5, 30): with every
attempt to reduce transgression to the sentimental movement of
restoration and return. Such nostalgia would have the "suspicious
and lugubrious" (5, 540) stupor of an idealizing aestheticism: "the
European's sickly taste for an exotic color" (5, 30)—"like a film about
'primitive' countries" (1, 530)—a numbing abstraction from present

9. Bataille's (not unambivalent) critique of the surrealists tends to focus, among
other things, on the naiveté of their appeals to transcendence (the "sur") which would,
in his view, obscure contemporary social conditions (with its concomitant technical
rationality) thus leading to various regressivities and archaisms. For the clearest elab-
orations of this argument, see "La 'vieille taupe' et le préfix *sur* dans les mots *sur-
homme* et *surréaliste*" (2, 93–112), "La Valeur d'usage de D. A. F. de Sade" (2, 54–69),
"La Religion surréaliste" (7, 381–95), and "Le Surréalisme en 1947" (11, 259–61).
10. "Despite appearances, I am opposed to the tendency that seems to prevail
today. I am not one of those who see in the abolition of sexual taboos a way out" (Notes
to *L'Impossible,* 3, 511ff.).

conditions which only masks an accommodation to the status quo. It would occlude the historic specificity of the given with the passive longing for the past, hypostatizing present circumstances by the very appeal to bygone days. History itself would prevent such an easy overcoming. The radical impurity of beginnings and ends—the ambivalent birth and death of "history"—should prohibit any temptation to regress. "The nostalgia for a bygone world is . . . based on a shortsighted judgment . . ." (7, 126).

> Even if we do have a paradoxical nostalgia for it, we can only by some aberration regret the loss of the religious and royal edifice of the past. The effort to which this edifice responded was only an immense failure and if it is true that the essential is missing from our world . . . we can only go further, without imagining, even for an instant, the possibility of a return back. [8, 275]

From what would one escape? It is too late to speak of leaving. Has not the "experience" of fascism itself blurred forever the line between effervescence and utility, organizing lumpen uselessness into the efficiency of state service, fusing charismatic sovereignty with the mechanical rationality of order, marking the final penetration (to speak Habermasian) of *Zweckrationalität* into the lifeworld of pure *dépense?* (1, 339–71). Such blurring indeed would erode the last enclave of uncontaminated spontaneity—implicating the body, the unconscious, desire, sexuality itself within the restricted circuit of the commodity exchange. A blurring which would paralyze—as Adorno and Horkheimer saw all too clearly, Marcuse not clearly enough—all hope of exit and mock every fantasy of regression as being the collusive daydream of the herd. Making "Auschwitz" henceforth (as Bataille puts it, with an almost Adornian pathos) the very "sign of man" (11, 226), the decisive rubric of our day. Turning the present into a "field of ashes" (5, 40), without an option of escape.

To what would one return? Historic precedents are neither conceivable nor provided. There is no historic form of sovereignty which is not already implicated in the machinations of profane rationality. Even the most "primitive" potlatches of the Tlingit and Kwakiutl were already contaminated by the calculus of acquired rank and power (Bataille does not, despite appearances, share Mauss's idealizations of the communifying bond of archaic "generosity.") Early potlatch was already caught up in the rational circuit of exchange. Tribal *dépense* proves to be a "comedy" (7, 73) of compensation and control, an insurance policy underwritten by the machinations of a "crooked will" (7, 75). For the Pacific chieftain indeed is guaranteed to win through losing—gift summoning countergift—stockpiling prestige and honor in return for the dilapidations of the fiscal reserve. "He enriches himself with his contempt for wealth, and what he shows himself to be miserly of is the power of his own generosity" (7, 72).

Nor is prehistoric "nature" a nostrum. If it is true that, in his invocation of "ends in themselves" (1, 305), Bataille would seem to invoke the most classical split between the natural and the cultural— the immanent entelechy of *phusis* pitted against the exteriority of *techné* (Aristotle); the apparent "purposelessness" of the flower pitted against the functionality of the artifact (Kant); the wasteful effusions of the songbird pitted against the niggardly efficiencies of the craftsman (Schiller)—he is unsentimental in his attachments, and dismisses every yearning for archaic Nature as being just "poetic fulguration" (7, 294).

Despite appearances. It is true that our meager acts of effervescence are said to be just "the expression of the Earth and its laws" (2, 155)—the very laws of "cosmic energy" which one would ignore, warns Bataille, at one's own peril (7, 33). True, too, that "communication" at times seems modelled on the labyrinthine bondings of molecular existence (1, 433ff.). And it is true that the undulations of expenditure seem to suppose a "link between lovemaking and light-waves" (5, 283)—"perhaps arbitrary," demurs Bataille, but no less telling.

But this is not the "cosmic *Lebensphilosophie*" some might imagine.[11] For natural immediacy is not an option. "In this kind of situation there is no recourse to animality" (8, 196). The unfettered immediacy of natural existence (apparently unquestioned by Bataille)[12] is neither possible nor desirable for humanity. For one thing, such immediacy remains "unfathomable" (7, 294). For another, it lacks all verve. The soggy indifference of "life" ("like water in water" [7, 295]) in fact is devoid of sacred tension. The animal (unfettered by work and prohibitions) knows not the joyful horror of transgression; it knows just the "slumber" (7, 313) of instinctual life. Libertarian appeals to

11. Jürgen Habermas, *The Philosophical Discourse of Modernity* (Cambridge: MIT Press, 1987), 235.
12. On evidently Hegelian grounds. The epigraph to *Théorie de la religion* cites Kojève (whose testimony is taken to be impeccable) on the difference between the immediacy of animal hunger and the mediated "negativity" of human desire.

nature would only neutralize "sin" as wholesome spontaneity (fun sex, healthy appetite): Genet and Sade, Baudelaire and Proust knew rather the awful attraction of forbidden fruit. For the violation of taboos is not a "return to animal violence" (10, 68): transgression (dialectically?)[13] preserves the very prohibition it would surmount. To evade such a "dialectic" by taking refuge in immediacy indeed would only reinforce one's immersion in the snares of work. "Nature" itself would be in this sense just the adaptive phantasm of servility. The very appeal to nature (as Horkheimer also saw) would in fact just bespeak its most perfect domestication.

> The theme of nature, which could seem to be a more radical force of opposition, would itself only offer the possibility of a provisional escape. (Love of nature is in any case so easily reconciled with the primacy of utility . . . that it has become the most commonplace— and the most harmless—means of compensation for utilitarian societies.) There is clearly nothing less dangerous, less subversive, and even in the end less wild than than the wildness of rocks. [9, 206]

Sacred experience never presupposes an original plenitude to be reestablished. "Humanity" as such is defined by an irrecuperable loss—a loss which brings only the intangible "gain" of a certain lucidity (7, 126ff.), and which can only redouble itself in the folds of time. "Clear consciousness is searching for what it has itself lost, and what it must lose again in the very act of drawing near to it" (7, 315). No "lived experience" could restore that. The infamous "present" of Bataille's celebrations would appear to falter. (Certainly the "standing" of the *nunc stans* would appear to slide.) "Only the possibility of pure repetition prevents us from perceiving the primacy of the present" (9, 196)—Bataille here speaks perhaps more precisely than he knows. For experience as such, in fact, would have the foldedness of the most "pure" of repetitions. The "return," were it indeed possible, would be precisely to a time that never was: "Religion in general was a response to the desire that man always had to find himself, to recover an intimacy *that was strangely always lost*" (7, 123, emphasis mine). In such circumstances, "life" could never be an answer to the lateness of the event. Death is that lateness. What it restores is just the absence of life's self-presence to itself.

13. On Bataille's apparent appeal to the operation of *Aufhebung,* and its possible overdetermination in *L'Érotisme,* see Derrida, "De l'économie restreinte à l'économie générale," op.,cit., 404.

The power of death signifies that . . . [life's] intimacy reveals its blinding consumption only at the moment when it ceases. . . . It is through its absence that intimate life—which had lost the power to fully reach me, and which I essentially regarded as a thing—is fully restored to my sensibility. [7, 309]

V.

Experience of non-experience. . . .

—Blanchot, *L'Entretien infini*

Expérience is not, in short, *Erlebnis*. It is neither the certitude of feeling nor the plenitude of sensation which Benjamin—like Hegel—rightly criticized as being the spurious claim to an immediacy in reality denied. (By the 1930s, the ideological stakes of just such a claim had become abundantly enough clear.) Nor—despite a certain fascination on Bataille's part (justly, if prematurely, suspected)—is *l'expérience intérieure* the *inneres Erlebnis* which Jünger will come to identify with the essence of war, and which announces itself, typically, as the heroic certitudes of pain and labor.[14]

Adorno called *Erlebnis* "an outmoded and . . . deficient expression."[15] Indeed he flatly inscribed it within the horizon of the culinary—that circle of consumption which defines our immersion in Marx's "realm of necessity" (the restricted circuit of self-preservation). Benjamin was to trace such an "experience" of immediacy to the specific degradations of our modernity. *Erlebnis* would be that clammy sensation of proximity which marks our radical alienation from the depths of history—the collapse of spatial distance through the frenetic jostlings of the crowded city, the collapse of social distance through the uniformities of wage labor, the collapse of temporal

14. See Ernst Jünger, *Der Kampf als inneres Erlebnis, Werke,* (Stuttgart: Ernst Klett Verlag, 1960), vol. 5. Despite moments of swaggering, and despite being drawn to Jünger's own descriptions of the decomposing corpses of the battlefield in *La Limite de l'utile* (7, 251–53), Bataille seems to denounce such heroics as being ultimately a conformism and servility. "Heroism is an attitude of flight" (5, 347). On Bataille's distinction between militarism and authentic "war," see *La Part maudite,* 7, 51–65.

15. Theodor Adorno, *Ästhetische Theorie* (Frankfurt: Suhrkam Verlag, 1973), 362.

distance through the jerky accumulation of empty moments—the "catastrophic" occlusion of (auratic) distance through the amorphous homogeneity of the given.[16] Such a sensation of "lived experience" would be just the failure of authentic memory. The capacity for historical reflection would be sterilized with the atomization of the present. Death itself would be "eliminated."

It is a point Heidegger, too, in his own way, was to make, when in *Sein und Zeit* he related the vitalist "stream of experience" [*Erlebnisstrom*] to the homogenous flux of accumulative now-points—to a modality, that is to say, of the inauthentic (*SZ*, 388). Such a stream could only isolate the present as the empty unit of exchangeability. Creating (as he remarks later) the very need to ground perception in the self-givenness of the private subject (*US*, 129ff.). A givenness which would obliterate all the differences, yielding only the trivial self-identity of the immediate. ("The Greeks were lucky," he comments, "to have had no 'lived experiences' " [*N* 1, 95].)

Expérience is closer, no doubt, to Benjamin's *Erfahrung*: to that communifying "experience" already lost by the time of the industrial era, taken up or overwritten by the circuit of productivity and exchange. In reality, such experience had been lost long before it could ever begin. For Benjamin knew well that there was never a point of originary plenitude to be recapitulated or "reexperienced": *Erfahrung* had been from the outset already fractured by the passage of time itself. *Erfahrung*—the *experience lost*—is nothing other than the *experience of loss*. Experience reveals only the truth that there never was an "experience." Benjamin's Proust (though perhaps not Bataille's) knew this:

> [Proust] is pierced by the truth that none of us has time to live the true dramas of the existence that are destined for us. This ages us. Nothing else. The wrinkles and lines on our faces are the entries of the grand passions, vices, perceptions that called on us—but we, the masters [*wir, die Herrschaft*], were not at home.[17]

Such is the uncanny "too late" which marks the structure of lived time as such. It is a belatedness which disrupts the inevitability of every destiny, dislodges every claim to "mastery" [*Herrschaft*], disap-

16. Walter Benjamin, "Über einige Motive bei Baudelaire," *Gesammelte Schriften*, 1(2), 605–54.
17. Benjamin, "Zum Bilde Prousts," *Gesammelte Schriften*, op.,cit., 2.1, 320ff.

propriates every comfort of being "at home." Memory, then, assumes the involuntariness—*ungewolltes Eingedenken,* Proust's *mémoire involontaire*—of a seizure without closure. Reminiscence becomes the recapitulation of what never did, in the first place, take place. For Benjamin, such a loss had the power to counter every form of nostalgia, and fuelled the impatience for revolutionary change.

VI.

> But what is this experience [*Erfahrung*]? Is it the abdication [*Abdanken*] of thinking?
> —Heidegger, *Zur Sache des Denkens*

But Heidegger too, after all, began to speak of such an experience. It was to involve for him as well the general economy of the gift. A certain "turn" was first in order. A turn away, perhaps, from the erect proprieties of authentic Dasein and towards a general dispossession of the "ownmost" self. (After a while, perhaps, the erect "standing" of *Selbständigkeit* came to seem suspiciously close to the security holdings of accumulated stock [*Bestand*]—suspiciously close, that is, to the avaricious urge to self-elevation, meta-physics's founding gesture.)

It was to involve a turn toward (but these directionalities lose their meaning) a receding origin, the absent presence which precedes every relation of property/propriety and which calls for a radical "letting go" [*Gelassenheit*]. It will be a question of experiencing the tug of a Being no longer (or not yet) embroiled in the snares of productivity, prior to every manipulation and all control. No movement of regression could recuperate this. For what is to be appropriated is not the plenitude of a prior purity but rather the very experience of loss as such. For presence defines itself precisely as the withholding of the present: a "gift" which determines time itself as an epochal or self-suspended "sending," rather than as the serial string of accumulated now-points which could be collected or held intact. It thereby divests the present of its atomic integrity, unravelling the possibility of all exchange. As such, it undermines every structure of appropriation by refusing to render present that which it offers as (only) a gift.

Time is not. There is ("it gives") [*Es gibt*] time. The giving which gives
time is determined by the nearness which denies and withholds. This
nearness grants [*gewährt*] the openness of time-space and safeguards
[*verwährt*] what remains both refused in what has been, and kept back
in what arrives. We name the giving which gives authentic time
a reaching which opens and conceals. Insofar as reaching is itself
a giving, there is hidden in authentic time the giving of a giving.
[*ZSD*, 16]

"Es gibt Sein, Es gibt Zeit" [*ZSD*, 19]: such a "gift" would precede
the give and take of property, preceding, therefore, every "present" of
an accountable exchange. Such a "gift" would in fact displace (without mediating) the opposition between giving and receiving. For at
this level the relationship between "man" and "time" (or "Being")
would become the mutual extension of an excess rather than the
measured reciprocity of a debit-credit exchange. "Production" here
breaks down or falters, and with it every work relation known to
this day.

Is man the giver or receiver of time? And if he is the latter, how does
man receive time? Is he first of all man so that, after that, occasionally—that is, at some time or other—he receives time and enters into
relation with it? . . . Authentic time has already reached man as such
so that he can be man only by standing within [*insteht*] the threefold
reaching and by enduring [*aussteht*] the denying-withholding nearness which determines this reaching. Time is no product of man, man
is no product of man. There is [*Es gibt*] no production here. There is
only a giving in the sense already named, that of a reaching which
clears open time-space. [*ZSD*, 17]

Indeed such a "gift" would displace the very opposition between giving and withholding. For the "appropriation" [*Ereignis*] which defines
the "event" of giving would be just that self-withdrawal by which the
present is "kept back." "Expropriation," then, "belongs to Appropriation"—"Zum Ereignis gehört die Enteignis" [*ZSD*, 23]—and thus the
"own" becomes dispossessed. This introduces a "reserve" beyond all
avarice, and thus introduces the germs of a radical future beyond the
calculations of any "project." Beyond, that is, the projectile volunta-
risms of the *projet*. Towards a "waiting" [*warten*] which, "expecting"
[*erwarten*] nothing, "releases itself into openness" [*G*, 42], and thus
preserves the possibility of the radically new.

VII.

> My sovereignty welcomes . . . as the bird sings, and gives me no
> thanks for my work.
> —Bataille, *Méthode de méditation*

Such a gift would introduce, if not the restricted and restrictive pressure of the *potlatch*, still the burden of an unnamed debt or guilt. A guilt so infinite, perhaps, that no repayment could be thinkable. Once acknowledged, such a guilt would disrupt the very economy of exchange and the system of retributive justice which inevitably follows.

Such a guilt already had been registered at the edges of fundamental ontology. Had it been thought through (as Levinas once pointed out), it would have surely shattered the very appeal to self-recovery and self-mastery which had defined Heidegger's "project" at the outset. For the existential analytic had uncovered, as the constitutive structure of Dasein, a moment of radical obligation or indebtedness [*Schuldigsein*]: an unrepayable debt which Heidegger called, quite simply, "coming to owe something to Others" (*SZ*, 282), and which he located prior to every recuperative transaction of exchange. Such exchange transactions (as Nietzsche had already shown) could only determine time as the linear flow of empty now-points—i.e., the homogeneous "stream of *Erlebnisse*," in fact, that characterized the inauthentic, as we saw above (*SZ*, 291). The time of authentic "guilt," in contrast, would precede such a linear determination: time as such would be the gift preceding every accountable advance. It would be the opening of a responsibility prior to the law—prior to the restricted tallying of debits and credits which Nietzsche had identified as the sense of "justice" [*Gerechtigkeit*] and linked to the mercantile economy of revenge [*Rache*]. The premoral space of ethics: a site of incommensurability before the law.

"Guilt" in this sense would be the debt prior to the circuit of possessions—the restricted economy of the marketplace—and, as an opening to "the Others," would mark a sociality prior to all accounting and exchange. Only such a being as Dasein could be capable of such sociality. The peculiarity of its death—the "still outstanding" quality [*Ausstand*] of its ending—marks its finitude as the site of an obligation which will never be paid off (*SZ*, 241–46). Such a finitude would link death inseparably to the Others. (Bataille saw that, if Heidegger—at least not always—did not.)[18]

A debt so infinite that no thanks could ever be enough. Gratitude itself would be no answer to the incommensurability of the gift. In a restricted economy, gratitude [reconnaissance] would be just the mediating recognition which would discharge the debt by symbolic restitution, annuling the gift by reinsribing it within the intersubjective circle of exchange. In a general economy, an infinite gift would provoke a gratitude so radical that no payback could be thought.

In *Was Heisst Denken?*, Heidegger will define thinking as thanking, *Denken* as *Danken:* was "grateful" response to a gift which is itself nothing—nothing other than the ability to think, that is, to thank, as such. Thanking becomes simply the recursive, performative movement—"a thanking which does not just give thanks for something, but only thanks for being able to thank" (G, 65)—which knows no object for its gratitude and thus has nothing with which to pay back. Here the two moments of exchange—gift and countergift, endowment and thanks—become indistinguishable (if not mediated), introducing a radical indeterminacy at the heart of thought. For thanking would become itself a gift (requiring thanking . . .)—and thus the closed circle of compensation twists open into the erotic spiral of a surplus without end.

> How could we give more fitting thanks for this dowry [Mitgift], the gift of thinking what is most thoughtworthy, than by thinking over what is most thoughtworthy? So that the highest thanks would be thinking? And the deepest thanklessness, thoughtlessness? Authentic thanks, then, never consists in our coming with a gift and merely repaying gift with gift [vergelten Gabe mit Gabe]. . . . Such thanking is not a compensation [Abgelten], but it remains an offering. . . . [WHD, 94, 158]

18. "I have been the first to describe "communication" in its connection with *angoisse*," remarks Bataille in the notes to *Le Coupable* (5, 542)—a remark which indeed strikes to the heart of the entanglement between Heidegger and Bataille. For in raising the solitary "anguish" of *Sein-zum-Tode* to the communal "ecstasy" of the experience of *l'autrui-qui-meurt* (an experience disallowed by Heidegger in his prohibition of the *Ersatzthema* of the "Other's death"), Bataille seems to articulate a region of social experience unrecognizable to Heidegger himself. Just as the Heideggerean structures of temporality were perhaps inaccessible to Bataille. On the question of Bataillean community and its relationship to *Sein-zum-Tode*, see Jean-Luc Nancy, *La Communauté désoeuvrée* (see above, n. 8), together with Maurice Blanchot, *La Communauté inavouable* (Paris: Minuit, 1983).

SUZANNE GUERLAC

"Recognition" by a Woman!: A Reading of Bataille's *L'Erotisme*

"To give transgression to philosophy as a foundation . . . this is what my thinking undertakes . . . [la démarche de ma pensée]," Bataille writes in his conclusion to *Erotism: Death and Sensuality.*[1] In his 1967 essay Derrida proposed a now canonical account of the *démarche* of Bataille as a dual writing, one which works from a set of Hegelian concepts and subjects them to systematic displacement, the most prominent being the one from Hegel's concept of mastery to what Bataille calls "sovereignty." With sovereignty, Derrida affirms, there is a renunciation of recognition and meaning. No longer to seek recognition, he declares, is "the ultimate subversion of mastery."[2] The term "transgression" which Bataille uses to characterize eroticism (as well as poetry, laughter and sacrifice) has come to stand for this gesture of subversion which is in turn associated with a notion of the transgression of philosophy itself, or at least of its claims to

1. Georges Bataille, *Erotism. Death and Sensuality*, trans. Mary Dalwood (San Francisco: City Lights Books, 1986), 275. Subsequent references will be to this edition and will be given in parentheses in the text. I have altered the translation at times.
2. Jacques Derrida, *Writing and Difference*, trans. Alan Bass (Chicago: University of Chicago Press, 1978), 265 (original emphasis, translation somewhat altered). "[S]overeignty," Derrida writes, "has no identity, is not *self, for itself,* towards *itself, near itself.* In order not to govern, that is to say, in order not to be subjugated, it *must* subordinate nothing (direct object), that is to say, be subordinated to *nothing or no one* (servile mediation of the indirect object: it must expend itself without reserve, lose itself, lose consciousness, lose all memory of itself and all the interiority of itself . . . ")
[265]. I would like to emphasize that I am using Derrida's claims concerning the difference between sovereignty and mastery as a foil. Although I will emphasize the proximity of sovereignty to mastery (or the structure of recognition) in its form, the operation of the "dialectic" in Bataille radically distinguishes it from the force or effects of the Hegelian dialectic.

YFS 78, *On Bataille,* ed. Allan Stoekl, © 1990 by Yale University.

mastery. Bataille's insistence on the intimacy of eroticism and philosophy, however—" . . . the supreme philosophical question coincides with the summit of eroticism" (273)—and his portrayal of transgression as a *gift* to philosophy (the gift of a foundation) reminds us what a delicate notion transgression is and, at the same time, how close a reading *Erotism* can withstand.

Bataille begins his discussion of eroticism with what he calls a "philosophical detour," a schematic opposition between continuity, or fusion, on the one hand, and discontinuity, or separation, on the other. Eroticism is characterized as a movement from the latter (back) to the former. Given this point of departure, one might expect the sacred orgy (extreme case of loss of separateness through fusion) to become the privileged erotic experience, an exemplary operation of sovereignty. Bataille takes us by surprise, therefore, when he suddenly declares the orgy to be "necessarily disappointing" (129) and proceeds to focus exclusively on a heterosexual eroticism *à deux*, a gendered scenario of relation to an erotic object. The orgy, it seems, involves too radical a loss of separateness: "Not only is individuality itself submerged in the tumult of the orgy, but each participant denies the individuality of the others. All limits are completely done away with . . ."). Although radical fusion may, as Bataille declares, be the ultimate meaning of eroticism, the presence of an erotic object is required, at least initially. In eroticism it is a question of losing oneself knowingly, it seems, and not too completely after all.

While there are various instances of, or occasions for, sovereignty in Bataille's writing, it is in relation to eroticism—"clé des comportements [key to sovereign experience] souverains"—that the notion of transgression is most systematically developed. It is also here that specific theoretical constraints on the elaboration of sovereignty come into play. These emerge in relation to the erotic object whose theoretical status problematizes any simple account of the difference between mastery and sovereignty as it occurs through eroticism.

Man is the erotic, not the rational animal, Bataille responds to the philosophical tradition. At the same time, however, he wants to posit man as religious animal. In order to do so, he must delimit the animal and human realms which tend to be associated, if not identified, in discussions of sexuality. It is for this reason that Bataille defines eroticism as the *conscious* activity of the sexual animal, thereby placing an emphasis on lucidity which is absent, or less insistent, in accounts of other modes of sovereignty such as poetry or laughter. It is for the sake of this lucidity that erotic experience is staged as a relation to an erotic object and that, as Bataille puts it in "L'Histoire de l'érotisme," a dialectic is necessary.[3] The erotic object—the beautiful woman prostitute—guarantees this dialectic, and, in so doing, enables a certain consciousness.

The object of desire, Bataille writes in "L'Histoire de l'érotisme," is "the mirror in which we ourselves are reflected" (*OC*, 100). The woman performs this reflection to the extent that she operates as a sign. "Ordinarily a man cannot have the feeling that a law is violated in his own person which is why he awaits the confusion of a woman, even if it is feigned, without which he would not have the consciousness of a violation. . . . It is a question of marking, through shame, that the interdiction has not been forgotten, that the *dépassement* has taken place in spite of the interdiction, in consciousness of the interdiction" (134). The woman's shame, real or play acted (*jouée*), is read as a sign of transgression and to this extent signifies eroticism itself. Whereas the orgy gives an experience, or event, of negation of limits, it does not give it to consciousness and to this extent it does not give it to us as meaning. The erotic object does. It is a "paradoxical object" precisely because it is " . . . un objet *significatif* de la négation des limites de tout objet . . ." [an object which signifies the negation of the limits of any object].[4] In the possession of the erotic object man comes into consciousness—of loss, of death, and of himself as erotic subject.

The erotic object must be not only a woman, but a woman as object, or, in other words, a prostitute. In "L'Histoire de l'érotisme" Bataille contrasts the hypothetical erotic object of the theory (or fiction) of eroticism with actual experience. In real life, Bataille writes, autonomous women are at least as desirable as prostitutes, even more so. It is "customary" to wish for "the movements of more real beings, existing for themselves and wanting to respond to their own desire" instead of the "figures figées" [frozen figures] of " . . . beings destroyed as ends in themselves . . . " (*OC*, 124). The

3. Bataille, "L'Histoire de l'érotisme," in *Oeuvres complètes* (Paris: Gallimard, 1976), vol. 18. It is in a note that Bataille writes, concerning the question of the erotic object, "Mais une dialectique est nécessaire" (549). Subsequent references to this text will be to this edition and will be given in parentheses, marked *OC* (my translation).

4. Bataille, *L'Erotisme* (Paris: Minuit, 1957), 143, my emphasis. Subsequent references to the French text will be to this edition and will be given in parentheses, marked B.

passivity of the prostitute, however, is necessary for philosophical reasons. In relation to autonomous, desiring women (woman as subject) Bataille writes, man "cannot avoid struggle which would lead to destruction" (*OC*, 124.)[5] It is in order to avoid such struggle that, Bataille concludes, "we [i.e., men] must . . . place this object equal to ourselves, to the subject, in the frame of the dead object, of the infinitely available object . . . " (*OC*, 124). The prostitute is portrayed as a work of art, something like a living still life, a *nature morte*.

It is just here that we find the note already mentioned concerning the *necessity* for dialectic. And it is here that we can begin to see the paradoxical proximity of Bataille to Hegel—or of sovereignty to mastery. From what has been said so far it should be clear that there is a version (or fiction) of Hegelian recognition in eroticism. A determinate erotic object is required because a dialectic is necessary to yield self-consciousness of man as erotic animal. The dialectic yields a kind of meaning even in its nondiscursiveness, its silence. It is precisely to avoid the kind of struggle to the death which occurs in Hegel's master/slave dialectic that the woman must not be a desiring subject, that she must be placed within the frame of the dead object. Yet even with the precaution taken, we are not free of the subordination associated with mastery. The sovereign moment of erotic possession subordinates object to subject. Does this mean that Bataille's thinking is still dialectical? It is perhaps more exact to say it is dialectical *again*, in a repetition which renders the pertinence of the dialectical movement difficult to decide, and does so in a systematic, or rigorous, way. The discrepancy between Bataille and Hegel, between sovereignty, as it operates in eroticism, and mastery is less a formal or conceptual difference than a temporal or rhythmic one.

Bataille takes a step back from Hegel or, to be more precise, Kojève.[6] But it is a choreographed step in a paradoxical dance. In the Hegelian struggle for recognition, the positions of master and slave are designated when one subject concedes victory to another, sacrificing his autonomy in order to survive. Instead of being killed by his

5. The French text reads, " . . . si nous nous trouvons devant de tels êtres, même entièrement soucieux de répondre à ce désir qui n'est pas le nôtre, nous ne pouvons nous empêcher de lutter dans le sens de la destruction" (*OC*, 124).

6. Michel Surya writes in his biography, *La Mort à l'oeuvre* (Paris: Séguier, 1987), that the real discovery of Hegel for Bataille came through Kojève and that Bataille conscientiously attended Kojève's lectures on Hegel. Surya cites Bataille to the effect that he would leave Kojève's lectures "rompu, broyé, tué dix fois." See 196–99.

opponent he undergoes "dialectical suppression"; his life is spared but his status as subject is annulled. To be a slave means to be considered no better than a thing,[7] to be reduced in Kojève's words, to the status of "living cadaver" (K, 22). The master, on the other hand, succeeds in finding satisfaction or *jouissance*—"il réussit à venir au bout de la chose et à se satisfaire dans la jouissance" (K, 22). In Bataille the woman—the erotic object—is cast in the role of the already *aufgehoben* slave while the man enjoys the role of the master who, having already vanquished the slave, can take the things of this world for his pleasure. Bataille begins the dialectical relation to the erotic object where the Hegelian master/slave dialectic leaves off.

In Kojève's version of the Hegelian story the slave will eventually regain his autonomy through work. He can do so because, in the intense anxiety of death which prompted his capitulation to the master, he crossed the threshold from animal "sentiment de soi" [feeling of self] to human self-consciousness. For Bataille the equivalent of this anxiety of death is erotic desire. Since the woman as erotic object does *not* desire, however she does not undergo this anxiety and cannot enter into the historical, dialectical, progression toward autonomy. Thus what Kojève found tragic about the Hegelian recognition scene—the fact, as he put it, that the master is not "recognized by another man,[8]—is not simply comic for Bataille.[9] It becomes the particular virtue of eroticism: "recognition" by a woman!

To take the question of recognition seriously we must look more closely at the "mechanism" of eroticism, the dynamic equilibrium—*jeu de balance*—of *l'interdit* (interdiction/the taboo) and transgression, and at Bataille's presentation of it. The point of departure for the argument of *L'Erotisme*, the "philosophical detour" of the categorical opposition between continuity (or fusion), and discontinuity (or separation), is a version of the Hegelian opposition between identity and difference (or negativity). This initial opposition is put into play with others: violence and reason, nature and culture, the sacred and the profane, and, finally, the dual operation interdiction/transgression. According to one line of development in Bataille's text, the imposi-

7. Alexandre Kojève, *Introduction à la lecture de Hegel, Leçons sur la phénoménologie de l'esprit* (Paris: Gallimard, 1947), 23. Subsequent references will be to this edition and will be given in parentheses, marked K (my translation).

8. This is because, by the time recognition occurs, the slave has already been reduced to the status of mere thing.

9. See Bataille, "Hegel, La Mort et le sacrifice" in *Deucalion* 5 (1955): 21–43. Translation included in this issue; see "Hegel, Death and Sacrifice," 9–27.

tion of interdiction upon the violence of nature inaugurates a human world of work, consciousness of death, and restricted sexual activity. It marks the passage from the animal world to the human order. However, just where Hegel would place his anthropogenic scene of the struggle for recognition, Bataille's theoretical elaboration splits in two.

In the first place Bataille substitutes an unconscious negativity of interdiction for the Hegelian negativity of consciousness which is opposed to continuity or identity. In so doing he introduces a new dimension into the Hegelian story of the dialectic of human history, a structural difference (or difference in level) between the sacred and the profane. Bataille refers the reader to Roger Caillois's analysis of the sacred in *L'Homme et le sacré* and credits Caillois with the discovery of the very mechanism, the *ressort* of eroticism: the dual operation of interdiction and transgression. The reference to Caillois, however renders Bataille's use of the word "sacred" (or of the opposition sacred/profane) ambiguous since Caillois both analyzes an ambivalence of the sacred and opposes this primitive, ambivalent, sacred to a modern, monovalent one. Bataille mixes both these versions of the sacred together. The result is that sometimes the opposition between sacred and profane coincides with an opposition between transgression and interdiction, whereas at other times both transgression *and* interdiction are said to belong to the world of the sacred in its ambivalence. Bataille switches at will from one framework to the other.

Consistent with the Hegelian, chronological, line of development Bataille suggests that the imposition of interdiction upon the violence of nature both sacralizes that violence and opens the domain of reason, the realm of history or culture. In this context transgression involves a periodic, and controlled, introduction of the force (or violence) of the sacred into the profane world of reason, one which rejuvenates the system. This implies a correspondence between the opposition sacred and profane and that between transgression and interdiction. Here, then, Bataille conflates Hegel-Kojève's anthropogenic story of dialectical passage from animal to man (or desire to self consciousness) with an anthropological narrative of the emergence of culture from nature. At other times, however, Bataille presents interdiction and transgression as two moments of an ambivalent sacred, two emotional responses to the violence of nature. Interdiction marks the moment of *recul*, the step back from, or refusal of, violence prompted by a feeling of horror. Transgression occurs as a *rebondissement*, a return of (or to) violence produced by positive emotions of attraction or fascination. With this formulation (75) Bataille emphasizes the irrational (emotional) nature of interdiction itself, and, in this sense, the irrational foundation of the domain of reason itself, set up by interdiction on the authority, of feeling.[10] It is in the context of this elaboration that transgression and interdiction are translated into operations of expenditure and accumulation. The economic formulation depends upon an emotional "logic," equivalent, on the order of feeling, to affirmation and negation in Hegel's logical order. The emotional ambivalence is so intense, Bataille writes, that the only clear distinction between interdiction and transgression is an economic one: "Getting and spending are the two phases of this activity. Seen in this light, religion is like a dance where a movement backwards [recul] is followed by a spring forwards [rebondissement]" (68–69). The mechanism—the *ressort*—of eroticism is a dance. The word *ressort*, as the Robert dictionary indicates, includes both the meanings of *recul* and *rebondissement*. The dance is thus Bataille's version of Hegel's *aufheben*. Only here, instead of a sober dialectical synthesis, the vertigo of the dance yields a "un accord plus profond" [deeper harmony] (69). By substituting interdiction for the negativity associated with work, and the woman, "living cadaver," for the position of the slave, Bataille appears to have elided the scene of recognition altogether. Instead, he has postponed it. His version of the scene of recognition—eroticism as relation to the erotic object—occurs at a second time, a *reprise* of the dialectical turn which yields the experience of the sacred.

Bataille places interdiction, the negative moment in the development from animal to human in the diachronic (Hegelian) story, in a dialectical relationship with its *contrecoup* [counterpart], *transgression*. "There is no need to stress the Hegelian nature of this operation," Bataille writes in a note to his text concerning the operation of interdiction/transgression, "which corresponds with the moment of dialectics expressed by the untranslatable German verb aufheben (to surpass while maintaining)."[11] In other words, he superimposes this

10. This would be one, banal, sense in which transgression could be said to operate as a "foundation" of philosophy.
11. This note is cited in Derrida's essay. I have used the translation by Alan Bass in the English text of that essay, in *Writing and Difference* (Chicago: University of Chicago Press), 275. The note occurs on page 36 of *Erotism*.

dialectical mechanism, this *ressort,* onto the Hegelian development of the negativity of consciousness and the passage from the condition of animal to human being, a story he suspends before the scene of the struggle for pure prestige. Bataille interrupts one Hegelian development with another, or, to be more precise, with the same movement at another moment of development. He syncopates Hegel.

Throughout *Erotism* Bataille calls attention to the ruses of his text, to the "changes of emphasis" and the posturing of various theoretical gestures and tones. He even explicitly signals the superimposition of primitive and modern versions of the sacred which operates through an alignment of continuity/discontinuity and nature/reason (or animal/human) with the sacred/profane and transgression/interdiction oppositions as they are taken from Caillois. This joins the two theoretical stories precisely through the ambiguity introduced by the two versions (primitive and modern) of the sacred, and hence of its relation to the profane. Transgression, Bataille writes, "is complementary to the profane world, exceeding its limits but not destroying it. Human society is not only a world of work. Simultaneously—or successively—it is made up of the profane and the sacred, its two complementary forms. The profane world is the world of interdictions. The sacred world depends on limited acts of transgression. . . " (67–68). Here the word "sacred" is used in its modern, monovalent modality, in opposition to the profane. Bataille then shifts to the other track, though not without signaling the move: "This way of seeing is a difficult one," he acknowledges "in that *sacred* has two contradictory meanings simultaneously. Basically whatever is subject to prohibition is *sacred.* Interdiction, *l'interdit,* designating negatively the sacred thing, has not only the power to give us . . . a feeling of fear. . . . This feeling can change to one of devotion. . . . Man is at the same time subject to two movements: one of terror, which rejects, and one of attraction, which commands fascinated respect. Interdiction and transgression correspond to these two contradictory movements . . . " (68). To operate this slippage from monovalent to ambivalent sacred, Bataille can rely upon the ambiguity of the word *interdit* which refers both to the rule, or the action, of exclusion, and to the object rendered taboo.

Bataille finesses the double inscription of the words "sacred," and the double movement of his argument so elegantly, that we hardly notice it despite the signal he provides. In "L'Histoire de l'érotisme," however, the dance with Hegel is much more explicit. The steps are traced out more boldly. Whereas in *Erotism* Bataille characterizes the complementarity between profane and sacred worlds as simultaneous *or* successive (my emphasis), here he depicts the double movement of interdiction and transgression as "almost simultaneous" (*OC*, 66). In this elaboration Bataille takes as his point of departure Kojève's definition (after Hegel) of history as the dialectical progression of the self-creation of man as negation of the givens of nature. From here[12] he goes on to propose that, in a second moment, the cultural world, a function of the negation of the natural world through the imposition of interdiction (his correction of Hegel's story), itself becomes the horizon of the given which impinges upon the autonomy of the subject and against which the subject revolts. This is the moment of transgression, where what was previously negated returns (no longer in submission to the given) as desirable (*OC*, 69). It is in this context that Bataille describes the two movements of interdiction and transgression as "almost simultaneous"—a negation and its *contrecoup*. "This double movement", he explains, "does not even imply distinct phases. I can, for the sake of exposition speak of it as two moments, *en parler en deux temps*. But it is a question of a totality, *ensemble solidaire . . .* " (*OC*, 66). One cannot speak of one without the other just as one cannot separate the ebb from the flow of the ocean tides. "The duplicity of eroticism," Bataille writes, "is unintelligible as long as the totality of this double movement of negation and return is not grasped" (*OC*, 66).

The double movement of interdiction/transgression, however, does not just involve a moment of negation and one of return but rather a double movement of negation *and* return. At the very least it is a question of two moments of negation: the first (interdiction) a negation of nature yielding the passage to culture and the second (transgression) a negation of culture as horizon of the given yielding the passage to the sacred—man as religious animal. The dizzying character of this ambiguity, however, has to do with its temporality. The two points of view concerning the duplicity—the successive and the simultaneous—correspond, respectively, to a situation within

12. "History has been [a bien été] the (perhaps unfinished) exploration of all human possibility [de tout le possible de l'homme] founded on the negation of nature," he writes, ". . . this is the meaning of the infinitely renewed quest for the totality of the possible [c'est ce que signifie la quête infiniment renouvelée de la totalité du possible"] (*OC*, 66).

history on the one hand and at the end of history on the other. Thus the rhythm of point and counterpoint, of ebb and flow, involves not just two moments, but two times, or two temporalities: the profane temporality of history (and of work) and the sacred one in which time stops. The double movement is sequential in that, as Bataille puts it, to say yes, one must have been able to say no; logically, transgression cannot precede interdiction. It is simultaneous, however, because in the instant there is no before or after. Transgression, *la fête*, opens a mythic time which is not linear. Finally, the two movements are both simultaneous *and* sequential to the extent that they collapse the two moments of Hegel's scene of recognition: the anthropogenic moment (the self-consciousness of the master) and that which comes at the end of history, the self-consciousness of the sage—the subject of absolute knowledge.[13] In "L'Histoire de l'érotisme" Bataille is explicit about the relation between this thinking of eroticism and a Hegelian notion of the end of history. "History, to my mind, will have finished" he writes "when the disparity of rights and of level of subsistence are reduced: such would be the conditions for an ahistorical mode of existence of which erotic activity is the expression" (*OC*, 163). At the end of history, Kojève writes, the sage is content to retrace the path already traveled. This is what Bataille does in his study of eroticism, his "erotic phenomenology," (*OC*, 524).[14] Eroticism involves not the mastery of the lord but the sovereignty of the sage. It is to this moment of the subject of absolute knowledge that Bataille has postponed his version of the scene of recognition: man's relation to the erotic object, the beautiful woman prostitute. "By what right," Kojève had asked, "can we affirm that the State will not engender in man a new desire, other than that of Recognition, and that it will not consequently be negated one day by a negative or creative action

13. In an essay entitled "Postulat initial" which appeared in *Deucalion* 2 (1947), Bataille writes (speaking of eroticism, laughter and poetry): " . . . The negation I am introducing only takes place once the circle is closed, beyond the domain of history and of action . . . the instant can only be "major" when man has nothing left to do, when he has found Hegelian satisfaction and when his insatisfaction is no longer linked to active negation of any determinate form, but to the negation that no activity can resolve, of the human situation" (157, my translation).

14. Bataille writes that his study is a "phenomenology of the spirit, as it appears in erotic existence" (*OC*, 524). In a passage excised from Bataille's text, but provided in an editorial note, we read: "This book . . . simply takes up again, in a limited domain, the development that Hegel undertook in the *Phenomenology of the Spirit*." This, he adds, involves "a method not without rigor" (*OC*, 524).

other than that of struggle or of work?" (K, 468). Eroticism is Bataille's answer to Kojève's question.[15]

Eroticism involves a struggle for pure prestige in the etymological sense of the Latin *praestigium*, given by the Robert as illusion or seductive artifice. The "recognition" which results from this struggle operates through a fiction of death, not simply a fictive death as in the case of the dialectically suppressed slave, but a fiction, illusion, or seductive artifice of death as absolute recognition—or recognition of the absolute. The fiction of death does occur by default in this dialectic for want of the real thing; it is its positive result—its meaning. The *figure figée* of the prostitute, the beautiful erotic object, is essential to the staging of this fiction.

"The dialectic has a positive result," Hegel wrote, "because it has a specifically determined content, because the result is not . . . empty and abstract nothingness, but the negation of certain specific determinations" (cited in K, 477). Clearly the problem with the orgy is that it involves an abstract negation, in Hegel's sense. It is the beauty of the erotic object which lends concreteness to the erotic encounter. Beauty designates the erotic object to desire, and in this sense, it is the meaning, *le sens* of the erotic object, a meaning constitutive of value (131). In a woman's nudity, Bataille writes, "the potential beauty of this nakedness and its individual charm are what reveal themselves . . . the objective difference in fact, between the value of one object and that of another" (131). Beauty provides the specific determinations negated in the act of erotic possession.

In his essay "La Notion de dépense" Bataille specifically mentions the importance of the prostitute—the *fille perdue*—in the creation of those nonproductive values generated through potlatch and other modes of gratuitous expenditure or *dépense sans réserve*. Potlatch, too, is a struggle (or rivalry) for pure prestige, one achieved through the generation of what Bataille calls the *propriété positive de la perte* through which nonutilitarian values such as honor, rank, or glory, are acquired. Woman is at the center of eroticism as Bataille puts it, because of her status as object of exchange.

"The decisive element in the distinct constitution of erotic objets is a bit disconcerting," Bataille concedes in "L'Histoire de l'érotisme," "it presupposes that a human being can be considered as a

15. "Questioning has meaning only as elaborated by philosophy," Bataille writes in his conclusion to *Erotism*, " . . . the supreme questioning is that to which the answer is the supreme moment of eroticism—that of eroticism's silence" (275).

thing" (OC, 119). He goes on to discuss various modes of subordination or alienation, passing in review man's domestication of animals
and the master's domination over the slave before arriving at the
question of relations between women and men. Of the slavery of
Hegel's master/slave dialectic Bataille writes, " . . . the fiction
thanks to which our ancestors regarded their fellow men as things is
full of meaning," (OC, 120). Aside from slavery, Bataille writes in a
charmingly ambiguous turn of phrase, "men have generally tended to
see things in woman/ consider women as things [voir les choses dans
les femmes]" (OC, 120), because, before marriage, girls were considered to be the property of their fathers or brothers. It is because of the
fact that women, unlike the maenads, enjoy this reified status, because they could be considered to have the form and determination of
an object, that they can function as objects of erotic desire. Whereas
the maenads "fled in disorder, the object of desire . . . ornaments
herself with the greatest care and offers an immobile figure/face
[figure] to the temptation of he who would possess her" (OC, 121).
The problem with the orgy is that its participants, like the maenads,
cannot be captured in order to be exchanged—or to function as the
support of a figure or a fiction.

    Bataille's study is a history of eroticism in the sense that it ex-
plores the dialectical development of the contradiction, the dual operation, of gift-exchange associated with the prohibition of incest. The
duplicity of eroticism, the dual operation transgression/interdiction,
corresponds to this economic contradiction. Bataille opens "L'Histoire de l'érotisme" with a rambling discussion of the theory of Lévi-
Strauss concerning the prohibition of incest. On the one hand, he
says, the theory emphasized the expenditure [dépense] associated
with sexual interdiction because of the exchange of women. He calls
the prohibition of incest "the law of the gift" because it sets in motion the movement of "generosity" associated with the circulation of
women in exchange. At the same time, however, it had implications
for the restricted economy of productive exchange to the extent that
women were also a source of labor. The ambiguities of the theory of
Lévi-Strauss, Bataille writes, "correspond to the double aspect of the
'gift-exchange'" (OC, 29). It is in this sense that Bataille describes
potlatch as "at once beyond calculation and the epitome of calculation" (OC, 39). Bataille regrets that Lévi-Strauss did not emphasize
the relation between the exchange of women (or the potlatch) and the
structure of eroticism. Testily he states that the anthropologist

"would no doubt not go so far as to say what I say: that it is a question of a dialectical process of *development*" (*OC*, 36, original emphasis).

Bataille's dialectical development of the insight he shared with Lévi-Strauss involved a superimposition of various stories concerning a struggle for pure prestige. He combines elements from Hegel's analysis of the struggle for recognition, which requires the fiction of the servile man as object, with the anthropological stories concerning the potlatch as struggle for pure prestige and of women as objects of exchange. In other words, he combines elements of the formal structure of the master/slave dialectic with one anthropological story of interdiction (the prohibition of incest) and one of transgression, the potlatch that includes the gift and sacrifice. If the Hegelian fiction of slavery is "full of meaning" for Bataille, it is because it provides the point of articulation for these overlapping stories.

The woman, the erotic object, is thus a paradoxical object in another sense as the locus of intimacy between the restricted and general economies. To the extent that the relation to the erotic object includes elements of the Hegelian scene of recognition, there is subordination in the sovereignty of eroticism. There is possession in a nonreciprocal relation. On the other hand, erotic possession belongs not to the restricted economy of utility but to the general economy of expenditure. The woman gives herself to the man. Interdiction as law of the gift thus repeats the "double movement" Bataille attributes to the dual operation of interdiction/transgression. Interdiction (of incest) precedes eroticism as relation to the erotic object because it is necessary to the constitution of that object. This movement corresponds to the first line of development of Bataille's theory, the story of history which follows the path of Hegel-Kojève. At the same time the woman as erotic object is necessary for transgression which provides the "recognition" of erotic sovereignty, that is to say in the transgressiveness of erotic possession *per se.*

In other words, then, there is no pure origin of transgression, or of the economy of expenditure. It seems that the dance of interdiction/transgression goes all the way back—or circles round. There is no transgression which is not mediated by interdiction, no *rebondissement* without a moment of *recul*. But neither is interdiction primary, for the historical narrative refers us back to a (violent) animal sexuality from which we step back with horror: "To the extent that the tumultous movement of the senses occurs," Bataille writes in "L'Histoire de l'érotisme," "it requires a step back, a renunciation, the step back without which no one would be able to leap ahead so far. But the step back itself requires the rule, which organizes the dance and assures that it will spring forth again indefinitely" (*OC*, 36). If woman is at the center of eroticism, as Bataille writes, it is as the paradoxical object which marks the limit between law and transgression, or their interpenetration.

In *Erotism* Bataille figures the dual operation of interdiction/ transgression through the image of the chrysalis. The emotions of desire and anxiety associated with interdiction and transgression ". . . are, in the life of man, what the chrysalis is to the final perfect creature *l'animal parfait. L'expérience intérieure* of man is given at the instant when, bursting out of the chrysalis, he feels that he is tearing himself, not something outside that resists him. He goes beyond the objective awareness bounded by the walls of the chrysalis and this process too, is linked with this reversal *renversement*" (39). Intermediate form between the larva and the *imago,* the chrysalis figures the intermediate stage between animal existence and the emergence of the "perfect animal," the religious animal, from the limits of historical time. The image thus figures both the story of interdiction as entry into history (passage from larva to chrysalis or from man to animal) and transgression as a leap out of history at the moment of the *imago* or image. Elsewhere in Bataille the appearance of the image on the walls of the Lascaux caves marked the emergence of civilized man from the "larval" state of animal existence.[16] There what Bataille called "the sacred moment of figuration" was a sign of the beginning of history and of art. The figure of the chrysalis, therefore, accommodates Bataille's, syncope, both moments of his *ronde* with Hegel. It does so, in particular, through the insistence of the image or of figuration *per se*. It both duplicates and delays the image through the hesitation of the implied moment in the figure, or in the metamorphosis of the chrysalis, the imago.

We have suggested that the dialectic of the erotic object is necessary to Bataille's theory of eroticism as the support of figuration or fiction—the fiction of death in particular. We can perhaps learn something more about what fiction means in Bataille, or how it operates, by meditating on the figure of the chrysalis. If the chrysalis figures a movement toward sovereignty, and sovereignty, as Bataille writes in the text on Lascaux, is a fact of "he alone who is an end in himself"

16. "Lascaux ou la Naissance de l'art" in Bataille, *Oeuvres complètes* 9, 32, and 36.

(*OC*, 76), then clearly, the chrysalis is an image for man as erotic
animal. If, however, woman is always "at the center of eroticism," she
is also at the center of this image, although in a manner which by-
passes what the image gives us to see and operates through the language of the figure. For another word for *chrysalide* is *nymphe* which,
in a first meaning, refers to a mythological goddess, or rather, as the
Robert specifies, "her image in the form of a naked young girl." In
addition to the zoological meaning (synonymous with chrysalis) the
dictionary also gives an anatomical meaning: "the small lips of the
vulva." The synonym of the chrysalis, then—the nymphe—signifies
the woman's sex, and clothes or figures it, if you will, with the image,
the form, of nakedness.

In its form, Bataille writes, eroticism is fictive. The fiction is what
ensures the lucidity or consciousness necessary in order to distinguish eroticism from mere animal sexuality, and to erect man as
erotic animal and religious animal as well. The woman—the erotic
object—is essential to eroticism in order to render it *saisissable*, in
order to figure it or present it to consciousness through the mediation
of visual form. It is the play of signifying operations within eroticism
which distinguishes it from animal sexuality. Yet what is figured
through the dialectic of the erotic object, what is seized by consciousness, is, precisely, loss or expenditure. With eroticism we are
left with a fiction which does not represent anything but which must
nevertheless be staged or performed—a fiction of death. Its appearance requires the presence of the "paradoxical object"—the
beautiful woman prostitute—an object which signifies the absence
of any object.

With the metaphor of the chrysalis we have the sex of the woman
hidden within the figure of metamorphosis. The chrysalis names one
moment of the process which it also "figures," though only as an
accumulation or juxtaposition of latent figures—the larva and the
imago—which serve both to veil and to reveal one another. The metamorphosis, as image, passes not into another image of something, but
into the word image *per se*, the imago. The linguistic level introduces
a latent figuration which gives us the image, to the extent that it
names it—imago—but does not give us anything to see. Likewise the
image of the woman's sex (or of the naked girl) is veiled by the linguistic alibi of the synonym, *nymphe*. This corresponds to the way
beauty operates in Bataille's account of eroticism where it is associated with nakedness. Nakedness is a revelation of beauty which re-

veals the "individual charm" of a woman—"the objective difference, in fact, between the value of one object and that of another" (131). At the same time the beauty of the nude woman serves as a veil. It exerts a charm which seduces the man into desiring the woman's non-beautiful parts—the nymphe in the anatomical sense.[17] In the figure of the chrysalis, the nymphe as image, that is to say explicitly as image, figuration of the mythological goddess through the image of the naked girl, clothes, as it were, the naked fact of the woman's sex with an image of nakedness, a kind of seductive artifice, or prestige.

The positive result of the dialectic of erotic sovereignty is a fiction, one "invented expressly": "We approach the void" Bataille writes, "but not to fall into it. We want to become intoxicated with dizziness and the image of the fall is sufficient" (OC, 94). But this is an image, like the word "imago" which is not, in itself, an image *of* anything. The positive result of the dialectical movement of interdiction/transgression is neither discursive meaning nor loss of meaning but rather a fiction, a *fiction voulue* and a seductive illusion, a *praestigium* of death.

17. "The beauty of the desirable woman suggests her private parts, the hairy ones, to be precise, the animal ones. . . . Beauty that is a negation of animality and awakens desire ends up by exasperating desire and exalting the animal parts" (143–44).

JONATHAN STRAUSS

The Inverted Icarus

> In clear consciousness, I devoted myself to the conquest of an inaccessible object.
>
> —Bataille

In Bataille's writings there appears and reappears a network of terms that play comparable roles, and one would be tempted to say that they have similar meanings were not the very possibility of their having any meaning at all in question, were these not words which, in the context of Bataille's writing, put the very possibility of meaning itself at risk. These are terms which rupture a text, which interrupt its connections, which disrupt its sense, and which designate concepts of an alterity so radical that it cannot be identified and of a foreignness so complete that it can never be known. These are the figures, the masks of something that can never be seen face to face by a coherent subject, and they include erotism, the sacred, the sun and other celestial bodies, the sovereign, the fascist leader, the proletariat, and a certain essence of humanity that informs public places. The latter represent something which for Bataille is fundamentally other, which, in an absolute sense, is heterogeneous, and Bataille, who returns ceaselessly to this subject, is continually confronted with the difficulty of bringing to words that which transgresses reason and which falls beyond the knowable and the identifiable.

In the article "The Psychological Structure of Fascism," Bataille introduces the idea of an absolute heterogeneity into an analysis of fundamental human social structures, and to mark the fact that he is designating an idea that has never been fully expressed and which cannot easily be accommodated by existing language, he puts the word *heterogeneous* into italics whenever he wants to refer to his particular concept of radical alterity. The word *homogeneous*, when understood in the context of this alterity, is treated similarly. Initially

YFS 78, *On Bataille*, ed. Allan Stoekl, © 1990 by Yale University.

because it is more accessible to human understanding[1] and then ultimately and inevitably for reasons we shall examine, Bataille employs the *homogeneous* and its terms to articulate the *heterogeneous*. The former is described in the fascism article as a closed system of communication and exchange in which all deficits are recompensed by gains and in which there is no useless expense or pure loss. Everything, insofar as it is *homogeneous*, is interchangeable and substitutable:

> *Homogeneity* signifies here the commensurability of elements and awareness of this commensurability.
>
> Every useless element is excluded, not from all of society, but from its *homogeneous* part. . . . A useful activity has a common measure with another useful activity, but not with activity *for itself*. ["Psychological Structure," *VE*, 137–38]

As a concrete example of that common measure, that unifying communicability of disparate and different elements which constitutes the principle of the *homogeneous*, Bataille cites money (ibid.).

The *heterogeneous*, on the other hand, falls beyond common measure, and in respect to the *homogeneous* element of society it remains incommensurable and altogether other.[2] Unlike the *homogeneous*, the *heterogeneous* bears itself as its own end and purpose, existing in itself and for itself.[3] Those expenditures which do not reappear as a profit elsewhere within the closed system of *homogeneous* exchange, those losses which cannot be recouped as an equivalent utility and whose purpose lies only in themselves, whose only purpose is to be loss, will be understood to represent the *heterogeneous* element of society. This *other* aspect of society finds expression in "luxury, mourning, war, cults, the construction of sump-

---

1. "A psychological description of society must begin with that segment which is most accessible to understanding—and apparently the most fundamental segment— whose significant trait is tendential *homogeneity*. Georges Bataille, "The Psychological Structure of Fascism," in *Visions of Excess: Selected Writings, Selected Writings, 1927–1939*, ed. and introduction Allan Stoeckl, trans. Allan Stoeckl, Carl R. Lovitt, and Donald M. Leslie, Jr. (Minneapolis: University of Minnesota Press, 1985), 137. All essays from this edition will henceforth be cited in the text, title, *VE*, page numbers. All translations are slightly altered.

2. "*In summary*, compared to everyday life, *heterogeneous* existence can be represented as something *other*, as *incommensurate*." Ibid, 143.

3. "An existence valid in itself (*heterogeneous*)," ibid, 139. "This concentration in a single person intervenes as an element that sets the fascist formation apart within the *heterogeneous* realm . . . this agency is an existence *for itself*." Ibid, 143–44.

tuary monuments, games, spectacles, arts, perverse sexual activity (i.e., deflected from genital finality)" (Bataille, "The Notion of Expenditure," *VE*, 118). As a figure for this useless expenditure, Bataille returns repeatedly throughout his writings to the image of the endlessly burning, self-consuming and self-sacrificing sun.

Although it is absolutely excluded from the *homogeneous* system, if not from society itself, and although it remains irrecuperably alien to the network of equivalent exchange, the *heterogeneous* nonetheless affects this system, imposing on it the very coherence and structure which allow it to function. In its more elevated and manifestly imperious form, as the head of an army for instance, the *heterogeneous* articulates the *homogeneous* mass of humanity, ordering an otherwise undifferentiated populace into the "geometrical regularity" ("The Psychological Structure of Fascism," *VE*, 150) of an army's rank and file; in the person of the sovereign, the *heterogeneous* not only directs the *homogeneous* but also gives to it a reason and a meaning which it cannot offer itself.

> The inability of *homogeneous* society to find in itself a reason for being and acting is what makes it dependent upon imperative forces . . .
>
> . . . since the king is the object in which homogeneous society has found its reason for being, maintaining this relationship demands that he conduct himself in such a way that the *homogeneous* society can exist for him. ["The Psychological Structure, *VE*, 146–50]

As it is the nature of the *heterogeneous* to organize and to give itself as end and reason both to itself and to its other, so conversely is it the nature of the *homogeneous* to be attracted, to tend towards another. When Bataille first introduces the concept of the *homogeneous* he refers to it as "tendential *homogeneity*" (ibid., 137). Later, in the same article, he more explicitly writes that "unification, the principle of *homogeneity*, is only a tendential fact" and that this pure tendency, which as the very principle of the *homogeneous* is its identity and existence, "requires being *for itself*, namely the specific mode of *heterogeneous* existence." Indeed, the common element of society must receive existence itself from its other, since the *homogeneous* alone is incapable "of finding in itself a motive for requiring and imposing its existence" (ibid. 147). This tendential aspect manifests itself within *homogeneous* society in the role of the productive individual, who is valued not in himself but for what he produces and who therefore ceases to exist for himself, becoming a "function, arranged within measurable limits, of collective production (which makes him an existence *for something other than itself*)" (ibid. 138). Through his commensurability, the productive individual loses himself as reason for being and is alienated from his 'own' meaning. This same loss of an existence "for itself" operates within the *homogeneous* community as a whole, and the latter derives its organization from its tendency towards an other which bears its end in itself. Within this article's conceptualization of social and economic forces, the reason for society's existence is to be understood as the *heterogeneous*.

This attractive *other* is more than merely the organizing principle of the *homogeneous* as such, it is also the epitome of that which is human.[4] However, the very activity by which the *heterogeneous* manifests its existence, that very attraction which it exercises over the community which it articulates, and which in turn figures the *heterogeneous*, serves also to obscure the latter much in the same way that dust motes cover the disturbances whose movements they reveal:

> Beyond these limits [of personal human destiny]—there where human meanings begins—existence matters to the extent that [human beings] attract and, apart from this attraction, they are less than shadows, less than specks of dust. And the attraction of an isolated human being is itself still only a shadow, a pitiful fleeting apparition. It is but the tentative incarnation of THAT WHICH ALONE IS HUMAN LIFE, which has no name and which the agitation of countless multitudes obscurely demands and constructs, in spite of appearances to the contrary. Who knows what bitterness and sanctity are exhaled in this agitation, which is horror, violence, hatred, sobs, crime, disgust, laughter, and human love. Each individual is but one of the specks of dust that gravitate around this bitter existence. The dust makes it impossible to see the condensation around which it orbits . . . ["The Obelisk," *VE*, 214]

Human meaning, itself nameless, begins just beyond the swirl of humanity which expresses it, but which mis-states it, which falsifies

---

4. In the margins of "The Psychological Structure of Fascism" Bataille wrote "The heter[ogeneous] is comparable to that which one calls *life* in the cell. Thus, if life is the movement of the whole, the heterogeneous is the *moved*." *Oeuvres Complètes*, ed. Denis Hollier, presentation by Michel Foucault (Paris: Gallimard, 1970), vol. 1, 348n. Henceforth cited in the text as *OC*.

human sense in manifesting it, in giving it face and figure in the person of an attractive individual or in the movements of a crowd. This disfiguring expression of a radically and inexpressibly alien meaning of human existence is described not only as a dust mote, but also as a shadow, the same word which Bataille uses to describe the individual himself, and the intelligibility of this passage lies partially in the repeated hesitation between these two tropes. Not only does this hesitation suggest a practical acknowledgement that no single trope is sufficient to express the relation of humanity to its meaning and that any metaphor for that meaning must fail, but the reference to shadows also evokes a third, unspoken, metaphor. What casts the shadows is never specified. In the context of this passage they are, as Bataille writes, "nothing but shadows," images of something which itself will never be known, which remains nameless. But the shadow which is "only a shadow" and is yet a figure, or expressive disfigurement, of something else, is also shadow itself, and necessarily evokes the source of light that makes of a shadow an image. The gravitating dust motes are shadows cast by an unspoken and attractive sun or other condensation of light which their figural logic "demands and constructs" and which they obscure by expressing. However, simply to construe the *other* as the sun merely constitutes one more figuration, and the text in this way specifically rejects the obvious identification of human meaning with solar clarity. In a reasoning reminiscent of negative theology, this passage indicates that the best metaphors will be the most deceptive, the clearest the most obscuring. Unlike a Nicholas of Cusa, however, Bataille does not take this to mean that the worst metaphors will therefore be the most accurate, and it is only in following Bataille's further, and fundamentally incomplete working out of the problematics of representation and obscuring that one can appreciate the specificity of his attempt to bring the unspeakable and unidentifiable into his writing. This appears most clearly in those passages and texts which address issues of writing itself.

As the *heterogeneous* is the *raison d'être* of the society of communication and exchange, its reason and meaning, so does it play a similar role in the exchange of reason and meaning themselves. The realm of science is a privileged aspect, one of the "eminent functions" ("The Psychological" *VE*, 141) of the *homogeneous* order, and consequently constitutes an expression—although a fundamentally falsified one—of the *heterogeneous*.

The idea that scientific reason functions as an inclusive and homogenizing force found expression in an early article by Bataille entitled "Figure humaine" [Human Face], which presents the concrete specificity of the "I" and its figuration in the physical appearance of a human individual—especially its striking and somewhat repugnant manifestation as a person attired in a manner that has gone recently but decidedly out of style—as a moment that cannot be recuperated into the abstract and universal sphere of a rational order. In a footnote denouncing Tristan Tzara's acceptance of the idea that the absence of a relation is in itself a relation, Bataille, using the specific example of Hegelian dialectics, describes abstract reason as a powerful assimilatory force intent on accounting for and incorporating anything alien to it.

> As early as 1921, when Tristan Tzara recognized that "the absence of system is still a system, but the most congenial," although that concession to insignificant objections remained at the time without apparent impact, the imminent introduction of Hegelianism could be foreseen. In fact, it is an easy step from this acknowledgement to the panlogism of Hegel since it is in conformity with the principle of the *identity of opposites:* one could even suppose that given that initial act of cowardice there was no longer any way to avoid panlogism and its vulgar consequences, i.e., the sordid thirst for every integrity, blind hypocrisy, and finally, the need to be useful to anything determinate. ["Figure humaine," *OC*, vol. 1, 183. (My translation.)]

This article, which represents an early attempt, in face of an all-embracing philosophical system, to free a space for an irreducibly alien element within Occidental society and science, situates the irreconcilable *other* in the specificity, the vagaries, and the monstrosities of the realm of nature. Bataille again questions the possibility of a reconciliation between panlogism and Nature in a later article entitled "The Critique of the Foundations of the Hegelian Dialectic," which attempts to delimit the experimental foundations of Hegelian dialectics. There again, he insists that philosophy has remained unaccountable for Nature and that the latter in fact constitutes, even in Hegel's own estimation, the end of philosophy. To support this contention, Bataille quotes from Hegel's *Philosophy of Nature*, writing that "Hegel himself was the first to indicate cautiously that it was precisely nature which by its 'impotence to actualize the Notion sets limits to philosophy'" ("The Critique of the

Foundations of the Hegelian Dialectic,) *VE*, 106–07). And yet, according to Bataille, the *Philosophy of Nature* itself represents a continued effort on Hegel's part to incorporate an avowedly irreconcilable Nature, a Nature which is the limit or end of philosophy, into the dialectical structure. It is this least promising aspect of Hegelianism, the part which, according to Bataille, left Hegel himself ultimately unsatisfied, that eventually became the foundation for the Marxist appropriation of dialectics.

> The very elements that suddenly become, for Marx and Engels, the method's foundations are precisely those that offer the most resistance to the application of this method, and not only by definition, but above all in practice. In spite of the trouble taken by Hegel to resolve the difficulties encountered in the *Philosophy of Nature*, this part of his work left even him unsatisfied. ["The Critique," *VE*, 107]

It was a dissatisfaction which survived Hegel himself. Engels's eight-year labor to develop a dialectical theory of nature ended in a failure which he was forced to acknowledge in the second preface to the *Anti-Dühring*, and which Bataille analyzes at length in the "Critique." Bataille's article itself, which ends with the outline for a potential "dialectic of the real" based on what were at the time recent psychoanalytic insights, constitutes yet another attempt to found dialectics in experience, on precisely those elements "which offer the most resistance to the application of this method." Within the intellectual filiation of Hegel, Engels, and Bataille, the task of philosophy remains the appropriation of its own end, of its own term and terms: it is the task of self-limitation, and in this strict sense, of self-determination and self-definition. It is philosophy's task of self-appropriation and self-grounding, the attempt to give itself that which the *homogeneous* can never give to itself, which it must seek elsewhere: its principle and its existence ("The Psychological," *VE*, 146–47). There is an essential difference, however, when Bataille undertakes the labor which he has inherited from Hegel and Engels. He undertakes it with a certain lucidity, with an awareness of its underlying futility.

The theme of reason as a labor of assimilation and identification reappears in the article "The Psychological Structure of Fascism," where scientific reason is construed as eminently *homogeneous*. The relation of science—which, as an assimilatory force, constitutes in principle a process of inclusion—towards its other is at first described as an essentially passive nonrelation, in which the *heterogeneous* remains unincorporated simply because it is unincorporable, and Bataille writes that "the very term *heterogeneous* indicates that it concerns elements that are impossible to assimilate; this impossibility, which has a fundamental impact on social assimilation, likewise has an impact on scientific assimilation" (ibid., 140–41). Bataille continues to uphold the idea of a *homogeneous* passivity in face of the unassimilable alterity of the *heterogeneous* by describing the relationship between science and the irreducibly other as a *de facto* censorship ["une censure de fait"] rather than as an active one. And yet there is a change of nuance when the exclusion of the *heterogeneous* from the field of science is then compared to the mechanism of censorship which psychoanalysis situates between the Conscious and the Unconscious. Bataille's insistence on this analogy leads him finally to declare that "it would seem that the Unconscious must be considered as one of the aspects of the *heterogeneous*" (ibid., 141, 143). But the censorship of the Unconscious is scarcely a passive structural impossibility of communication between two radically different realms, and psychoanalysis has traditionally seen in the censor of the unassimilable a powerful and dynamic force. Indeed, the entire idea of dreams and the dream-work reveals an energetic labor to exclude or distort the unspeakable, to keep it in silence through a network of deceptive (mis)representations and figures.[5] In this regard, by following this psychoanalytic analogy, the relation of science to its other seems less to resemble a static structural impossibility than the sort of dynamic of representation and occultation analyzed in the passage already cited from "The Obelisk."

The problematic of a homogeneous science and an unassimilable *other* remains essentially intact in "Figure humaine," the "Critique" of Hegelian dialectics, and the article on fascism, but in the latter the focus shifts from the irreconcilable opposition between the natural order and Hegelian dialectics, which had figured in "Figure humaine"

5. The dynamic censorship between the Preconscious and the Unconscious is said by Freud to generate the associations between dream elements: he writes, for example, that "whenever one psychical element is linked with another by an objectionable or superficial association, there is also a legitimate and deeper link between them which is subjected to the resistance of the censorship," *The Interpretation of Dreams*, trans. and ed. James Strachey (New York: Avon, 1965) 569. It is the distortion of the original thoughts and associations under the pressure of censorship that constitutes the type of thinking which is the dream work and, ultimately, the dream. Cf., 544n. and chapter 7 passim.

and the "Critique" to the opposition between a single, fundamental, *homogeneous* order manifesting itself in the complementary forms of science and society and a *heterogeneous* force whose determination has grown significantly more problematic than can be accommodated by simply and specifically identifying it with Nature. In the fascism article, Bataille writes, referring to science and society, that "these two types of assimilation have a single structure: science has for its object to establish the *homogeneity* of phenomena and is, in a sense, one of the eminent functions of *homogeneity*" (ibid., 141). But this task of assimilation, of identification and homogenization, is always first and foremost the attempt to assimilate what will always remain irreducibly alien, and Bataille concedes that the object and crux of any sociological study, including his own, remains essentially undetermined: "The entire problem of social psychology rests precisely upon the fact that analysis must be brought to bear on a form that is not only difficult to study, but whose existence has not yet been the object of a positive determination" (ibid., 140). That indeterminate form, he will explain in the following paragraph, is the *heterogeneous*, the form which can never be assimilated into science. What is striking then is not that Bataille should concede that the object of his inquiry has not been positively determined, but that it has *not yet* been so determined. In short, Bataille undertakes the task of determining, or assimilating, an object which his own reasoning demonstrates to remain absolutely undeterminable and he undertakes the task *as if* the heterogeneous *could be assimilated.* At this moment the figure of Bataille at work on "The Psychological Structure of Fascism" bears a striking resemblance to that of Engels, engaged for eight years in an ultimately futile attempt to reconcile the natural world with Hegelian logic: it is the figure of the philosopher caught in an interminable task of assimilation whose sense and direction lie specifically in that which can never be assimilated.

At the opening of his article on the psychological structure of Fascism, Bataille writes that "The psychological description of society must begin with that segment which is most accessible to understanding—and apparently the most fundamental segment—whose significant trait is tendential *homogeneity*" (ibid., 137). The significant aspect of the accessible part of society—the aspect which is not only important, but which *signifies*, which has a sense—is the *homogeneous* insofar as it is directed towards another, to the extent that it tends towards, or intends, the *heterogeneous*. The *homogeneous* means the *heterogeneous*. And so the psychological, or in general the scientific description of society is an attempt to get at the *heterogeneous*, to identify and determine it. Science and human understanding mean something else, they are alienated from their meaning. Science and human understanding, philosophy and panlogism have always only spoken of one thing: what they couldn't say.

In *L'Expérience intérieure*, Bataille writes:

> There is in the understanding a blind spot which recalls the structure of the eye. In the understanding as in the eye it can be detected only with difficulty. But while the blind spot in the eye is inconsequential, the nature of the understanding dictates that the blind spot have in it more sense than the understanding itself. [*OC*, vol. 5, 129]

It is precisely what science cannot see, what it obscures, that point to which it has blinded itself but which in exchange allows it to see everything else, that is the meaning of science. The heterogeneous,[6] then, is that which cannot be known face-to-face by the homogeneous, that which is always only represented, whether it be in writing or society. It is that towards which human activity always tends and which it always expresses; as the for-itself [the *pour soi*] ("The Psychological," *VE*, 147); it is the eternal object of that which refers to an other, it is the referent par excellence. Yet the heterogeneous can never be represented, is always obscured, as if in a cloud of dust, by that which would designate it, is always mistaken by a writing which remains within its own terrestrial limitations and must inevitably fall short. Human signification—"there where human signification begins"—is the concealment of that for which it longs. It is a blind spot which constitutes the original representation, the paradigm of representation and the condition of possibility of all further representation: the sign of what shall never be known. But, as becomes apparent in the article "Rotten Sun," this blind spot is also the after-image of the sun, although of a sun which has perhaps never yet been seen.

Philosophy, sociology, and science in general are futile but pointed labors. The fact that they were not only pointed, but were actually labors was of great importance. In remarking that Marx and Engels

6. Outside the "Psychological Structure of Fascism," Bataille often uses the word heterogeneous without placing it in italics, and even in that article he is not consistent (cf., for example, 143). When discussing the concept of the heterogeneous or in reference to the fascism article, I will place it in italics, otherwise in roman.

had attempted to found their appropriation of the dialectical method on Nature, Bataille stated that the latter resists "the application of this method, and not only by definition, but above all *in practice*" ("The Critique," *VE*, 107, my emphasis). Bataille had already made a very characteristic use of this distinction between definition and practice in an article for the *Critical Dictionary* in the journal *Documents*. Instead of simply giving a definition of its heading, his entry on the word "Formless" destabilizes the very idea of definition by refusing, out of a respect both for the formal requirements of a dictionary and for the implications of the word "formless" itself, to give a finite meaning to the word. It is not only the sense of the word "formless" which is at stake, it is sense itself, because "formless" exceeds the limits of sense, the limits which in giving sense also give recognizable form.

> A dictionary begins when it no longer gives the meaning of words, but their tasks [*besognes*]. Thus *formless* is not only an adjective having a given meaning, but a term that serves to bring things down in the world, generally requiring that each thing have its form. What it designates has no rights in any sense and gets itself squashed everywhere, like a spider or an earthworm. In fact, for academic men to be happy, the universe would have to take shape. All of philosophy has no other goal: it is a matter of giving a frock coat to what is, a mathematical frock coat. On the other hand, affirming that the universe resembles nothing and is only *formless* amounts to saying that the universe is something like a spider or spit. ["Formless," *VE*, 31]

There is a particular problem with the word "formless," because to define it would be to betray its sense. "Formless" is precisely that which is beyond the limits, which has no term, and which exceeds definition. To give it a meaning would not be to take its meaning seriously, to make the word redundant. Mathematicians, philosophers, and presumably lexicographers would dress the world up in a frock coat, have the unspeakable cut a figure, and the task of philosophy is precisely this figuring. Unlike Tzara, for whom the lack of system is still a system, Bataille refuses such a formalization of the formless and turns instead to put definition itself into question and to set the dictionary to work in a new manner. It is through the very idea of work itself, specifically the novel idea of a task of words, that Bataille attempts to evoke something that lies beyond all systems, including language. The labor, the *"besogne,"* of a word which none-

theless still has a sense exceeds formal thought and philosophy, and
the word "formless" in its labor, reveals the possibility of an indeterminate universe, or a universe which can only be designated as
"something like." "Not only by definition, but above all *in practice*"
the word "formless" reveals the goals and ends of philosophy, what
Hegel described, in *The Philosophy of Nature*, as the "limit" of philosophy.[7] This raises the possibility that there is active, as it were, in a
writer's work something which he may be conscious of or even trying
to express but which cannot be demonstrated, defined or expressed as
sense: looking for a certain labor of the words would be the only way
to read this aspect. It is this novel, this revolutionary aspect of language that we will look for in Bataille's writings.

The heterogeneous is that precisely which cannot be represented,
which is always necessarily misrepresented, and which is nonetheless the meaning of all philosophical discourse. Bataille identifies it
with the human act of sacrifice: "The loveliness of a starry sky, its
ragged grandeur have the purifying beauty of a sacrifice"; ("La Limite
de l'utile," *OC*, vol. 7, 190). "The peoples of ancient Mexico brought
man into union with the glory of the universe . . . the Aztec people
saw . . . the unity of sacrifice and light, the equivalence between the
heady offering up of oneself and glories no less heady" (ibid., 192). Yet
the very nature of sacrifice is representational, for a sacrifice is in its
essence the representation of that which one can never see and which
nonetheless constitutes the self, which is, in this sense, the heterogeneous of human consciousness: sacrifice represents the death of
the self. Bataille, inscribing the representational nature of sacrifice
into the Hegelian dialectic of master and slave, writes that:

> In order for Man to reveal himself ultimately to himself, he would
> have to die, but he would have to do it while living—watching himself
> ceasing to be. In other words, death itself would have to become (self-)
> consciousness at the very moment that it annihilates the conscious
> being. In a sense, this is what takes place (what at least is on the point
> of taking place, or which takes place in a fugitive, ungraspable man-

7. Denis Hollier has written of the necessary limitlessness of the Bataillean dictionnary, its wasting of sense, and of the way these two principles are implicit in the
article "Formless," which "instead of closing the dictionnary on itself . . . opens it to
the loss of sense, to infinite incompleteness." This idea of infinite incompleteness will
be very useful for understanding Bataille's idea of the task, or *besogne*, of words. *La
Prise de la Concorde: Essais sur Georges Bataille* (Paris: Gallimard, 1974), 63, (my
translation).

ner) by means of a subterfuge. In the sacrifice, the sacrificer identifies himself with the animal that is struck down dead. And so he dies in seeing himself die, and even, in a certain way, by his own will, one in spirit with the sacrificial weapon. But it is a comedy!

At least it would be a comedy if some other method existed which could reveal to the living the invasion of death: that finishing of the finite being, which *his* Negativity—which kills him, *ends* him and definitively suppresses him—accomplishes alone and which it alone can accomplish. . . . So it must be, at all costs, that man live at the moment that he really dies, or that he live with the impression of really dying. . . . This difficulty reveals the necessity of *spectacle*, or of *representation* in general.[8]

Even in sacrificial acts of automutilation it is this representational subterfuge which is at play, because there is in the intentional ablation of a bodily part a significance that goes beyond the pain that the operation inflicts: there remains, inscribed on the person of the automutilator, a permanent loss, a subsistent breach in the unity of the self. This "rupture of personal homogeneity, the projection *outside the self* of a part of oneself" ("Sacrificial Mutilation and the Severed Ear of Vincent Van Gogh, *VE*, 68) introduces into the integrity of one's person an alterity, a decisive nonbeing, but a nonbeing that cannot simply be thought of as the opposite of being and which can only be marked through the continuity of the body which it disrupts. What this disruptive somatic writing marks is precisely that other which, in falling beyond every symmetrically continuous system which apprehends nonbeing in terms of being and other in terms of the same (for example the panlogism of Hegel referred to in "Figure humaine"), subsists as resolutely unknowable. The sense of this "projection *outside the self* of a part of oneself" is ultimately the projection beyond oneself of oneself. For this reason, Bataille sees in automutilation, as well as in the vomiting by which a participant might react to a gruesome ritual, a representation of the constitutive death of the self. The participant, he writes, "is free—free to indulge in a similar disgorging, free, continuously identifying with the victim, to vomit his own being just as he has vomited a piece of himself or a bull, in other words free to throw himself suddenly *outside of himself*" (ibid., 70). This sacrificial substitution of a part for the whole of the self is expressed by the deranged painter Gaston F., whose case is analyzed

8. Georges Bataille, "Hegel, Death and Sacrifice," in *Yale French Studies* 78, trans. Jonathan Strauss, cf., pp. 9–28.

by Bataille in an article on Vincent van Gogh and who, apparently incapable of bringing himself to suicide, in its place bites off one of his own fingers. "It did not seem very hard," the painter explained, "after contemplating suicide, to bite off a finger. I told myself: I can always do that" (ibid., 62).

As sacrifice is the disruptive writing of the death of the self, so is writing a futile waste of the self. There is a certain identity between writing and sacrifice. They both mean something which cannot be expressed, and yet they both also somehow participate in that inexpressible other. In the fragments for the article "La Limite de l'utile," Bataille again speaks of the task of writing, its "besogne," using the same word he had already employed in the article "Formless." This time, however, it is no longer the task of the words themselves that is in question, but instead the labor of the writer. After a passage in which he has imagined the "depths of space," the "ragged grandeur of the nebulae," and the "measureless irony" that separate them from human existence, Bataille turns his attention towards himself in the act of writing:

> For an instant I remain dazzled by the splendor of the sky: at that very moment my thoughts resume their course. The very sentences that I am writing [j'écris], the task [besogne] which I am pursuing, quickly lead me back to the horizon of ordinary labors. I must take that part of life which has fallen into me from the sky and make it enter into the continuity of *down-to-earth* considerations . . . My life takes place at the heart of an immense universe, from which I experience a feeling of agonizing greatness: yet scarcely [à peine] have I perceived my greatness when a comic feeling leads me back to my smallness . . . In the sky, the myriad stars do not work. They do nothing which might subordinate them to a use, but the earth demands toil from every man and constrains him to exhaust himself [s'épuiser] in endless labors. ["La Limite de l'utile," OC., 189–90]

Writing constitutes part of the interminable labors that distinguish the human from the celestial and in which man destroys (s'épuiser) himself. There is a self-destructive aspect to the act of writing, especially to that endless and futile task of writing the incommensurable which Bataille undertakes here, in his "ironic" descriptions of celestial glory, and throughout the whole of his work, aligned as it is towards a moment of radical and unincorporable alterity. To the extent that both a futile interminability and a destructiveness mark it, a sacrificial quality—in the specifically Bataillean sense of sacrifice as a useless expense of the victim[9]—deforms this labor, this ambivalent and perhaps somehow ironic aspect of words which is at once the very work of philosophy and the end of philosophy endlessly pursued by philosophy. Bataille describes his writing as the "task" through which he wastes himself and as the index of his baseness in comparison with the splendors of the sky, yet this literary undertaking constitutes not only a sacrifice but also a representation of the self: Bataille writes, "I write." In writing the sentence: "The very sentences that I am writing, the task which I am pursuing, quickly lead me back to the horizon of ordinary labors," Bataille represents himself in the act of self-immolation, writing himself to death, constrained "to exhaust himself in endless labors," and thereby performs an act of self-representational sacrifice. The text becomes a representation of the writing, the self-sacrificing Bataille, who, like lucid Engels working at the *Anti-Dühring*, acknowledges the interminability of his labor but continues, conscious of the futility of his undertaking. The representation of the sacrifice of the self, the subterfuge, is itself also that same self-sacrifice. When representation becomes sacrifice in this way, it collapses the subterfuge that distances the partners in the sacrificial couple. The text at this moment can be said to become heterogeneous. At the moment of the "j'écris," it is no longer the same text. It is another text.

The heterogeneous enters precisely at the moment when Bataille asserts the terrestrial nature of writing and with an irony that, as Bataille makes clear by contending, in reference to the celestial, that "the depths of space always hold a measureless irony for our dusty attempts," ("La Limite de l'utile," *OC*, 189–90) is inherent in manifestations of the heterogeneous. In speaking of the sun itself, Bataille refers to a certain ironic instability in its nature, a tendency to reverse limits:

> All this leads one to say that the summit of elevation is in practice confused with a sudden fall of unheard-of violence. The myth of Icarus is particularly expressive from this point of view: it clearly splits the sun in two—the one that was shining at the moment of Icarus's elevation, and the one that melted the wax, causing failure and a screaming fall when Icarus got too close. ["Rotten Sun," *VE*, 58]

9. Cf., the section "Discourse Gives Useful Ends to Sacrifice 'Afterwards'" in "Hegel, Death and Sacrifice," . . . 25–26.

There is a similar doubling and instability of opposites in the lines following the "j'écris" passage. Bataille first writes, "For an instant I remain dazzled by the splendor of the sky: at that very moment my thoughts resume their course. The very sentences that I am writing . . . lead me back. . . ." A few sentences later he explicates the movement implicit in those lines. Retaining the present tense, but altering some of the details of the first description, he writes, "scarcely have I perceived my greatness when a comic feeling leads me back to my smallness" ("La Limite de l'utile," *OC,* 190). Here, in the second version of the same event—the one written after the moment, which was itself a moment of self-description—Bataille implicitly, but clearly affirms the existence of a human glory analogous to that of the sun, and he perceives it in himself. In the first version, however, Bataille asserts that it is the glory of the sky that dazzles him, and the moment of self-perception reveals a comically laborious writer. The two versions are not inconsistent, rather it is the glorious sun that is doubled. Bataille stresses the indissociability of greatness and humiliation: as soon as the celestial overwhelms him, he becomes aware of his own abjection, and this single moment is described as a glorious self-perception. The moment of solar greatness is its opposite: the fall of Icarus, but an inverted fall of Icarus, who at his lowest moment— "the task I am pursuing"—is swept upwards in an act of self-immolation. Indeed, the fall of Icarus, the futile expenditure of self in the raptures of freedom, which contrasts so fiercely with the science and self-preservation of his father, was already a sort of fall into the sun. "The Icarian being who goes to seek the fire of the heavens," Bataille writes in the article on Van Gogh, "is, however, nothing other than an automutilator, a Vincent Van Gogh, a Gaston F" ("Sacrificial mutilation," *VE,* 70).

Among the fragments for the article "La Limite de l'utile," the moment of the "j'écris" intervenes as a rupture in the continuity of the writing, as a mutilation of the text, and as an irruption of the sun within the drudgery of reason. It is the end of philosophy coming not as a term but as an interruption of the task that is immediately and interminably resumed. It is the lucid vision of the futility of the task that makes of the task its own end, that makes of it a writing to death and a labor of death. "Death," writes Bataille, quoting Hegel, "—if we wish so to name that unreality—is the most terrible thing there is and to uphold the work of death is the task which demands the greatest strength." "Hegel, Death and Sacrifice," 14. The word "work" however, appears neither in the original German nor in the translations by Hyppolite and Kojève which Bataille cites. In this lucid interruption of the Hegelian text Bataille reads death as a sort of labor that can be undertaken, that ironically inverts the lowly work of philosophy into the Icarian, ecstatic immolation.

The apparent inconsistency of the "j'écris" passage responds to the duplicity of the sun, a duplicity which reappears in other solar descriptions and which is inherent in the heterogeneous. For it is in the specific nature of the heterogeneous to be for itself, and to limit itself to the modes of being or not being. It never appears as that which comes or moves between being and not being or as that which merely ought to be [*devoir être*], a mode which is restricted to the homogeneous:

> Yet, the pure *having to be* [*devoir être*], the moral imperative, requires being *for itself*, namely, the specific mode of *heterogeneous* existence. But this existence precisely escapes the principle of having to be and can in no case be subordinated to it: it immediately accedes to *Being* (in other words it produces itself as the value *being or not being* and never as a value that has to be). ["Psychological Structure," *VE*, 147]

This mode of the "ought to be," of the "devoir être," also implies a duty ["devoir"] to being itself [*être*], which means also a duty to the *heterogeneous*, since the latter participates directly in being. This servile and futile relation to being itself we have already seen under many guises, or as many guises, since it is always as a disguise or a figuration that the homogeneous appears, but what is striking here is this insistence on the heterogeneous as either being or not-being. The heterogeneous is broken between two radically different modes, without having, in itself, a communication between them. It is one or the other, which is to say that the heterogeneous, because it is or is not, is also other to itself, but only because it is or is not and has no being-in-between. The *other*, according to Bataille, is itself in principle always already disrupted, fragmented.

Bataille's work of writing, and his writing itself, is punctuated by moments of lucidity that cannot be integrated into the laborious and homogeneous aspect of the text, but rather elevate that latter aspect to the status of sacred, self-sacrificial, and heterogeneous. In this irremediable state of rupture, interrupted by the presence of an *other* writing, the text can no longer be thought of as integral. It is opened by missing parts, by mutilations, and by absolute absences. Bataille's text itself, if taken seriously in the same way that Bataille takes the sense of the word "Formless" seriously, is fragmentary insofar as it is heterogeneous, and is heterogeneous to the extent that it is fragmentary. Bataille himself wrote often about this condition. He describes erotism, in his book of that title, as a transgression, a breaking of social limits. In *L'Expérience intérieure*, he asserts, "I write for the reader who, in entering my book, would fall into it like a hole and would never come out," ("L'Experience intérieur," *OC*, 135) and "you could never become the mirror of a dismembering reality without having to *break yourself* . . . " (ibid., 113). In the article "Hegel, Death and Sacrifice," there appears the following passage, where the expression "absolute dismemberment" represents a quotation, which Bataille has analyzed extensively, from the Preface to Hegel's *Phenomenology of Spirit:*

> If I envisage death gaily, it is not that I too say, in turning away from what is frightening: "it is nothing" or "it is false." On the contrary, gaiety, connected with the work of death, causes me anguish, is accentuated by my anguish and in return exasperates that anguish: ultimately, gay anguish, anguished gaiety cause me, in a feverish chill, "absolute dismemberment," where it is my joy that finishes dismembering me, but where dejection would follow joy were I not dismembered all the way to the end, immeasurably. ["Hegel," 25]

A turning not away but toward death, when the self looks its absolute other dead in the face, withdraws the absolute other from the categories of abstract negation ("it is nothing") and misrepresentation ("it is false"), and instead dismembers the very principle of the self itself. Here the I and the text become fragmented and different, heterogeneous, like the rising and setting sun, the irruption of madness in creativity, the tearing away of a finger, the rise and fall of Icarus.

DENIS HOLLIER

The Dualist Materialism of Georges Bataille*

> . . . where there is nothing which an obsession to lay bare the
> reverse side of thought does not consume.

a) AWAKENING

The light of day is the space of thought. But this space is too hospi-
table to thought for something essential not to escape from this con-
formity. Day only gathers thoughts subservient to the day; the
insubordinate ones never come to light; they darken like the night. It
could be that the awakening brought by daylight is no more than the
dream of an awakening, and that thought, offered almost without its
knowledge to the diurnal order, is awakened only to maintain indirectly a deeper sleep. Thought feels at home in a clarity which gives it
an impression of mastery, a deceptive one since it does not master its
own ends. It thus moves in an illusory world where transparencies
reflect one another and disappear, without anything ever happening
which would offer a handle for thought to grasp on to and recover
itself again, really awakening it.

The *awakening* of thought is not its *exercise* because, in this
exercise, thought is blinded by the good toward which it gropes. The
exercise of thought correspond to a distracted attraction to moral
good. Its *awakening* begins with the contradictory and paralyzing
consciousness of evil, of something which suspends thought because
it cannot be thought and willed at the same time. Thus to the *exercise*
of thought, which is a *morality*, since it presupposes even a naive
submission to the good as the condition of its possibility, its *awakening* is opposed, which provokes a moral *demand* by which the opposi-

*This is a shortened and revised version of an article published in *Tel quel* no. 25
(Spring 1966). By permission of the author.

tion of good and evil comes to consciousness. "The essence of morality, says Bataille, is a questioning about morality; and the decisive move of human life is to use ceaselessly all light to look for the origin of the opposition between good and evil."[1] It is as though one had to choose between letting oneself be directed toward the good (one might say that in this sense the good itself, the motor of the will, is not willed) and a suspension of the *exercise* of thought in an *awakening* which would place one "beyond" the opposition between good and evil which it would simultaneously bring out; the choice would thus be between *doing* good and *knowing* what it is. This tells us already that, in Bataille, dualism will not oppose Good and Evil, but morality (where one does the good) and a moral rigor which is beyond good and evil.

Bataille always longed for a "lived experience" in the incandescence of which "knowing" and "doing" would come to merge, from within which the future would rise as though the present, having opened up, would expand and flow into it, as though the future were this very drifting of the present and no longer an escape out of the present as the structure of the project would have it. A lived experience which, by tying "the terms of dialectical development" to the "elements of real existence," would effect the "synthesis—at once decisive and impossible—of consciousness and the unconscious, which is for Bataille the ultimate possibility of *that which is.* Such a synthesis is what interested him most in psychoanalysis: it occurs, according to him, at the "moment of the brutal efficacity of analysis," a moment which he strangely describes with Heidegger's words for death: the "possibility of the impossible."[2]

This synthesis requires thought to withdraw from objects and projects to become the restrained, maintained tension of a purely intensive thought, awakened to itself. This is what philosophy would consist of if only philosophy agreed to "tie reflection to such an object as would exclude the possibility of its sleeping." "What does it mean to philosophize, Bataille asks, if not to push reflection to such a degree of tension that daily existence feels like sleep and the effort of

1. "Du rapport entre le divin et le mal," *Critique,* (March 1947). I quote from Bataille's *Oeuvres complètes* (*OC* 11: 199). This article is a review of Simone Pètrement's book on dualism which I discuss later (see note 4). Cited henceforth in the text as indicated above.

2. The citations in this paragraph are taken from two articles: Georges Bataille and Raymond Queneau: "La Critique des fondements de la dialectique hégélienne," *La Critique sociale,* (1933); *OC* 1: 277–90.

the philosopher, awakening?"[3] Such an awakened thought has to tie its reflection to insomnia-producing objects—such as eroticism, death, and thought itself—which resist being thought, and from which thought is always tempted to accept exclusion, objects into which it collides and against which, failing to fall asleep, it loses its footing. And that is why at its most acute moment of awakening, thought is moral rigor, for "moral philosophy, not metaphysics or science, is the only thought process which responds head-on, which confronts the silence of our death" ("Du rapport . . . " *OC* 11 : 199).

Rational thought plans, unifies, leading—in accordance with the principle of identity—to a monism which is its first and its last, its only word; it reduces everything by translating it into terms of equation and everything soon slumbers under the light of the Same. The *awakening* of thought, in which thought occurs as a heterogeneous event, as a break in homogeneity, thus prompts dualism, which represents for Bataille the awakened (and divided) thought about awakening. This thought has obvious philosophical flaws, but these are the price one must pay for the rupture with monism, the price for the committed dissatisfaction. On the subject of dualist philosophies, Bataille wrote: "It seems to me that the point at which the attention *awakens* here completely is that which merits this exasperating tension, which becomes irritated at any possibility of reduction. But would awakening be awakening if the one who was awakened were once to find himself *satisfied* with what he discovers? If he didn't prolong further and without concern the *interrogation* which is awakening?" (Ibid., 202). It is no longer sufficient to open one's eyes and greet the day; it is necessary to open them unto the night, to the point of opening up the day to the night and the night to the other night. In Bataille's many stories of the eye, one must always "open the eyes farther."

b) DUALISM

Bataille never failed to acknowledge the seduction dualist thought and its often heterodox expressions exercised over him. Furthermore, seduction itself—as opposed to reason and reckoning—is what both dualism and Bataille yield to, the means they use to communicate between themselves as well as with us. The forms historically taken

3. "Le Dernier instant," *Critique*, (October 1946); *OC* 12: 116.

by dualism are numerous, but there are no perfect ones; it is part of the definition of dualism that ultimately, they must remain unsatisfying. Dualism itself, as a doctrine, never relinquishes the untenable position it imposes upon the one enticed by it, keeping him in a never resolved dissatisfaction. According to Bataille, this simply results from the fact that one must choose between a perfection which, satisfying the mind, definitely puts it to sleep, and the awakening which requires an ever unresolved dissatisfaction. Among the many oppositions upon which dualisms were constructed (that of Good and Evil, of the intelligible and the sensible, of the transcendent and the immanent, of the high and the low, of virility and femininity, of vision and discourse) the opposition between the profane and the sacred is the one we must truly consider fundamental here.

Let us recall, from Simone Pètrement's book (which Bataille praised enthusiastically),[4] what is generally understood by dualism: the term designates a mode of thought, bordering on philosophy, religion, and mythology, of which Manichean Gnosticism is considered to be the most striking manifestation. At the core of this philosophy, one finds, according to Pètrement, "not the opposition of two gods, but the opposition of God and Matter, [Matter being] a second principle, with its distinctive nature, different from that of the spirit, and not derived from it" (12–13). As for God: "the gnostic God is 'the Stranger', 'the Unknown', 'the Abyss', 'Silence', 'the God who is not'." Never, perhaps, has the remoteness of God, the absence, the void in which he must be sought, been so exclusively the object of a theology" (15). A theology then of the absence of God, which easily evokes Bataille's atheology: "must dualism then necessarily be a sort of atheism? It is however certain that it has relations to mysticism or at least to a profound religious feeling" (91).

Rather than a system of thought in the strict sense, dualism is an attitude of thought: dualism is not a dualist system but a will to dualism, a resistance to system and homogeneity. Obviously an untenable attitude in the long run. For system cannot help being monistic and, since the *exercise* of thought is spontaneously systematizing and monistic, dualism results from the will bracing itself against this tendency, thought itself taking a stand against the movement proper to reason and its tendency toward conciliation, toward

4. Simone Pètrement, *Le Dualisme dans l'histoire de la philosophie et des religions* (Paris: Gallimard, 1946).

reduction. Thus the radicality of original dualism degenerates into a metaphysical position; that is to say it "refines" itself and corrects ("perfects") its founding heterogeneity into the antagonism "of contrary and symmetrical terms," whereby it does not take long to become a system in which duality holds only the place of a thesis, an affirmation among others: it has already become monism. For, to be true to its inspiration, dualism must remain "imperfect," "surprising," "extravagant"; instead of positing two principles in conflict within *the* world, it posits two worlds. Or at least—"since, having nothing in common, they are not comparable and cannot be counted"[5]—dualist thinking exerts its tension in maintaining the hiatus of this duality, in maintaining it as pure interval, pure separation, pure disjointed *in-between.* "Of course," Pètrement comments, "it seems absurd to suppose two worlds. The notion of the world is the notion of totality. How can one suppose two *totalities?* Language itself refuses this expression." Dualism's resistance to expression, a resistance imbedded in language itself, condemns it to a perpetual imbalance, discomfort, a perpetual limping and *sliding:* never do the two "totalities" let themselves be grasped simultaneously, never are they side by side, next to each other, because they both equally claim to be everything, to contain everything. One is the contestation of the other: they have no other common ground than their mutual exclusion. "This shows," says Pètrement, "that it is not a question of metaphysics." According to Bataille, it is a question of ethics. Commenting on her book he insists on dualism's ethical dimension, a paradoxical ethics which starts beyond the line of demarcation between Good and Evil. "My will to transcendence prolongs, if not the desire to find the Good, at least a longing for moral truth, which is the unappeased passion par excellence within us" ("Du rapport . . . ," *OC* 11:198).

These two worlds cannot exist simultaneously because by definition there is only one world; they will thus have to succeed one another. But in what form? How will the passage from one to the other happen? From the world of Good in which the will reigns, how will one pass to the world of Evil? Not by willing since the will is what produces the Good. How can one escape from the will? Can one will not to will? One does not choose between Evil and the Good but

5. Pètrement, op. cit., 111. And also: "To posit terms as contraries is to render them inseparable; to posit them as principles of the same totality is to reunite them in the same totality."

between two "goods," since choice and will cannot have any other
object but one which they consider to be good, the good alone being
an object. Evil, on the contrary, which is the negation of objecthood,
eludes the will. Here, choice is suspended and replaced by seduction.
This opposition is most clearly delineated in Bataille's article on
Baudelaire, in *Literature and Evil:* "[Baudelaire], had no will power
but an attraction moved him in spite of himself. Charles Baudelaire's
refusal was the most profound form of refusal, since it was in no way
the assertion of an opposite principle. . . . Evil, which the poet does
not so much perpetrate as he experiences its fascination, is Evil since
the will, which can only desire the Good, has no part in it."[6] One
should not content oneself, however, with saying that in wanting the
Good, Baudelaire (for example) really wanted to spice up Evil, or vice
versa. It is true that "if the luminous intensity of Good did not give
the night of Evil its blackness, Evil would lose its appeal" (ibid.,
"Proust," 152; OC:9:257) [142]).

But Good's complicity with Evil, far from being a double game
[*double jeu*] of the will, resides in the structure of being itself which
thwarts [*déjoue*] the will. For the contrast (the spice) would not come
into play if the will did not fully desire the Good: how would it lend
itself to a game which it had itself staged? The Good is not what the
will has to pretend to want in order indirectly to attain Evil and
experience the refined pleasure of transgression: transgression is in
fact only possible for the one who desires the Good without any
ulterior motive, with all of his will. It is even this very lack of distance
on the part of the will devoted to the Good which delivers it to
transgression. Bataille develops the same argument in his analysis of
Proust's sadism. "If pink has to be contrasted with black in order to
suggest desire, would this black be black enough had we never thirst-
ed for purity? had it not tarnished our dream *in spite of ourselves?*"
Thus "if [Proust] was virtuous, it was not in order to obtain pleasure,
and if he obtained pleasure, it was because he had first wanted to
obtain virtue" (ibid., 158, 154; OC 9:269, 268 [143]). Evil is then, in a
way, the Good which has become a source of pleasure. It starts with
virtue being seduced by the Good itself. Evil results from the merging

6. Georges Bataille, "Baudelaire," *La Littérature et le mal* (Paris: Gallimard, 1957),
61; OC 9: 207. [The English translations here are from *Literature and Evil* (trans.
Alastair Hamilton, Marion Boyers Ltd., 1973, 1985), 57. Translator]. All English translations have been provided by the translator and will be indicated in the text by
brackets.

of sensibility and reason in existence. That is to say, when after having unconditionally desired the Good, the will arrives at the extreme point where it can no longer want (for there is nothing conceivable left, no *object* that is better) and nevertheless remains unsatisfied, aware that there still is place for something which is not itself, which is beyond the Good and imposes itself without being wanted; when the will which had wanted nothing but the good, which had wanted everything to be Good, notices that there is a residue before which it remains helpless, a residue which has total power over it since, at this extreme point, will becomes so vulnerable that it can only yield, although it is aware that it was precisely this which, in wanting, it did not want. Such is transgression: that point where the will, reduced to impotence before the irreducibility of a residue, can only, though without wanting to (for there is nothing left to want), yield, knowingly, to what it did not want; Good itself somehow, being compromised in the passivity of pleasure, veers toward Evil without lucidity of consciousness diminishing. Evil is consciousness in pleasure, a passing consciousness that cannot *last.* Its place is the punctual trespassing flash when the interdiction is crossed: to dwell on the other side of interdictions, to claim to remain in evil (as Genet, according to Bataille, would have it) is nonsense (cf., *La Littérature et le mal,* "Genet," 203; *OC* 9:300). Evil does not exist independently of the interdiction which is the limit of the Good; beyond this limit reigns only another Good; not Evil. Evil never reigns.

In gnostic dualism, Bataille was seduced by a contradictory materialism which he opposed to the physicist's mechanical and rational materialism which, because it is monistic, he called a "doddering idealism." Thus Bataille's attitude can be portrayed as a *dualist materialism:* an "impossible" attitude, as distant from theology as it is from even an atheistic humanism which he named atheology. In his first article about Gnosticism, "Le Bas matérialisme et la gnose," written in 1929, Bataille interprets the recurrent representation in Gnostic iconography of a headless animal as an affirmation of atheological materialism. "The severed ass's head of the acephalic personification of the sun undoubtedly represents, even if imperfectly, one of materialism's most virulent manifestations."[7] This is the point where the two parts of Bataille's theoretical work merge; the *Somme Athéologigue* and *La Part maudite.*

---

7. "Le Bas matérialisme et la gnose," *Documents,* 1930; *OC* 1: 220–26. [The English translation is from "Base Materialism and Gnosticism," *VE,* 48–49. Translator].

c) THE SACRED AND THE PROFANE

God's absence is no longer closure: it is the opening of the infinite. *God's absence* is greater, it is more divine than God (I am thus no longer *I*, but an *absence of I:* I was waiting for that conjuring away and now, beyond measure, I am gay).[8]

Even if Bataille's references, with their sometimes scientific claims, can be bothersome, the opposition between the sacred and the profane is the matrix of his thought, notably of what we have called his dualism.

Let us posit an initial definition: existence is profane when it lives in the face of a transcendence, it is sacred when it lives in immanence. However, matters become complicated as soon as one asks what in the profane world is transcendent and, in the sacred world, immanent. Indeed, to the first question one must answer that it is the sacred itself which is transcendent for the profane: the profane is defined by the absence of the sacred from which it is separated, this separation constituting its distinctive mark.

But what is the sacred? Let us clarify the question because, as we shall see, it is ambiguous: what is the sacred from which the profane is separated and which transcends it? It has many names of which the most commonly used are God, or the State, or total Man; but what is fundamental here is less what is posited as transcendent (these abstract entities) than the very separation as a structure of existence. It is thus profane existence itself which produces separation, institutes itself as separate from the sacred, and the transcendence by which it defines the sacred in fact characterizes the profane itself.

"Everything leads one to believe," says André Breton, "that there exists a certain place in the spirit where life and death, the real and the imaginary, past and future, the communicable and the incommunicable are no longer perceived to be in contradiction to one another." Bataille quotes him and continues "I shall add: Good and Evil, pain and joy."[9] But he does not add: the sacred and the profane. Dualism

---

8. "L'Absence de mythe," in *Le Surréalisme en 1947* (Paris: Maeght, 1947); *OC* 12: 236.

9. *La Littérature et le mal*, "Emily Brontë," 29; *OC* 9: 186. [*VE*, 28].

Breton's sentence comes from the *Second Manifesto of Surrealism*, it is thus one of the aftermaths of "Le Bas matérialisme," Bataille's article on Gnostic Dualism which Breton attacks in his 1930 manifesto. His being the main target of this manifesto did not prevent Bataille from often referring to Breton's formulation. See also the conclusion of the essay on Genet, which is the last page of the final essay of *La Littérature et le mal*, 226 [*OC* 9: 316; [204].

starts precisely here, with the fact that there is no point, either in the spirit or elsewhere, where the sacred and the profane cease being perceived as contradicting one another, even if at times they have to coexist and seem to be superimposed on one another. Moreover, this very point, this instant of the fusion of contraries defines the sacred as such and distinguishes it from the profane: the sacred confuses that which the profane opposes or distinguishes.

There are then indeed *two* worlds, the profane in which we live, and the sacred in which we die, the world of the presence of I, and the world of the absence of I, of my absence, the world where I am not, where there are no I's. "*The world we die in*, says Bataille, is not the 'world we live in'." This world is opposed to the world we live in like the inaccessible to the accessible."[10] The opposition thus is not between this world and then the other world, but the world of identity and its alteration; the world of thought [*la pensée*] and its expenditure [*dépense*], the world of measure and its immoderation [*démesure*]. The sacred does not so much contradict the profane, as it differs from it by a difference which is the alteration of its identity.

It is a strange relation which ties together these two worlds with no common ground, whose unthinkable and impossible coexistence cannot be described in terms of an addition or a totality, never amounting to a total. This situation appears clearly in Bataille's textual operations involving the name of "God," the profane name of the sacred. Even if it is the highest name, God remains nevertheless just a name and from this perspective, a tributary of language, it remains bound to the profane world. Doubtless, insofar as it is the *highest word*, God is the key word which permits (like a weak point in the system which has called upon it to achieve its closure) the sacred to be evoked, but the profane *name* of the sacred, as soon as it turns away from this profane status, reveals itself to be the *absence* of God. But let us stop at this passage.

In Bataille, the name of God refers to what is the keystone of the profane world, the world in which things are what they are. God is the one who guarantees the identity of the self, who guarantees compensations proportional to merits, justice, balance, stability of meanings in language; tied to the isolation of individuals in separate *selves*, it is the supreme self whose idea enables human *selves*, despite their separation and their limits, to communicate among themselves.

---

10. "Ce Monde où nous mourons," *Critique*, August–September, (1957); *OC* 12: 457.

These exchanges obviously escape the direct and sacrificial communication of the sacred; they are indirect and result from a compromise between the integrity of individuals and the desire they have to open themselves to one another. Yet this keystone which, at least partially (from the fact that God is present under the guise of a word), belongs to the profane system itself, is considered by the profane system—which it thus sustains, or which is sustained through its mediation—as contaminated by the sacred world. Starting with this keystone, the profane world is able to edify itself into a quasi-architectural system (hierarchical and specialized parts working together to give solidity and cohesion to the whole). But this results in an architecture which hangs upon that which it rejects; the top of the edifice remains somehow heterogeneous to it, since, like a key, the name of God serves as much to close the profane world as to open it. It is as much that which separates the profane from the sacred as that which links it to it, and if the obverse of it is profane, its reverse is sacred. The name of God introduces the equivocal dimension of the presence—absence whose ambiguous play will contaminate all language. For this name which posits the divine as transcendent is the absence of God: *absence of his presence;* but its reverse, or the sacred (as distinct from the divine), is also a mode of the absence of God, this time however in the *sense of the presence of his absence* and of the immanent experience of this absence. This passage from the obverse to the reverse is what Bataille calls the *sacrifice,* that is the putting to death of God by man, which both consecrates the dead God and deifies his human murderer, the perpetrator of God's absence.

d) MAN

> He who does not "die" from being only a man will never be other than a man.[11]

The truth of the universe is expenditure, which is not graspable, never fully thinkable. The incompatibility between thought [*pensée*] and expenditure [*dépense*] is radical, similar to that between conscious

11. *L'Expérience intérieure* (Paris: Gallimard, 1954), 49; *OC* 5: 47. [We are using the English translation, *Inner Experience*, trans. with introduction by Leslie Anne Boldt (New York: State University of New York Press, 1988)].

and unconscious. Thus, since expenditure is ultimately the unthinkable par excellence, thought itself is the suspension of expenditure.

This is the topic of "Corps célestes," an essay published in 1938, a first version of the pages which *La Notion de dépense* will devote to cosmology. In it Bataille refers to Eddington, the astronomer associated with the theory of the expanding universe; but his reading of it transforms it into an interpretation of the world that would rather deserve the name of expending universe.[12] There is one truth in the universe; it is expenditure, which is never thinkable. But it is visible, perceptible, for the sun brings it as its own—if blinding—evidence, the sun which, fire and flame, is nothing but the incessant expenditure of energy with no compensation whatsoever.[13] Yet, although this is the general law of the universe, one single point of the universe, a cold spot in the furnace, oddly insists on ignoring it: the Earth (the planet of thinking beings), a blind place in this luminous, bulging immensity, an avaricious planet, somber and cold, isolated in a prodigal, luminous, and boiling universe. While the universe, in the boundless movement which it communicates to all of its parts—so completely that it is scarcely possible to continue speaking of parts, so intrinsically alien is it to any separation—, is uniquely this very movement, the endless manifestation of an incessant disappearance, the total loss which is radiance, on Earth, on the contrary, the parts are jealously isolated, the mass becomes atomized, the particles claim for themselves an autonomy in which they withdraw, independent of the totality which gathers them.[14] Symmetrical to the cosmic

12. "Corps célestes," *Verve*, (Spring 1938); *OC* 1: 514–20. The article was illustrated by a series of paintings by André Masson representing galactic explosions. [Translated as "Celestial Bodies," in *October* 36, (Spring 1986), special issue on Georges Bataille, ed. and trans. Annette Michelson, 77].

13. Bataille's sun always split into two, between light and heat, between rays and flames (which become ashes). It is thus always necessary to make the distinction between Platonic sun and that of Prometheus-Van Gogh; between the sun which illuminates and that which consumes; between that of erection ("le dur désir de durer,") [the hard desire to endure] and of ejaculation. For Bataille, the shift from one to the other is dramatized in the central episode of the myth of Icarus, the passage of the sun "that was shining at the moment of elevation" to the one "that melted the wax." (Soleil pourri," *Documents*, 1930; *OC* 1: 231–32). ["Rotten Sun," *VE*, 57–58].

14. "Earth, as a heavenly body, differs indeed from a star insofar as it is cold and does not shine. . . . The surface of the planet is formed not only of molecules, each uniting a small number of atoms, but of much more complex compositions, some crystalline, other colloidal, the latter leading to the autonomous forces of life, to plants, to animals, to men, to human society. . . . Cold Earth cannot keep the atoms of

cornucopian overflow, a general devouring movement prevails on Earth. The scientist (at once earthly body and thinking being) claims for himself the status of an exception to his own theory.

Thus it is as though the Earth's surface were the theater of a reversal in the general movement of the universe. The first movement, unbounded, is that of *"communication"* between beings, the second, hierarchical, that of what Bataille describes as the "composition of beings."[15] Since the autonomy of isolated beings increases in proportion to the degree to which they are composite, to the complexity of their constitution, composition is a movement which produces a hierarchical and pyramidal system of beings, at the summit of which Bataille places human society, the most complex of all organisms, with language and discursive knowledge working as "biological binder" (the equivalent for society to what tissues are for bodies). We can translate this fact into terms whose meanings we have already established. For example, with matter—the formless matter of Bataille's "base materialism"—we can identify the generalized movement of cosmic expenditure and with form, its miserly anthropocentric denial. Matter, the complex labyrinth of uncomposed beings, is the base of the pyramid. We could also say that matter which is spent—matter is in fact just another name for expenditure and "dissimilation"—is in this way, above all, relentless exteriorization, a pure outside, while autonomous organisms whose lives are characterized by absorption and assimilation only exist by virtue of the *separation* between an outside and an inside.

But earthly bodies (such as scientists), even if they ignore the general movement of the expenditure of energy, are not independent of it, for they consume and accumulate its energy. While resisting expenditure, they remain no less integrated into the cosmic movement of energy, saving what is spent, absorbing what is produced, internalizing what is externalized.

The Earth is thus a cosmic *hole* in which the truth of the universe (expenditure, communication, glorious manifestation) gets drained, sucked in, sacrificed. But the Earth and man—since the culminating point of the will for autonomy is the epistemological species, the

her surface within the power of an almost zero radiation, and the 'movement of the whole' which forms around her moves in a direction contrary to that of the movement formed within a star with high temperature." Corps célestes," OC 1: 514–20. [77].

15. "La Communication," *L'Expérience intérieure,* 122–28; OC 5: 110–15, [93–98], and "Le Labyrinthe," 106–22; OC 97–110. [81–93. Translation modified].

inhabitant of Earth's surface—forget what makes their autonomy possible (the very prodigality they interrupt), and quickly claim to be the truth, the meaning of the universe. By claiming that the universe is meant to bestow itself for them, they turn away from their aleatory origins. "All that we recognize as truth is necessarily linked to the error represented by the 'stationary earth'" ("Corps Célestes," *OC* 1:516 [76]). And, since anthropocentrism is the main feature of systems of thought which are unable to expand, to decenter themselves far enough to conceive of the excentricity of expenditure, "the crowning achievement of this [devouring] tendency is anthropocentrism" (ibid., 518 [77]). Anthropocentrism, indeed, represses dehumanizing and decentering excesses; it is committed to saving "the world we live in," a world organized around the human subject, against the world of expenditure, which Bataille also calls "the world we die in," "a world for nobody, a world from which subjects have been evacuated, the world of the non-I."

But here is precisely the point where the reversal occurs, where man's avaricious reversal of the law of the universe will itself be reversed. Even man, ultimately, has to enter into communication and expenditure. To start with, in Bataille's description of man, the accumulative drive itself is so strong, that it becomes a virtually unrestricted, unbounded, endless and aimless force which increasingly comes to resemble its opposite: unrestricted expenditure. A greed without reserve, a greed that loses its limits, becoming excessive, unquenchable. "The greater their wealth, the more they proliferate. Their productive force produces only new productive force. . . . Men," Bataille continues, "began . . . to observe the greed which drove them as a curse."[16] In "Corps célestes," man's greed, the very compulsion to produce and to accumulate, is what Bataille calls man's accursed share. Thus, the movement that opposes expenditure, rather strangely, was originally described with the very terms which will later characterize expenditure itself. The curse which first referred to what cannot be spent will later refer to what cannot be saved. In this specific case, the logic of the shift is dependent on the concept of avariciousness, which requires limits. In becoming infinite, greed loses its meaning, it becomes excess instead of greed, a

---

16. "Corps célestes," *OC* 1:519. In *Le Bleu du ciel,* Dirty's excesses are identified with her voraciousness.

greed expanding into expenditure. Infinite avarice and infinite prodigality become indistinguishable.

This shift or reversal reflects a hiatus which is essential in Bataille's theory of expenditure, a theory which, submitted to a sort of theoretical stuttering—the characteristic rhythm of dualism—cannot be uttered in one breath. It takes several attempts to get it out.

Thus, as a first step, man discovers the law of the universe, but in so doing, he escapes it, he distinguishes himself from it. The motor does not move. The thinking of expenditure is tax deductible, it is not itself an expenditure. Instead of donating, it collects data. Denying the cost of information (that one has to expend oneself in order to know), science is the intellectual, ideological version of the earthly refusal of expenditure. The planet is not the only version of an immobile ground. Scientific discourse is another one, an intellectual and abstract form of anthropocentrism which the Copernican revolution did not succeed in demolishing. Thus writes Bataille: "Even if human existence is really in the process of discovering the universe that sustains it, this existence must acknowledge the universe as a spectacle external to it or else deny itself" (ibid., 516 [76]). The existential problem of science is that of an Oedipus who risks being swallowed by the sphinx precisely because he found the right answer. Contrary to Brecht's *Verfremdungseffekt*, this distancing is essentially a strategy that prevents the beholder from being absorbed by the show. Man resists entering the spectacle, he resists identifying with it. He does not recognize himself in it. Were he to acknowledge himself "as spectacle viewing itself," he would risk losing his life.

Yet, at the heart of this cosmology, there is a contradiction between the existential position of the subject and his knowledge, the gap between what man knows and what he is. A cold minded and cold hearted vulcanologist, he develops a theory of an expanding universe from a position which is based on the refusal of expansiveness. Man withdraws from the game, he shirks expenditure. He does not participate in the play of the world, imagining that he is an exception, that he rests on safe, solid, stable ground in a world invaded by movement.

A first form of the break with anthropomorphism is a blind one, the Dionysian surpassing of the theoretical (Apollonian) attitude. This first way out is an explosive one. The vulcanolgist moves out to Pompey. He replaces reserve with self-sacrifice, with "the need to give, whether one's own self or one's possessions." "Through loss man can regain the free movement of the universe, he can dance and swirl in the full rapture of those great swarms of stars" (ibid., 520 [78]). But the situation to which such a break leads cannot be described as the "spectacle viewing itself." This time, however, it is for the opposite reason: the ex-beholder is blinded, and even destroyed by his proximity with the show, his participation in it. Entering *dépense*, he lost *pensée*. At least, this is what Bataille says in "Corps célestes." However, it is not what happens in it: "Corps célestes" is an essay which is about blindness without being blind itself. It escapes the alternative between the two exclusive positions of a thought that distances itself from any expenditure and an expenditure which excludes thought.

In the final analysis, the major interest of Bataille's theory of expenditure might not be of an economic or anthropological order but, rather, of an epistemological one. Its interest stems less from its theoretical content than from what it does to the space of knowledge. A memorable discussion in Paris followed the publication of *L'Expérience intérieure,* during which Bataille was grilled by the most important philosophers of his time, Sartre included. One of his last answers is literally a turning upside down of Lucretius's *Suave mari magno.* . . . It is hard to decide if it relates to the actual setting of the exchange, Bataille the self-taught eclectic being examined by licensed philosophers, or whether it is a description in general terms of his philosophical position. Lucretius describes man's pleasure at witnessing the storm which imperils others from the solidity of the philosophical shores, a position in many regards analogous to what Bataille, in "Corps célestes," called the error of "stationary earth." But, in answering the various philosophers who had questioned him during the discussion, Bataille reverses the image: "Placed before you, I feel myself to be the contrary of him who tranquilly watches the dismasted vessels from the shore, because in fact, in spite of everything, I cannot imagine anyone so cruel that he could notice the one who is dismasted with such carefree laughter. Sinking is something altogether different, one can have it to one's heart's content."[17] Bataille's cogito, thus, reads: "I sink therefore I am."

In the violent expenditure of self, man must "perceive that he breathes in the power of death" ("Corps célestes," 5:20 [78]). This philosophical raft of the Medusa is the allegory of a thought that has

17. "Discussion sur le péché, *Dieu vivant,* 1945; *OC* 6: 358.

left behind the world we live in, the philosophical world of the exercise of thought, of thought as *exercise,* for the world we die in, the world of thought as *awakening.* A thought which sustains itself beyond the loss of the subject, when thought keeps going even after its subject has been spent. Expenditure here is not so much an object to be thought of, as it is the mode of thought when there is no subject left to think it. Thinking expenditure, for a subject, means first of all thinking of a scene from which he has been evacuated. It means to push self-sacrifice at least to the point of the loss of ego, entering a space where the ego, having become expendable, is endowed with the glory of not being there.

Translated by Hilari Allred

II. The Political and Social Imperative

MICHÈLE RICHMAN

Bataille Moralist?: *Critique* and the Postwar Writings

The significance of the review *Critique*, founded in 1946 and directed by Georges Bataille until shortly before his death in 1962, remains a relatively unexplored area of his career.[1] This lacuna is all the more surprising given the acknowledged centrality of such journals to French intellectual life, especially during the half-century spanning the twenties to the early sixties. Régis Debray[2] has argued that since the Dreyfus Affair, the locus for intellectual activity has shifted from the university (1890–1919) to publishing houses (in conjunction with the journals that they subsidized between 1920 and 1960), and most recently to the media, dominated by television. Each setting fosters a subspecies of the "homme de lettres" and a distinctive mode of writing that correlates with a particular public image. Thus, until the daunting task of writing a global cultural history of the last fifty years is accomplished, the best introduction to the period will continue to be studies which use the focus on a review as springboard for investigating the complex overlap of social, political, and intellectual circles that sociologically characterizes the life of the Parisian intelligentsia.

That Bataille, from the perspective of his own writing cycles, was

1. Works consulted regarding the founding and early history of *Critique* include Jean Piel, *La Rencontre et la différence* (Paris: Fayard, 1982); Pierre Prévost, *Rencontre Georges Bataille* (Paris: Jean-Michel Place, 1987); Michel Surya, *Georges Bataille: La mort à l'oeuvre* (Paris: Librairie Séguier, 1987). All references to works mentioned will henceforth appear in the text. The author expresses her gratitude to Jean Piel for sharing his personal recollections during an interview in Paris, Sept. 1983.

2. For further discussion, see Régis Debray, *Teachers, Writers, Celebrities: The Intellectuals of Modern France* (London: NLB, 1981), translation of *Le Pouvoir intellectuel en France* (Paris: Editions Ramsay, 1979).

YFS 78, *On Bataille,* ed. Allan Stoekl, © 1990 by Yale University.

especially keen on gaining recognition for *Critique* is evidenced in his 1952 avant-propos to to the essays collected under the heading *Literature and Evil* (9).[3] Tracing their inspiration to a "tumultuous" youth heady with the adventures of Surrealism and exasperated with the "suffocating limits" of what was then designated literature, Bataille notes that these essays, though the product of "mature reflection," nonetheless remain faithful to their revolutionary impulse. Noteworthy is the fact that they first appeared in *Critique*, a review whose "seriousness," he underscores, explains its considerable success (9, 171–72).

Confirmation of Bataille's opinion had been provided by the national journalists' guild in 1947, when it awarded first prize to *Critique* as the best journal of the year. But the autobiographical statement is also important because it locates the relation between the pre- and postwar periods somewhere between continuity and rupture. Certainly a study of *Critique* cannot ignore Bataille's participation in a number of small and ephemeral, but influential reviews during the 1920s and 1930s. Not only did *Documents* and *La Critique sociale* publish the first writings Barthes judged the best of Bataille, but their respective subversive orientations imparted to the early essays a virulence unmatched in the later works. Similarly, the enterprise of *Critique* could be compared to other prewar activities of a collective nature organized at Bataille's initiative, such as "Acéphale" and the *Collège de sociologie* (1937–39). But in comparison with the radical politics of *La Critique sociale* or the surrealist eclecticism of *Documents*, *Critique* presents a subdued, even scholarly, image. Yet an important element of these earlier projects strikes the reader of *Critique* immediately: its exceptional diversity. Virtually every area of postwar research is represented, whether physics, economics, political economy, philosophy, religion, literature, art, history, anthropology, or psychoanalysis.

The corollary to *Critique*'s eclecticism is its international perspective. Given the historical insularity of French translation practices, coupled with the scarcity of paper in the postwar years, *Critique* provided an invaluable service by reviewing untranslated foreign language works. Regardless of linguistic or financial barriers to the actual acquisition of the books discussed, readers of the first

---

3. Georges Bataille, *Complete Works 9*, ed. Denis Hollier (Paris: Gallimard, 1979), 171–362.

issues could benefit from discussions of Heidegger, British economic policy, Italian social history, or the political economy of the United States. Challenging any lingering postwar Eurocentrism, the editors clearly opted for a global orientation. They understood that despite immediate pressure to focus on reconstruction, French political life would henceforth be determined by France's place within the new international order dominated by the two superpowers. Domestic policies, not parties, are evaluated in terms of their impact on the planned economy of an already highly centralized State. Restricted by an editorial policy that precludes letters to the editor, *Critique* effectively avoided polemical confrontations or intervention into the political arena. Major historical phenomena are addressed through the mediation of historical studies under review. The review format undoubtedly reinforced the absence of a clear political profile, as stipulated by Bataille, according to his longtime collaborator and successor, Jean Piel.

It is therefore important to consider the significance of the review in terms of the consequences of Bataille's choice of a more public, if not political, forum. In contrast with the "underground" profile of the twenties and thirties, when he often published under a pseudonym and shifted from one short-lived journal to another, the formation of *Critique* brought Bataille into the intellectual and cultural spheres constituted by the other prominent journals of the postwar period: the Catholic *Esprit* (founded in 1932); the Communist Party's intellectual organ, *La Nouvelle critique*, and Sartre's *Les Temps modernes*. Though now part of the Parisian intelligentsia's major league, Bataille's brilliant team of professors, émigrés, and autodidacts nonetheless tended to play on the sidelines, overshadowed by the more timely, more successful group led by Sartre. But unlike his earlier deliberate marginality, Bataille's position here can be appreciated as dictated in large part by the hegemony enjoyed by existentialist thought until the early sixties. History tells us that many of the writers and issues subsumed under the "poststructuralist" rubric that began to prevail shortly after Bataille's death had been first promulgated in *Critique*. Although Sartre's positions were thus usurped and superseded, this sequence of events remained unforeseeable for Bataille. Not only did he remain concerned with the influence exerted by existentialism, his writings provide evidence of a sustained intertextual dialogue with Sartre as well.

These three aspects of *Critique*, its eclecticism, internationalism, and its institutional status, will guide our appreciation of the relation of the review to the development of Bataille's work. Clearly, what must be appreciated is just how effective Sartre was in dictating a general problematic common to all intellectuals according to existentialist terms. Correlatively, whether in the case of Sartre or Bataille, the review must not be viewed solely as providing institutional support for the ideas of one man. Rather, the fact of collaborating on a review generates what Barthes called an *écriture*,[4] a historically determined language shared by all participants united in its psychic as well as intellectual community. To what extent is such a notion applicable to *Critique*, otherwise distinguished by its lack of a set project or program?

The starting point for our response will be Bataille's opening review article of Henry Miller in *Critique*,[5] where the social, political, and, most important, "moral" ramifications of the notion of *dépense* are explored. The central weakness imputed to Miller is that he did not challenge the patriarchal order on which he ultimately remained dependent in such a way that the glorious "instant" of expenditure not be dismissed as a gratuitous act of self indulgence, committed by a minor subordinate to the dominant values of work, profit, and accumulation. Thus emerges the main issue to which Bataille continuously returns: the reinterpretation of the instant of *dépense* as the basis for an alternative ethic. Whether it surfaces in discussions of artistic activity or is perceived in the political flirtation with nuclear disaster that marks politics in the atomic age, the characterization of unlimited expenditure remains constant: total and unequivocal, the impulse to give, to relinquish, or to sacrifice all in a violent annhilation of self-consciousness and conscience, such is the destruction of an order of property implied by *dépense*. Bataille's notion defies discourse (science), work, and action (politics). Writing for *Critique*, he pursues the consequences of such an extreme notion within the confines of the historical moment in two directions: one examines the conditions or circumstances in which the established order appears to tolerate and even encourage some mode of gift-giving. These examples open the way to concrete propositions that extend such possibilities and challenge the traditional obstacles to their implementation. At a complementary level of analysis, he examines manifestations of *dépense*

4. Roland Barthes, *Le Degré zéro de l'écriture* (Paris: Editions du Seuil, Bibliothèque méditations, 1953).
5. Georges Bataille, "La Morale de Miller," *Critique* 1 (1946): 3–17.

among writers and artists by considering the effects of such transgressions on the individual's internal moral order. And it is in the articulation of the two dimensions that Bataille seeks totality or a *vue d'ensemble*. Common to both meditations, however, is an emphasis on the inevitability of dependence, whether it be on the domain of rational calculations, or the system of interlocutors to whom the writer is intertextually tied. In sum, the notion of *dépense* must undergo a *mise-en-discours* that garners support from the context of the review's seriousness at the same time that it undermines the very system of representation ostensibly providing its legitimation.

The persistence of this issue will be traced through a series of review essays that use contemporary works by Camus, Simone Weil, and others as departure for speculations closer to Bataille's concerns than those under review. The effort to relate the morality of expenditure to the practices of the State will be considered by means of the exchanges among Bataille, Jean Piel, and the economist François Perroux. Finally, the content of the review itself will be evaluated in terms of its position vis-à-vis the other intellectual journals within a field of activity dominated by *Les Temps modernes*. By complementing this reading of Bataille with recent studies of *Esprit* and *Les Temps modernes*,[6] I hope to demonstrate the constraints as well as conflicts which played a determining role in the contest for influence and power during the final years of Bataille's career, and which were to have enduring effects for subsequent intellectual activity.

The obligatory "presentation" of *Critique* in its inaugural issue is brief, and not very illuminating with regard to the pages to follow. More revealing is Bataille's first review article of Miller's *Tropic of Capricorn*. Miller, in California at that point, had published *Capricorn* in Paris (1934) and had just been convicted for one month to two years in prison, besides being levied a fine. Bataille takes up Miller's defense against American puritanism and its judicial strong-arm, but also warns against French bourgeois morality. The latter's disapproving intellectual guardian in this case was Maurice Nadeau. In '46 Nadeau referred to Miller's "monstrous immorality," while conceding to the superficiality of his own judgement. Bataille takes up the

6. Works consulted include: Michel Winock, *Histoire politique de la revue Esprit (1930–1950)* (Paris: Editions du Seuil, 1975); Anna Boschetti, *Sartre et 'Les Temps Modernes': Une entreprise intellectuelle* (Paris: Editions de Minuit, 1985); Howard Davies, *Sartre and 'Les Temps Modernes'* (Cambridge: Cambridge University Press, 1987). References to page numbers will be made in the text.

morality tack and declares Miller a "saint" despite some fuzzy thinking ("molles vérités") that nonetheless eventually lead to arcane se-
crets. In this autobiographical quest—"à la recherche de la valeur
morale perdue"—Miller counterposes boyhood memories to the
model of adulthood guided by the search for profit. He refuses to
accept a system where earning bread becomes more important than
eating it. The outstanding experience Miller provides, however, is
that of the neighborhood gang, *la bande,* where generosity, devotion,
loyalty, and a sense of justice and equality are no less significant than
within social milieus organized by work.

The lesson Bataille draws from Miller's "do-nothings" is that the
tacit opposition between child and adult, or minor versus major, must
be revised according to evidence that such oppositions seem to obtain
only in the recent history of Western bourgeois-capitalist societies.
The possibility of hierarchies based exclusively on merit, work, and
production are relatively alien to archaic cultures. For readers of "La
notion de dépense" and *L'Expérience intérieure,* Bataille is clearly
reworking familiar territory. Less expected, however, is the sudden
repudiation of Miller on the grounds that he has not overcome the
minor/major distinction and that he cultivates the irresponsibility of
childhood through immediate gratification and through indulgence
in farces. Bataille argues that Miller's so-called adult identity is so
difficult to pinpoint as to be elusive.

Given the serious nature of such distinctions for Bataille, it is not
surprising to find his own arguments subtle to the point of equivocation: on the one hand, Miller allegedly prefers "abjection" to servitude, and condemns himself to near starvation. On the other, "this
awareness born from hunger not only inverts the principles of adult
society . . . it imparts to the derisory and laughable moments of play
the prerogatives of ecstasy, which is the highest point conceivable,
which is divine and which is also the suspension of conscience and
consciousness . . . " (9). Further on, differences are overlooked, so
that the considerable affinities between the two writers is exhibited
by means of a lengthy quote from *Capricorn* that bears uncanny
similarities to Bataille's "Oeil pinéal." It is thus all the more disconcerting to encounter Bataille's litany of reproaches to Miller: for his
recourse to a "gang" as the only model for community; for his exploi-
tative relationships with prostitutes as a substitute for erotic experience; for mystical tendencies; and, finally, for a propensity to flirt
with politics in an "ambiguous" fashion.

How are such criticisms to be taken? As a repudiation of Miller or as a reprise of the issues haunting Bataille—eroticism, unlimited expenditure, the need for community, the nature of inner experience, and the relation of all the preceding to politics? Overall, it is evident that Bataille is using the occasion to establish his own positions, including the projection of a very different persona from that of Miller. At the antipodes of Miller's freewheeling bohemian, one recognizes the "impeccable" Bataille. Most revealing, Bataille has taken up the traditional role of the French intellectual as moral arbiter vis-à-vis an order with which he maintains profoundly ambivalent relations.

Indeed, Bataille's final position on Miller underscores the ambiguities plaguing all artists. At best, great works are distinguished by the "éclat" of *dépense*—an ephemeral expenditure from which the work derives its aura. But the artist, as Bataille concedes, despite his aesthetic celebration of expenditure, nonetheless continues "to write, to publish, to read." On the surface, the statement of fact is not surprising, though it does inject a new element of realism when compared with earlier discussions. It will reappear in the evaluation of surrealism, where recognition of dependence on the domain of calculated rationality is claimed to be inevitable. The theoretical repercussions of this perspective are examined below. But the very words used by Bataille take on an added dimension by dint of their disturbing resemblance to those employed by Sartre in his negative review of *l'Expérience intérieure* in 1943.[7] Denying *dépense* any social redemption, Sartre insisted on a grotesque caricature of its collective potential. After harping on the disparity between the moral smugness of Bataille's uncompromising expenditure and the daily realities to which all must submit, Sartre challenged, "But is he sincere, for after all, M. Bataille works at the Bibliothèque Nationale, he eats, he reads, he sleeps and he makes love . . . " (175).

The subtext directed at Sartre interwoven in the Miller review erupts into overt antagonism the following year with Bataille's account of the study of Baudelaire that Sartre had published in early 1947. Excised from the reprinted version for the *Literature and Evil* collection, Bataille's opening sentence provides the best gauge of the intensity of his attack: "Few writings are more apt to irritate. It is

7. Jean-Paul Sartre, "Un Nouveau mystique," in situations 1 (Paris: Gallimard, 1947): 143–88. Originally published in *Cahiers du Sud* 262 (1943): 988–94.

with an undeniable rigidity and not without a certain perverseness that he has portrayed this stiffened, perverse and unsatisfied entity that is none other than Baudelaire himself" (9, 443). Bataille underlines the legal mode of Sartre's judgment of Baudelaire of the author, rather than a literary criticism that would seek to understand and appreciate. Existentialist criteria aside, Sartre's position merely repeats the literary criticism exemplified by Sainte-Beuve, where personal details of the author's life are enlisted to judge the work as well as to explain it.

At the center of Sartre's rejection lies the alleged choice of the poet which is supposed to account for every detail of his adult life. According to Sartre, following Madame Baudelaire's remarriage, her son perceived this severance from their earlier "mystical union" and its subsequent isolation as emblematic of his destiny. Taking up Sartre's closing sentence to the effect that "the free choice that an individual makes of him or herself is identified in an absolute way with that which we call his or her destiny." Bataille continues with a paraphrase of the statement's consequences: "Sartre wishes the condemnation to be definitive. Here we touch on the original choice that Baudelaire made for himself on that absolute commitment by means of which each one of us decides within a particular situation what he or she will be" (9, 442). In the early *Critique* review, Bataille's response is limited to pointing out the sources of closure in Sartre's perspective, especially those responsible for his blindness to that "obscurity" within, comparable for Bataille to a sacred domain intuited through poetry and the experiences of eroticism and laughter he deemed sovereign. Such a sacred part alternately termed *maudite*, sovereign, or heterogeneous, remains irreducible, despite the powerful counterforces of homogeneity and productivity represented by the Sartrean stance. More sharply, he points out the nature of Sartre's positions isolated from any philosophical tradition. The philosophy of engagement whereby an individual's entire fate is imputed to a single choice emanates exclusively from Sartre (9, 444–45). Most significant is Sartre's refusal to grant the Baudelairean mode of rebellion, consistent with a bohemian rejection of the bourgeois order, recognition as more than an adolescent revolt.

The refinement of Bataille's appreciation of the moral dilemmas inherent in the theory and practice of expenditure continues in the title of a review of Camus's *La Peste*—[8]"ou la morale du malheur."

8. Georges Bataille, "La Morale du malheur: *La Peste,*" *Critique* 13–14 (1947): 3–15.

Bataille announces his own position by means of a stunning rapprochement between Camus and Sade. Between them, he argues, lies the history of the modern State and the shared repugnance of the two authors for its legalization of murder in the name of capital punishment. Claiming to serve as protection against the unleashing of an even greater *malheur* or misfortune, this sanctioned killing is the outcome of a negative logic of calculation. For while it purports to substitute a rational alternative to the sacrifices of archaic tradition, the State merely robs the modern world of their passion while exacerbating the arbitrary and capricious nature of death in contemporary society.

The continuity with the moral dilemmas raised by Miller is considerable, given that Miller and his cousin had been accomplices to the murder of the chief of an opposing gang. The incident formed the basis for solidarity within their own group, as well as the most enduring experience of their early lives. What Bataille seeks to illustrate with the examples provided by Sade, Miller, and Camus, are precisely the consequences of the fact that the legalized transgression of the primary interdict on taking another's life is now exclusively controlled by the State. By so doing, it deprives the collectivity of its potential experience of sovereignty, in which the negation of the limits of the "real world" provided access to an experience of communication and solidarity otherwise sought through literature, poetry and, erroneously, politics.

Unlike his youth, however, Camus's rebellious adult undertakes his transgression with lucidity—the consciousness and conscience metaphorically represented by the Bataillian open eye. Returning to the surprising encounter between Sade and Camus, one finds the recurrent themes of power, violence, and the delusion of modern society that have reached a higher level of consciousness by repressing the potential for sovereignty. What Bataille emphasizes is the distinction between revolt and revolution. Where for Sartre, the first characterizes the "minor" attitude of Baudelaire or the adolescent within the father's house, the revolutionary individual is willing to challenge and overthrow that order. In his turn, Bataille rejects a revolutionary scheme wherein one order of power relations is replaced by another since the crucial disjunction between the movement of rebellion and the opposing inclination to submit others against their will (the very definition of power) is *not* guaranteed. In this, Bataille is consistent with a critique he levelled at Miller and will later forward against Genet: namely, the betrayal of sovereignty through coercion. Sade's orgies exhibit alternations rather than mutuality; yet they signal a propensity to sacrifice the subject within his/her own will to destruction. It is also possible to discern in these declarations a continued dialogue with existentialism when he asserts that "liberty is encountered only in crime . . . " (6). But most important is the refusal of all gain in the expression of passion Bataille seeks to elucidate: "Pure passion is naturally a form of revolt that never seeks legal power as its goal, but rather, that form of expenditure whose ruinous force destroys all power" ("Morale du malheur," 14).

Conversely, a morality based on denial is alien to the Bataillian experience of expenditure. This is why, despite a lengthy excursion through Camus's work, he ultimately rejects "la morale du malheur." Characteristic of a morality encountered in all moments of history, it implies an ascesis "avare et sans vie," that seeks to avoid death and suffering, incapable of the sovereign embrace "à hauteur de mort." Unlike the tragic figure of *Le Malentendu*, Tarrou in *La Peste* exemplifies the morality in question when he stops fighting for the victims and therefore ceases to love. After this capitulation, he proposes a swim to his friend in order to find "internal peace." Bataille then queries, "ought we learn to love nothing more desirable than a good swim?" (14).

The relationship between morality, sovereignty, and the role of the modern nation-state is further explored in the 1949 review occasioned by the posthumous publication of Simone Weil's *L'Enracinement*. Bataille's piece is entitled "La Victoire militaire et la banqueroute de la morale qui maudit," and his clearest sympathies lie with Weil's discussion of the problem of *déracinement* (especially through conquest), despite the fact that the awaited description of community is lacking: "The sense of rootedness designates an intimate collectivity, a milieu rich in poetry and beauty, which allows those who inhabit it to partake of a prodigious grandeur" (796). The important distinctions to be developed between the State and the community are thwarted by Weil's own predilection for "a collectivity struck by misfortune" (796).[9]

What Weil has yet to appreciate adequately are the problems raised by a coercive mode of loyalty and giving of self, one that is exacted by external forces rather than emanating from the surplus of

9. Georges Bataille, "La Victoire militaire et la banqueroute de la morale qui maudit," *Critique* 40 (1949): 789–803.

energy generated by collective encounters. Individuals are not only "enracinés," as she contends, they are also sovereign, which means without obligation: "loyalty comes from within in the same way as force" (800). Most important, the decline of good in contemporary society "is precipitated within the modern nation-state: the caricature of goodness demanded from the individual is a giving of self that is necessarily sad and therefore often begrudgingly granted" (801). This last citation underscores the preoccupation with the role of the State in Bataille's postwar essays, nowhere more evident than in his reflections on the possibility for gift-giving on an international scale. His major interlocutors regarding these ideas were Jean Piel and François Perroux, the economist. The considerable number of articles, essays, and exchanges among the three about the Marshall Plan, for instance, allow us to follow the germination of ideas destined for publication in 1949 under the title *La Part maudite*.

From the perspective of the issue of the morality of expenditure, the most important function of *Critique* was to provide a forum for Bataille's development of the theory of general economy. As evidenced in *La Part maudite*, Bataille's postwar speculations are distinguished from the 1933 "Notion de dépense" essay by his shifts to (1) a historical rather than ethnographic perspective, with special emphasis on the postwar reconstruction effort; (2) the role of the State in initiating and organizing large-scale gifts, as exemplified in the then-innovative Marshall Plan for foreign aid. The Plan demonstrated that huge sums could be distributed on a basis that was not exclusively economic and that it was therefore possible to generate relationships among nations that mark a significant departure from historical patterns. Although the compatibility of the Plan with Bataille's own projections can be documented,[10] its actual implementation sparked a polemic between him and his colleagues that is reflected in a considerable number of essays and exchanges at the time.

The first aspect of the Plan debated is the degree to which it does or does not reflect genuine disinterestedness. (According to the original disbursements, five-sixths of the total were to be in the form of an outright gift and the remainder in the form of a loan). Bataille, opposing Perroux's initially sanguine view, points to the American need to

10. Surya points out that as early as *Critique* 8–9 (Jan.–Feb. 1947), Bataille had formulated the outline of a project that Marshall did not promulgate until 5 June 1947 (Surya, 375).

flood the European market with adequate credits to guarantee the resumption of trade relations. Burdened with an accumulated surplus, the US was in search of new markets on which to unload its excess production. By skirting a psychological explanation, Bataille's approach remained consistent with the lesson of Mauss's essay on the gift, in which the motive for gift-giving, i.e., whether it is willed or obligatory, disinterested or egotistic, is settled by showing that it is amenable only to a holistic appreciation.[11] The gift itself is not an isolatable object because it participates in an elaborate system of prestations in which all kinds of institutions find simultaneous expression: religious, legal, moral, and economic. Similarly, it is impossible to discuss individual initiative since the self is always already engaged in some phase of the gift-exchange cycle. No matter how delayed in time or space, a seemingly isolated gesture is ultimately appreciated within the global network of reciprocal relations.

Bataille also underscored the political motivation of the American Plan: to gain a sphere of influence in Europe vis-à-vis national Communist Parties and the Soviet Union. The latter, having refused the terms of the Plan, isolated Czechoslovakia and Poland as well within the economic Cold War. This last repercussion of the Plan provoked the most complicated reactions within the *Critique* editorial circle. Although Bataille was never an official member of the French CP, nor an orthodox Marxist, he nonetheless refused to espouse a simplistic anticommunism and insisted on trying to "understand" it. Thus, at a time when many intellectuals were faced with having to reverse their own allegiances because of Stalin's excesses, Bataille was trying to clarify the degree of congruence between his own economic perspective and the potential for its realization inherent in the theory and practice of communism. Two areas in particular had to be explored: (1) its capacity for producing a viable community, such as he had begun to pursue prior to the war; (2) the alternative to capitalism regarding the consumption of surplus produced by every society. Steering between the Scylla of Stalinism and the Charybdis of kneejerk anticommunism, Bataille's essays are often argued in terms so idiosyncratic that their final position eludes even the most seasoned Bataillian reader. Predictably so, since Bataille envisioned the contest between the superpowers as entailing the most serious "mor-

11. For a comparison between Mauss and Bataille on the gift, see Michèle Richman, *Reading Georges Bataille: Beyond the Gift* (Baltimore: Johns Hopkins University Press, 1982), chapter 1.

al" issues facing humanity. An espousal of one was tantamount to a "leap into death," while any temporizing with the bourgeois ethic was anathema. The typically Bataillian predilection for putting ideas "à hauteur de mort" is thus translated into his goals for the entire review in this summary of his position provided to a *Figaro* interviewer in 1947:

> You see, I believe that there currently exists a desire to live events in a more and more conscious way. I think that it behooves Europe to demonstrate what is at stake in the contest between America and Russia. It is not a matter of exacerbating the conflict. But if humanity wishes to realize its potential, it can do so only by taking deliberate steps to a complete awareness of the conflicts that rend it asunder. [Surya, 372]

With François Perroux, Bataille engaged an economist in the debate over the potential role for gift-giving in the modern world. Despite their differences, Perroux's enthusiastic support for the gift as a viable force to be encouraged within a comprehensive view of the economy as inseparable from the social, undoubtedly did much to bolster Bataille's own point of view. Most important, Perroux's input could help to counter Bataille's insecurities as a generalist through the legitimacy of the specialist. In the introduction to *La Part maudite*, Bataille expressed the fear that he had taken on a subject so broad as to be "relevant to all and of interest to none."[12] Yet the nature of Bataille's reading public and the particular blend of esoterism and scholarliness found in *Critique* reflect the postwar conditions affecting the renaissance of the critical essay in the '50s. Enjoying a success unparalleled either in England or the United States, the contemporary French essay at its best proposes the same hybrid of introspection, moral imperative, and social analysis exemplified by Montaigne. Following the war, the French intellectual felt on one side pressure to participate in the social and moral reconstruction of a devastated nation; on the other, the innovations of the human sciences risked superseding the tradition of nonprofessional speculations of a general order.

The positive outcome of these forces is the new image of the intellectual forged by Barthes. Considerably influenced by Sartre's model of the social critic, Barthes responded to the urgency of the

---

12. Georges Bataille, *Complete Works* 7, ed. Thadée Klossowski (Paris: Gallimard, 1976), 20.

situation by formulating the category of *scripteur:* "The spreading influence of social and political facts into the literary field of consciousness has produced a new type of scriptor, situated midway between the activist and the writer, deriving from the first an idealized image of the committed man, and from the second, the idea that a written work is an act" (26). Moreover, Barthes's example demonstrated that the European sciences of man, concerned more with meaning and values than statistics, need not so much usurp Montaigne's model as help to recast it into an eclecticism worthy of his precedent.

The major victim of the extraordinary postwar push for modernization and its attendant upheavals in collective life, however, was literature, and along with it the prestige of the literary review exemplified by *La Nouvelle revue française.* The influence of American social science, especially quantitatively oriented sociology, was undeniable. Its impact was such that it encouraged the production and dissemination of knowledge primarily by means of the journal article. And this format had important repercussions on the development of the essay. Shorter than a philosophical treatise but nonetheless requiring some theoretical underpinning for its ethical *prises de position,* the essay furnished the ideal outlet for opinions of intellectuals formerly associated with literary writing. Thus, it has been noted that Bataille's preference for the essay partook of a general trend toward a mode of writing encountered in Barthes as well as Blanchot, all of whom

> set up other rules and formulae, for which the essay, article, and fragment are often the new form and new norm. Within this innovative appreciation of time and space, the format and unity of the book seek to recreate the connections otherwise dispersed among separate pieces: the book, during this period, is often a collection of articles, and the journal plays a considerable role in the elaboration and diffusion of knowledge.[13]

Despite the fact that most attention has been directed here to Bataille's formation of a so-called economic perspective, it is important to note that it is primarily expounded in critical essays that use literary texts as their point of departure and that the lead essay of the journal almost always addressed some aspect of literary writing. This

13. Francis Marmande, *Georges Bataille politique* (Doctorat d'Etat, Paris VIII, 1982), 227.

is especially significant because the greater popularity of *Les Temps modernes* until the early 60s is in part explained by its drawing on Sartre's successes in both literature (including the theater) and philosophy. Blanchot, for instance, close friend of Bataille and frequent contributor to *Critique*, published parts of his novels in Sartre's review.

Indeed, it is the acknowledged centrality of art to modern philosophy that provides Bataille with the appropriate context in which to forward his most explicit statements regarding the moral foundations of his theory of a general economy. The immediate occasion is a two-part review of several undistinguished general treatises related to the existentialist vogue, in which he begins to synthesize the various components of his position. Significantly entitled "De l'existentialisme au primat de l'économie,"[14] it recapitulates the major steps of the postwar trajectory marked by the inevitable allusions to existentialism against which much of the economic perspective was directed.

The most important reference here, however, is not Sartre, but the work of Emmanuel Levinas, just emerging from its Heideggerean antecedents. Levinas's determination of being as the "il y a"—an "ineffable" experience primarily accessible through art—is the starting point for Bataille's own thoughts regarding the nature of art as an economic phenomenon. Unlike the prewar vituperations against the facile side of literature and poetry, the latter is now touted as exhibiting a sovereign dilapidation of energy. Rather than dismiss its expenditure as mere "gaspillage" or waste, poetry, like most of art, must be recognized as a positive *dépense*. Beyond this basic argument, Bataille appropriates the terminology of Levinas's ethic of the other in order to develop the remaining dimensions of the general economy: the consequences of sovereignty for intersubjective relations; the repercussions of *dépense* for a more general theory of economy that posits *intimacy* as the "object" of knowledge; finally, how this general economy depends on a philosophy of "interiority" whose basic unit of analysis is a collective subject.

Pointing to the diminished interest in objects per se as a characteristic of modern art, Levinas sought comparisons between it and his own notion of the "il y a" which Bataille paraphrases as "an imperson-

14. Georges Bataille, "De l'existentialisme au primat de l'économie 1," *Critique* 21 (1948): 127–41.

al, anonymous, but inextinguishable *consumption* of being" (129). Moreover, Levinas's experience transcends interiority and exteriority: neither subject nor object, opposed to both as well as to the distinction between "existence" (the general and universal) and "existants" (individual beings and specific things), since within the "il y a" situation, the "existant" is dissolved into "existence." Particularly significant for Bataille is that Levinas refers the reader to several pages of Blanchot's *Thomas l'Obscur* as corresponding most effectively to the elusive notion he seeks to explore.

The brief introduction to Levinas is necessary for the contrast Bataille sets up between it and Sartrean existentialism. By equating existentialist knowledge with that which "is," i.e., accessible through knowledge and the "objective" qualities of things, Bataille concludes that even science is preferable, since "existentialist philosophy transforms us into a thing even more consistently than science, which at least leaves intimacy intact" (130–31). Similarly, the sacred element within religious rituals or, more contemporaneously, the license of poetic play, allow for intuitions of the mysteries eluding the existentialist who never escapes reduction to the level of "things." Like Bataille, Levinas credits French sociology for providing illustrations drawn from other cultures to illuminate the "il y a." But whereas Levinas has in mind the notion of a "pre-logical" mentality that Levy-Bruhl described as primitive fusion or participation, Bataille takes up the terminology of Levinas on the transcendence of existants into existence in order to appreciate the overcoming of subject and object, relinquishes a part of his or her riches, "without any consideration for a return, and independently of any appropriation by the other," in such a way that the distinction between self and other ceases to obtain (138).

Parallels are then drawn with the specific example of the artist who provides a comparable experience in relation to the work of art as well as between the work and the consumer. In this way, Bataille responds to the question foregrounded in the Miller review regarding the paradoxical status of art and the relation of the artist to his product or work, once it is inserted within the exchange network of market relations: the fact of selling paintings is subordinate to the essential movement which goes from the "existant" to existence. The final statement is justified by the blurring of distinction between the artist and the work. Art is therefore different from other activity by its exemplary mode of consumption, expended in the sovereign instant that resists subordination to a meaning primarily determined by future use. Regardless of the fact that a poem is inscribed within a temporality, or that it is a source of remuneration for its author, it marks "an unlimited possibility to communicate *consumption* (through a repetition of language) and to ascribe to the author a part of the unproductive expenditure to which the reader is committed. Each time the meaning of consumption is nonetheless given within the instant: it is the opposite of work, whose significance is limited to the future use of the product" (137).

Curiously, what Bataille concludes from this affirmation of the nonproductive quality of art is that it must be appreciated as an economic phenomenon. Not in the conventional sense of acquiescing to the inevitable pressures of the marketplace, but because all activity, given that a consumption of energy is involved, necessarily entails choices on the part of individuals compelled to relinquish, expend, or invest into specific ends within a set of constraints outside the bounds dictated by any one person. What art "communicates" is precisely a positive dilapidation of energy beyond the satisfaction of any particular need. But to the extent it "is" such an expenditure, art is also an economic fact to which the economy ascribes a value, so long as it is willing to concede a meaning to the present.

If Bataille has managed to affirm a view of art at odds with the traditional values of moral instruction, formal effort, and future duration, he has yet to explain all the ramifications of a general economy. Most difficult to elucidate is his appreciation of the "dissolution" of the conventional subject in the process of expenditure, replaced by the possibility of a collective unit which, as Durkheim argued in his theory of collective action, is greater than the sum of its parts. As Bataille rightly insists, the conventional "rational choice" theories of economics only deal with individuals devoid of "passions that unite." Although his extended reflections on the nature of community and collective experience cannot be reiterated here, the most evident way in which they are manifested in this context regards the question of so-called individual choice central to the polemic with Sartre. Similarly, Bataille underscored that in opposition to a regime where the "morality of unhappiness" is dictated by the criterion of utility, Camus conceptualized rebellion as a move toward transcendance inaccessible to isolated individuals.

Bataille's response to the "philosopher of liberty" is that Baudelaire's actions must be appreciated within a cycle of taboos and transgressions. The very actions or, in the case of the poet, his resistance to work in the traditional sense that Sartre deems most reprehensible, are precisely those transgressive gestures in which Bataille perceives true freedom. Central to Bataille's "morale," then, is the paradoxical phenomenon Mauss had challenged a generation of students to appreciate when he pointed out that taboos exist to be transgressed! Correlatively, Bataille argues that the violation of rules and interdictions heightens the awareness of their necessity. Such collective ritualization of experience beyond the boundaries of the quotidian, including festivals of destruction whose modern avatar is warfare, provide access to the heterogeneous domain of the sacred Bataille subsumed under the experience of sovereign expenditure. Never is the cycle rejected for inducing a mechanistic repetition. Rather, it offers possibilities that would otherwise remain closed to private experience or states of consciousness.

In the absence of collectively sanctioned excess, the taboo/ transgression pattern functions at the individual level. Where Sartre claims to have exposed the childishness of Baudelaire's attitude, Bataille therefore argues, "he had only discovered the conditions whereby an individual escapes his or her own self-imposed restrictions" (9, 441). Thus appear the conditions for the "hypermorale" Bataille attributes to such figures as Emily Brontë and the Marquis de Sade, who reach a higher state of consciousness by dint of their transgressions. The individual's moral stance is only worthy of consideration when it is recognized as the outcome of a process whereby "the real decision is the one obligating the individual to recognize himself destined to set up one part of himself against another: one cannot love oneself without being the object of some condemnation" (9, 193). What Sartre misses is Baudelaire's understanding that his choice in favor of poetry would lead to the life of a minor as judged by the traditional criteria of work and family, and was espoused in full appreciation of the consequences.

Sartre had condemned Baudelaire in the name of a paradoxical notion of existential freedom which Bataille argues does not fully take into account the nature and degree of constraints imposed on individual action. Consequently, the latitude of political action it seems to grant the individual is seriously curtailed in relation to what Sartre originally claimed. But Bataille also concedes that at the time of his initial reply to Sartre, he had not yet developed the full-fledged doctrine that was to emerge by the time of *L'Erotisme* (1957): "At that time I had only a vague notion of what subsequently became a developed doctrine. I was searching and Sartre's misunderstanding helped me. But I still did not know how to express my position clearly. It is only today (July 1956) that I am able to relate it to a total appreciation such as one finds in *L'Erotisme* (9, 441, in notes). The *vue d'ensemble* or "doctrine" of taboo and transgression is eventually elaborated on the basis of Bataille's enduring interest in social anthropology which is not in evidence, however, during the late 40s. Eclipsed by the post-war concern with gift-giving within the context of contemporary politics that contributed to *La Part maudite*, ethnography does not reappear until his review of Lévi-Strauss's *Elementary Structures of Kinship* in 1949.

This last observation, in which the strictly economic and political dimensions of the general economy appear at odds with the social aspects broached by anthropology, must not be taken as conclusive. For such an opposition runs counter to the appreciation of the Bataillian theory and practice of a general economy as it will be assessed in these closing pages. Especially relevant to this evaluation is the evolution of the Bataillian critical essay as it appears within the context of *Critique*. Indeed, the transgressions against the boundaries of disciplines and the hierarchical order of discourses constitute an essential quality of the Bataillian perspective that was transmuted into a distinguishing feature of the journal. Following the award bestowed on the review only a year after its inception, Bataille granted an interview to the *Figaro* in which he described its goals in the following terms: "human consciousness must cease to be compartmentalized. *Critique* seeks out the relations that exist between political economy and literature, between philosophy and politics." And in reference to an article by Alexandre Kojève (that had appeared in the reviews number 13–14), whom he qualifies as the most important philosopher of the day, "That article marks the confluence of literature, religion, and political economy" (Surya, 372).

Thus far, this study has demonstrated how *Critique* at the macro level, and the Bataillian essay at the level of individual writing practice, constitute something other than the sum of their parts that Bataille synthesized as a "morale." How this encounter among areas traditionally kept separate produces unforeseeable results can be appreciated in relation to the recurrent theme of the elusive "intimacy" induced by expenditures that destroy rather than preserve the objects consumed. The consequences of this position are twofold: on the one hand, it calls forth an alternative to philosophy's predominately "external" approach. In the review of Weil, for instance, Bataille draws together the issues of morality, sovereignty, and loyalty under the question of intimacy:

> That a moral exists is possible for the reason that one is not given to one's peers simply once and for all, from without, like a fact, or stone or tool. Rather, one appears as an intimacy, a sovereign presence, worthy of infinite respect and deriving sovereignty from a quality best evoked by the word prodigality. [797]

Second, as this last sentence, and the following one also taken from the same review illustrate, the Bataillian discussion of the morality of expenditure does not hesitate to veer off into a cosmological vision dominated by sun, sky, and star imagery: "It is only in the world that [it] can find a form of humanity, the truth worthy of wonder that is human existence, which in the immensity of Time and Space reveals a poetry charged with the violence of the storm" (802). What these brief citations help to illustrate are features of a writing practice that was to prove exemplary within the subsequent history of the essay form. Initially suffering from the lack of a clear-cut label and an even murkier set of values, including the advocacy of spectacular destruction and sexual aberrations as clues to a revolutionary "sovereign" perspective on human relations, Bataille's "morale" eventually acquired an identifiable set of positions and propositions which, taken together, contributed to the Copernican reversal to which he admittedly aspired.

Furthermore, by addressing what *Critique* designated to be the major intellectual issues of the day, Bataille was able to demonstrate the relevance of a theory of general economy beyond the immediate domains to which his own name might have consigned it. For this reason, it is possible to argue that the major impediment to a widespread recognition, i.e., an identifiable "philosophy" such as existentialism could claim to provide, was turned into *Critique*'s outstanding feature. By refusing the protocols as well as presuppositions of much of philosophy, Bataille set the pattern for a mode of critical practice that challenged the texts in question for the limits or contradictions they unwittingly exhibited. Camus "betrays" the tragic potential of one play in the compromised ethic of another work; Weil succumbs to a moral heroism based on denial; communism undoes its own possibility for a sovereign alternative to capitalism, and so on. Alternatively, Bataille's prose is studded with its own repertoire of striking images, key terms and notions, or what I have already likened to Durkheimian collective representations, whether the cosmological pineal eye, the munificent sun of *dépense*, the *part maudite*, or the categories of heterogeneity and sovereignty which have acquired widespread currency within contemporary critical idiom.

Indeed, the effectiveness of such transgressions is most evident in Bataille's legacy. In a major economic treatise,[15] Perroux argues the relevance of the gift for twentieth-century economies, with the proviso that it be conceived in a way other than the marginalized phenomenon of the "pseudo-gifts" encouraged by capitalism. Compatible with a market mentality, such pseudo-gifts cannot, and are never expected to rectify fundamental inequities. Nor can they promote new forms of sociability. Perroux's argument is formulated aggressively, in order to preempt the political dismissal of his proposals as naive or sentimental idealism. He then advocates a role for "transfers without any counterpart" (e.g., equivalence or return), as a means to foster social solidarity. He concludes with the following strong statement:

> A modern economy open to disinterested motives and the spirit of the gift has nothing in common with an economy in which charitable institutions and foundations abound. . . . We must not look to an economy that simply accommodates giving, but one whose vital institutions impose and facilitate the utilisation of disinterested motives to which have been restored their economic effectiveness. . . . [427]

Perroux's work can be situated within a post-Bataillian reading of economists who have sought to revitalize economic theory by injecting into it a qualitative dimension or an emotive level which considers behavior that does not conform to the so-called rationality of economic man.

More recently, Bataille's equation of *consumation* with communication, as a willed act of relinquishment or sacrifice that induces a sense of community whereby "I reveal to my peers what I am intimately. . . . All is transparent, open, infinite among those who consume intimately" (7, 63), is cited by Jacques Attali in his *Anti-*

15. François Perroux, *L'Economie du XXe siècle* (Paris: PUF, 1961; third edition expanded, 1969).

économique (1980).[16] Attali discerns in the Bataillian version of "consumation" an antidote to the eclipse of intimacy in the reductionist exchange of things characteristic of the *société de consommation*. As special adviser to François Mitterand, he confirms Pierre Birnbaum's hypothesis that there exists a direct link between Mauss's gift essay and subsequent theories of welfare from a socialist perspective.[17]

Ironically, it has been argued that Sartre, albeit in a very different idiom, also sought to synthesize an anthropology whose primary goal was the formulation and dissemination of a discourse on generosity and reciprocity (Davies, 1987). This position reinforces an earlier sociologically based argument that the professional competition between Sartre and Bataille was largely determined by their *proximity*, rather than the more predictable distance, within the intellectual field constituted by the major journals of the postwar period (Boschetti, 1985). Also benefitting from the impressive team he constituted for *Les Temps modernes*, Sartre's contentiousness toward Bataille can be interpreted as part of a more general strategy to eliminate his potentially strongest competitors. Although the greatest number of crossovers between any two reviews occur between *Critique* and *TM*, Bataille's group proved less formidable in the short run. The sociological explanation points to the generally marginal qualifications of most participants: in background (provincial or foreign); social connections (non-Parisian); education (l'Ecole des Chartes or the university versus l'Ecole normale supérieure). Similarly, the marginal nature of Bataille's thought in general has been underlined.[18]

It is therefore now appropriate to consider how it is that the ideas promoted within the context of *Critique*, most notably the ramifications of the general economy, were able to shift from a position of relative esoterism to the forefront of critical polemics in the mid- to late sixties. I propose the following configuration of factors as the basis for an explanation:

In arguing the importance of journals until their gradual usurpation by the mass media in the early 1960s, Regis Debray cited as an exam-

16. Jacques Attali, *Anti-économique* (Paris: PUF, 1980), 175. Attali, however advocates an experience of intimacy and communion which does *not* entail "sacrifice" of things and the work which produces them.

17. See Pierre Birnbaum, "Du socialisme au don," *l'Arc* 48 (1972): 41–54.

18. See Mario Perniola, *L'Instant éternel. Bataille et la pensée de la marginalité* (Paris: Meridiens Anthropos, 1982).

ple *Critique,* without which there would have been no "new" criticism. If we accept this assertion, which can be easily documented,
then it is relevant to consider Bataille's role in such a movement. We
recall that despite its impressive eclecticism, *Critique's* lead article
dealt with a literary work, and Bataille himself was frequently the
reviewer. We have also noted how, by bending the strictly critical
format, he was able to situate his own work in relation to major
contemporary literary figures. This strategic positioning of literary
matters was especially important in light of the longstanding French
admiration of literature's moral force. Its effectiveness as a unifying
factor was undermined, however, by the collaboration of Drieu La
Rochelle, wartime editor of *La Nouvelle revue française.* Having survived the surrealist onslaught, bellelettrism was dealt a blow comparable to the general social upheaval that ensued in the wake of
World War II.

Sartre's "Temps modernes" thus identified itself in relation to all
that was new and timely, if not daring and innovative, as a way to
break with and revitalize the traditional format exemplified by the
NRF. But even if the journal's commitment to literature allowed it to
publish new fiction, from which it derived the respect still credited to
most literature, the positions expounded by Sartre in the essays collected under the title *What is Literature?* (1948) reveal his reservations toward the growing tendency to privilege form over content,
and an even more vociferous resistance to the symbiosis developing
between literary criticism and the human sciences. What Sartre reas-
suringly exemplified was the strong French essayistic tradition, in
which the "man of letters" could offer pronouncements on virtually
every major issue of the day. His death marked the demise of an era in
which one individual could incarnate the moral conscience of an
entire nation through the claims of a generalist, an intellectual-at-
large whose formation was literary and philosophical.

Thus, despite Sartre's short period as a CP fellow traveler, the
overriding image projected by the journal touted for its commitment
to social issues was that of an independence from the major political
parties. Sartre's personal influence was based on moral grounds, and
like Bataille, his most intense passions were reserved for a critique of
bourgeois liberalism that refused to abide by the strictures of either
end of the political spectrum. While undoubtedly the more political
figure, Sartre shared with Bataille a rejection of the material reality of
capitalist civilization irreducible to the divergent means by which

they sought to escape or overcome it. Whence the important references to nineteenth-century authors as examples of evasion they alternately rejected or revised.

The model Bataille advocates is transgressive, where the collectivity accedes to a sovereign experience of *dépense* through the periodic violation of taboos which otherwise channel the expenditure of energy into production and accumulation. Although the "hypermorale" at the basis of such excess never loses sight of the inevitable necessity of the rational domain of calculated utility, this recognition need not defuse the intensity of the critical stance from which it emanates. A rebellion sparked at the fringes of social organization and which does not seek to appropriate power in the conventional sense, can nonetheless effect change at the level of social relations, the goal Bataille set for his own writing.[19]

When applied to literature, the transgressive model of the general economy revised nineteenth-century antibourgeois discussions of "art for art's sake" in relation to the marketplace by designating a symbolic mode of exchange in which art, like gifts, functions according to criteria different from those dictated by the restricted economy. In contrast with Sartre's condemnation or a defensive reaction to Baudelaire's refusal, Bataille insists on a Nietzschean affirmation wherein the politics of the general economy are espoused. Literature follows the example of the festival in this pan-economic vision, and resists the imposition of teleological ends by demonstrating its willingness to relinquish meaning in a sacrificial potlatch of the words of the tribe.

Certainly the approach to language manifested within the new criticism is crucial to effecting the break with its predecessors. To begin, it eschews the myth of transparency wherein one language ("parole") is shared by all speakers and, correlatively, that one individual could function as a universal spokesperson. The skepticism of the new critics derives from the class-based experience of French society and its reflection in the stratification of the codes by which we distinguish the various language communities, including their respective lifestyles and educational levels. Their theoretical sophistication was systematized by analytic instruments derived from the

19. For a discussion of the potential of "liminality" as a model for effecting social change and its relevance to Bataillian sociology, see Richman, "Introduction to the Collège de sociologie (1937–1939): Poststructuralism before its time," special issue on Bataille, *Stanford French Review* XII, 1 (Spring 1988): 79–95.

structural linguistics and ideologically oriented critical semiology honed in the Soviet and Eastern European cultures. Moreover, the rupture with prewar academic discourse was undoubtedly reinforced by the political experience of the 1930s and the social traumas of the war, where the fluidity of political careers demonstrated the absurdity of fixed labels—a dramatic lesson in the maximal disparities between signifiers and signifieds that could not be easily ignored.

Regardless of his oft-cited declaration that he makes a "classical" use of language, Bataille expressed his own wariness through his sensitivity to the "besogne des mots": i.e., the ways in which usage provokes and manipulates ideological associations that demand constant vigilance and counterwork. One critic (Marmande) has taken this position as the starting point for his political analysis, but I maintain that it is in the transgressive practice of Bataille's move toward a *vue d'ensemble* inspired by the theory of general economy, where he places in relation to each other issues otherwise maintained in discrete isolation, that the textual politics of Bataille's writing has been particularly influential.

The conclusion most relevant to this presentation of *Critique* to be drawn from the above is that literature, writing, and especially the formulation of alternative discourses, are not and cannot be accomplished in isolation. Barthes, responsible for reinforcing this acknowledgment through his notion of *écriture*, at the end of a career often viewed as progressively depoliticized, nonetheless qualified the fact of writing for a review as the "ethico-political" issue.[20] Although the production of a distinctive *écriture* was neither as systematic nor consistent within *Critique* as the *Temps modernes*, it is nonetheless possible to argue that the Bataillian point of view was shared and promoted by such stalwarts as Perroux, Piel, and Ambrosino.[21] Without their contributions, not to mention those of Blanchot, whose work provided the most striking example of profound affinities, *Critique's* foregrounding of the general economy would not have been possible.

It is ironic to note that Barthes's observation was based on his

20. For further development of this point, see Réda Bensmaia, *The Barthes Effect: The Essay as Reflective Text*, foreword by Michèle Richman (Minneapolis: University of Minnesota Press, 1987), chapter 14.

21. Regarding the role played by Ambrosino, for instance, Surya notes: "Le physicien qu'était Georges Ambrosino fut là beaucoup plus qu'un conseiller, il en fut l'inspirateur et le correcteur comme en témoigne une lettre du 28 novembre 1945" (384).

experience with the review *Tel Quel*, the major outlet for the elaboration and dissemination of many Bataillian notions in the decade following his death in 1962. Indeed, while *Critique* continues publication even today, that date marks the cessation of his direct influence.[22] According to Debray, it is also a turning point for French cultural life, in whose history before and after, Bataille's place as well as that of *Critique* must be fully appreciated.[23]

22. Piel dates the virtual end of Bataille's input to his last *Critique* article of 1958, "La religion préhistorique."

23. Earlier, different versions of this essay were delivered to a special session at the 1983 MLA entitled "Political Rereadings of the Forties," and to a Georges Bataille international colloquium in Amsterdam, June 1984.

JEAN-MICHEL BESNIER

Georges Bataille in the 1930s: A Politics of the Impossible

It is not easy to draw a map of the 1930s. This period in French history, which, to a great extent, extends to the present day, has progressively entered people's minds as that of a prewar while at the same time seeking to be experienced as that of the postwar. In such a context, one dominated by intellectual confusion and the muddling of political identities, Georges Bataille occupied a position both unique and typical. He espoused the characteristics of his epoch without, however, giving in to the generalized disorientation which reflected the disarray of intellectual references on the part of most of the period's actors and witnesses: a desire to break with tradition for those who lived the tragedy of the time as a chance to begin anew; a return to the security of certain dogmas for others, less sensitive to the tragic aesthetic than to a devotion to partisan commitment. During this confusing period, many Surrealists broke with the Communist Party in order to celebrate the virtues of violent "Refusal" [*Inacceptation*]. At the same time, Maurice Blanchot was led to rally for the "Young Right" and to proclaim "terrorism as a means of public salvation".[1]

To a certain extent, Bataille proceeds from this extreme fluidity of intellectual and political positions, from this irresistible expenditure of commitments and ideas. Like many of his contemporaries, he rejects the political establishment as well as apolitical resignation; he belongs to the camp of the "revoltés de l'inespoir" [rebels of hopelessness], to the camp of the activists of heterogeneity. The advantage

1. This is the title of an article by Maurice Blanchot which appeared in *La Revue Française*, (July 1936), and was reprinted in *Gramma* 5, (1976).

YFS 78, *On Bataille*, ed. Allan Stoekl, © 1990 by Yale University.

vantage of his position, relative to that of others, results from his rigorous formulation of the impossible situation faced by his generation: "If there is no longer a great machine in whose name to speak," he writes, "how do you call others to action, and for what end?"[2] This question is still asked (by Jean-François Lyotard, for example), but unlike the present day, which is generally unaffected by the vertigo of militancy, in the 1930s it was accompanied by a moving fascination for action. It was under these circumstances, then, that the evils of revolutionary projects were discovered: the reality of the Soviet regime and the rise of Fascism. The subsequent revulsion for "political machines" is understandable, but that is not a sufficient reason to abandon action. Given a choice between the risks of revolutionary action and the debilitating apathy of parliamentary democracy, there is no room for hesitation: ethics lie on the side of revolt and risk. The call of politics turns out to be stronger than the distaste for politics.

This is particularly clear with the Surrealists. For them, "refusal" becomes the absolute virtue, and Revolution—"any revolution, as bloody as you like"[3]—the most popular call to action. It became evident that historical impasses prescribe unbridled fury. The Revolution was, from then on, delivered from the transcendence which had been intrinsic to (whether they liked it or not) the "great theoretical machines": neither messianism nor eschatology, just rage in the gut and in the head . . .

It may be argued that, in order to attenuate the vehemence of this revolutionary decision, the reestablishment of the Reign of Terror called for by André Breton (in *Les Pas Perdus*) is only intended "for the spirit" and that, therefore, the Surrealists remained purely inoffensive idealists—"those pain in the ass idealists" as Bataille called them. That objection is valid, however, only if one forgets that Breton and his friends held on to the Hegelian directive to act so as to realize the ideal, to make that idealism satisfy the ontological argument and, thus, make it possible to create a new reality on the basis of thought alone. Moreover, Bataille's originality, which we shall see as exemplified by his "politics of the impossible," consists in his refusal of Hegelianism as a means of legitimizing the desire to revolt. In this

2. Georges Bataille, *Oeuvres Complètes* (Paris: Gallimard, 1970), vol. 6, 161. Henceforth cited in text as *OC*.
3. André Breton: "Any revolution, as bloody as you like. . . . : It would not be bad for the spirit to reestablish the laws of the Terror." *Les Pas Perdus* (Paris: Gallimard, NRF, 1924).

respect, he seems qualitatively more radical than the Surrealists, who had, in any event, more than one opponent in their race for subversive audacity.

The decision to work for revolution at any cost is in a way expressed in its pure state by the intellectual community which Roger Gilbert-Lecomte, René Daumal, Roger Vailland, and Josef Sima baptized "Le Grand Jeu" [The Great Game] in 1928.* This community of young men, who were all about twenty years old at the beginning of the thirties, put forth an image of revolt so extreme that it frightened even the Surrealists. André Breton tried first to bring them around, but then quickly rejected the group (after the famous meeting on the Rue du Château) for their "mysticism." These "Godseekers" obviously did not have their feet on the ground and their adolescence seemed all too uncontrollable.

Nevertheless, with them, one discovers just how far the feeling of being in a historical impasse was able to sprout revolt, the desire for a "Tout-Autre" [a completely different world]. "We are all backed up against a wall, writes Ribemont-Dessaignes, and even those who know what lies on the other side can see no way out except what is painted on the wall. There are only fake doors and windows. And they are no way out." Faced with a choice between absolute refusal and the world, violent and unconditional revolt appears to these adolescents as the only solution. That is what Daumal will explain later in *La Révolte et l'ironie:* "All that the adolescent understands is the hammering of his blood, the desire of his whole body for enjoyment. He wants either to understand or to destroy—and he will destroy. Off he goes into battle against the world; resolved to show the world that he defies its rule. He strives to respect nothing: he'll be sacrilegious, develop a taste for Black Masses, throw bombs in public meetings, insult great men, preach anarchy. He'll steal and murder. If, as is usually the case, he finds himself too weak for this violent revolt, he'll say 'I'm a coward, but that's the way it is.' "

Numerous are the texts which, in the three issues of the review *Le Grand Jeu* glorify "violent revolt" in this way.[4] Texts which owe nothing to, but instead anticipate, Breton's famous tirade: "The simplest Surrealist act consists of dashing down into the street, pistol in

* "Le Grand Jeu" is a term that refers both to the Tarot and, idiomatically, to an all-out effort. [—Translator's note]

4. *Le Grand Jeu* (Paris: Jean-Michel Place, 1977).

hand, and firing blindly, as fast as you can pull the trigger, into the crowd. Anyone who, at least once in his life, has not dreamed of thus putting an end to the petty system of debasement and cretinization in effect has a well-defined place in that crowd, with his belly at barrel level."[5] Upon closer examination, however, beyond this invocation of violence, what is at stake here is neither exactly a profession of nihilist faith nor an acceptance of some suicidal attitude. Their revolt is really in the service of an ideal. An unrepresentable ideal, of course—it is for precisely that reason that "Le Grand Jeu" challenges the principles of any revealed religion; but an ideal just the same, as it portends unspeakable "miracles" and promises "escape and liberation." Daumal sums up the ethics of violence—that is to say of the search for salvation through violence—expressed by the members of the "Grand Jeu" group: "To reject ceaselessly all of the crutches of hope, break all the stable creations of the law, endlessly torment each person with his desires and never be assured of victory: such is the hard and fast road of renunciation. Men must despair if they are to cast off their humanity into the vast tomb of nature and thus, leaving their human self to its own laws, find a way out." Nothing could be clearer: it is a question of "finding a way out" through violence. To revolt against hopelessness—against the wall of reality—is, at the same time, to give hope a foothold.

Is this merely an adolescent contradiction? In any case, logic hardly constrained these children of Rimbaud. Even as they unleash their desire to save the old world from destruction, they become mired in systems of thought which prove the vanity of action—that is to say, in this case, in Marxist determinism. Their revolutionary voluntarism is linked to a scientific belief in the fixed nature of things. Their determinism challenges the efficacity of human action by showing that everything has already been decided. This antinomy between human will and science is resolved by leaving it up to chance to decide when and where the ax will fall and whether the events are to be as people want them to be, or the product of an intangible chain of cause and effect.

"Le Grand Jeu" illustrates well the unsurprising shift which, against a backdrop of generalized confusion, collapsed the available philosophical options together and gave the thirties their unique configuration. For these rebels explicitly aligned themselves with the

5. André Breton. *The Surrealist Manifesto*, Trans. Richard Seaver and Helen R. Lane in *Manifestoes of Surrealism* (Ann Arbor: The University of Michigan Press, 1969), 125.

"determinist doctrine of history" which logically should make revolutionary action unthinkable. As Gilbert-Lecomte stated, contradicting Emmanuel Berl: "We affirm that we are Hegelians . . . Monists, absolute determinists"; and Daumal, contradicting Breton: "Nothing has yet been done with Hegel's principal idea: the perfectibility of human reason and its ultimate identification with the *Objective Spirit,* which creates the world by thinking of it. Nothing needs to be changed in the dialectic—Heraclitus's, Plato's, Hegel's, they are all the same—for it to come alive before our eyes, for the light of fatality to be a beacon for revolutions."

"Le Grand Jeu" is thus both wildly voluntarist and decidedly fatalist. This sums up the stagnation of this era which saw itself as the end of an age pretty well. It also explains, to some extent, how the most turbulent thinkers of the thirties, like Queneau and Bataille, could have sought wisdom alongside the most reasonable, such as Aron and Weil, in the classes of Alexandre Kojève, the Master who proclaimed the end of History while encouraging revolution.

That History is over, the final word spoken—by Hegel, Napoleon, Marx, or Stalin—does not seem to have necessarily called for the suppression of action—action racked and irresistibly haunted by the Other, the heterogeneous, or the Impossible. The formidable success of the lectures given by Kojève at the Ecole Pratique des Hautes Etudes between 1933 and 1939 is well known, as is the spell of his words which rendered obsolete the neo-Kantian discourse then dominating the French university system. With Kojève, Hegel arrived in France, and with him came tragic idealism, which alone measured up to the din of history and was capable of opposing the scientific idealism of the national academies.

To the calmest of his students as to the most turbulent, Kojève taught the inconceivable:

—That History is fundamentally tragic for it functions by means of struggle and war.

—But also that it is over and that one must read the present time as the conclusion of the process of History.

Kojève did, of course, produce a commentary on the *Phenomenology of Mind* and on its famous dialectic of master and slave, at the end of which will arise the era of universal recognition: a time of absolute equality when "citizens, as citizens, will have no specificity."[6] But

6. Alexandre Kojève, *Esquisse d'une Phénémonologie du Droit* (Paris: Gallimard, 1981), 578.

Kojève did not hesitate to present Hegel's commentary as "a piece of propaganda intended to shock people," just as he made it clear that Stalin was ushering in posthistory.

In short, conceived of as the place where conflict arises and dissipates, politics, according to Kojève, runs into its own impossibility and, in this sense, imposes the necessity of an "un ailleurs" [elsewhere]. After the war, in fact, Kojève abandoned teaching and his "propaganda" in order to enter the civil service, which manages the Universal for all eternity.

Le Dimanche de la Vie by Raymond Queneau is symptomatic of the effectiveness of Kojève's lessons. Valentin Brû, the novel's hero, sees himself as a man of the posthistorical era, or at least as a prophet of posthistory. His is the portrait of a hero who thinks of nothing but Jena—where History acknowledged its end with the Napoleonic victory and where Hegel (whose house Brû visits) wrote the final words of the *Phenomenology of Mind*. A zombielike hero, "useless" for lack of contradictions to bear—supernumerary in his regiment, a shopkeeper without conviction—Brû makes himself out to be a prophet (replacing his wife, a.k.a. Madame Saphire) and fools those around him, including his brother-in-law, who is flabbergasted that Brû's admiration of Jena allowed him to predict Hitler's revenge. . . . Brû's action is contemplation, for History has no meaning except when suspended. He forces himself to watch time pass and, in order to do so, he tries to empty his head, the only way to control time: "I think, he says, of the passing of time and, as it is identical to itself, I always think of the same thing, which is to say that I end up thinking of nothing at all." He is a parody of Kojève whose voice echoes in these oracles of the Sage: "There will be no postwar period. Or rather, after, there will be nothing. Or yet again, what will be is unthinkable. After such a war, there will be no afterwards."[7]

In the thirties, Kojève proclaimed in a captivating manner the historic impasse which was then felt confusedly by each individual. He showed the path of wisdom to these young rebels, who were beating their heads against the wall, in such a way that, if the Revolt should continue it would necessarily become Metaphysical, decidedly superhuman. In other words, it would be doomed to failure.

With Kojève, "Hegel becomes the evidence, and evidence is hard to bear." Among Kojève's transfixed listeners, Georges Bataille at-

---

7. Letter to Than Duc Thao, 10/7/1948. On the relationship between Bataille and Kojève, see J.-M. Besnier in *Le Magazine Littéraire*, (June 1987): 42–43.

tempted to test the end of History proclaimed by the Sage. Or rather he assumed the unbearable and painful paradox of the revolt within himself coupled with the knowledge that there was nothing more to do. A moving drama of irreconcilability lived by a man whose reason calls for his adhesion to the Hegelian system of universal reconciliation.

Bataille's letter to Kojève of 6 December 1937, in which he explains how difficult it was for him to accept the idea that there was nothing left for him to do, since "history is finished (except for the conclusion)," is often cited. He makes it clear, in that letter, that in order to retain his humanity—that is, not to sink into the lifelessness of Valentin Brû—it was necessary to struggle against the meaninglessness to which he was condemned by the end of History. To that end, he set his "ruptured existence" against the Hegelian system. The essential question therefore seems to be for him to know under what circumstances the "unemployed negativity," which the end of History forces him to be, will be recognized, and under what circumstances a need to act, which lacks a purpose, will be legitimated.

This is a crucial question which, indeed, ties together the paradox of revolt and fatalism and sums up, in my opinion, the tragedy of the thirties.

This paradox is apparent in Bataille's simultaneous adhesion to both Hegelian and Nietzschean thought. The coexistence of this double philosophical reference undoubtedly explains the dissipation of the pacifying effect of Kojève's teaching and the turn, within just a few years, to a combative Nietzscheanism. Put another way, Bataille let himself be convinced by Hegel at the very same time that he discovered, in Nietzsche, the expression of an absolute refusal of subjugation to any thought whatsoever. The "paradoxical philosophy" to which he subscribed, and which he described succinctly as "the sense of the impossible," goes together with a politics no less impossible: the unwillingness to submit what has been instituted to any recuperative dialectic.

Nietzsche is the guarantee of nonreconciliation needed by those who, at that time, refused to consent to the order of things. That in no way means that he became the object of a univocal reading—far from it. From the beginning of the thirties the avowed Nietzscheans are legion: there are those who read *Thus Spake Zarathustra* as an apologia for the use of brutal force and those who take it as encouragement to work for a Renaissance of civilization. Some find in *Beyond Good and Evil* a lesson of discouraging relativism while others echo its denunciation of democratic institutions and the rule of the masses. Finally, there are those for whom the struggle against fascism must begin by wresting the "hammer wielding philosopher" from the National Socialist fallacy. In short, the ethos of this time belongs to Nietzsche. In the upheaval of the prewar period, the German thinker resonates like the tonic chord of a generation clearly living out its disorganization. It is Nietzsche who formulates the encouragement to love "danger, adventure, (and) war," as well as the praise of those who "don't allow themselves to accommodate, mend, or reconcile."[8]

One can imagine the impact of Nietzsche's unbridled voice: to those who dream of destroying this worm-eaten world, it cries "eternal chaos" and thereby restores an infinite number of possibilities; to those who have lost hope in action, it says that the absence of meaning in the world is not to be confused with an acceptance of a necessarily demobilizing random chance, but that, on the contrary, it encourages an investment in this *terra incognita*. History is, in fact, innocent: "When you know that there are no goals, you know as well that nothing happens by 'chance.' "[9] Could there be a better reason for staying in the ring?

Nietzsche becomes a weapon of war. In this light, Bataille's rage when Hitler visited Elisabeth Foerster, Nietzsche's sister, on 2 November 1933, and when she dared to attest to her brother's anti-Semitism, is understandable. The falsification, recuperation, and subjugation of sovereign thought! Bataille devoted an entire number of *Acéphale* to making amends to Nietzsche. The stakes were obviously not only philological: it was instead a question of reestablishing the truth about Nietzsche (to point out the contempt that he felt for anti-Semitism). It was also, and above all, a move to preserve a Nietzschean point of view on politics, in other words an "elsewhere" beyond the categories of left and right, an attitude which could be opposed to Stalinism as well as to fascism. "Wresting Nietzsche away from the Nazis" was a way of denouncing the instrumental use of humanity (of any human being) which was incipient in National Socialism and would later burst forth in the established totalitarian regimes. It was a move to save independent action because it is the only weapon against the fascination of Nazism. It was necessary to make amends to Nietzsche because the cooptation of his thought for

8. Nietzsche, *The Gay Science*, paragraph 337.
9. Ibid, paragraph 109.

propaganda purposes is, in and of itself, the symbolic destruction of all free existence. The stakes were a measure of the urgency of the times: it was a question of escaping not only from political duplicity but also from the dizzying unification represented by Hitler, Mussolini, and Stalin. In sum, Nietzsche, as a figure, calls forth the need for a political stance that is up to the standards of life, that is to say, of tragedy.[10]

It was the "voluntarist" thought of Nietzsche that this generation needed most. Through it their rejection of both current politics and apolitical resignation found expression.

In the second issue of *Acéphale*, a magazine which was declared a wartime effort from its inception, Pierre Klossowski quotes extensively from Jasper's book on Nietzsche, in which Jaspers formulated the political possibilities opened up to him by Nietzschean philosophy. On the eve of World War II the idea of an "elsewhere," opposed to the status quo, is wedded to an awareness of the impossible as foretold by Nietzsche alone.

Bataille turns to the expression "politics of the impossible" in a letter to Jérôme Lindon, 9 January 1962,[11] in order to emphasize the necessity of subverting a politics which limits itself to "a discourse of the possible." This is a late echo of what Bataille had never ceased to proclaim since he first associated philosophy with political experience.[12] It even harks back to his commentary on Emmanuel Berl's article "Conformismes freudiens," which appeared in *Documents* in 1930. There Bataille announced his intention to take up sides politically, and he already began to attack the Surrealists, those "decadent aesthetes utterly incapable of even the possibility of contact with the lower classes" (*OC*, vol. 11, 94, 103).

Thus, the politics of the impossible announces its nature quite early in the work of Georges Bataille. It blends in with the project of establishing a "popular philosophy" which would be subversive insofar as it is motivated by a movement swelling up from the bottom. The impossible is, for this politics, the equivalent of the "heterogeneous" which texts contemporary to *La Critique sociale* set against the assimilating undertaking of the totalitarian states. The first issue

10. "L'existence, c'est à dire la tragédie," *Acéphale* 3, (Paris: Jean-Michel Place, 1980), 18.

11. Bataille, *Oeuvres Complètes*, vol. 3, 521. (This letter begins on page 519, the term is used on 520.)

12. Bataille, *L'Erotisme* (Paris: UGE, 1965), 277.

of *Contre-Attaque* translates it as "spontaneous movements of the masses." As Bataille then wrote: "Still, as astonishing as this may seem, one frequently notes, among militant revolutionaries, a complete lack of confidence in the spontaneous reactions of the masses. The need to organize parties has resulted in unusual habits among the so-called revolutionary agitators, who confuse the entry of the Revolution into the street with their political platforms, with their well-groomed programs, with their maneuvers in the halls of Congress."[13]

Nothing could be clearer: the politics of the impossible chooses revolution not as a goal to reach but as an unplanned uprising, what Bataille calls "la dépense pure" [pure expenditure]. And that includes even unbridled emotion, outbursts of violence which "carry the crowds out into the streets" and all that "from house to house, from suburb to suburb, suddenly turns a hesitating man into a frenzied being" (*OC*, 1, 403; *VE*, 162).

Contre-Attaque, the movement Bataille founded with André Breton in September, 1935, forcefully maintained that, in the face of fascism, one is held to the impossible. Henri Dubief, a witness to these times, remembers that "it was question less of organizing a defended retreat from fascism than of overcoming it by the mobilization of the popular masses, delivered from the structures of sclerotic workers' organizations."[14] After 16 February 1936, Bataille rejoiced: "500,000 workers, defied by little cockroaches, invaded the streets and caused an immense uproar. Comrades, who has the right to lay down the law? This ALL-POWERFUL multitude, this HUMAN OCEAN. . . . Only this ocean of men in revolt can save the world from the nightmare of impotence and carnage in which it sinks!" (*OC*, 1, 412; *VE*, 168). This is giving in to the "lyricism of the uncontrollable," as has been said; but more important, it is confidence in the "powerless power" which, resistant to all power and in that sense "impossible," characterizes the people, according to Maurice Blanchot.[15]

What governs revolutionary action, as Bataille sees it, is a politics

13. *Oeuvres Complètes*, vol. 1, 403–04. The English version is to be found in Bataille's *Visions of Excess: Selected Writings, 1927–1939*, ed. and trans. A. Stoekl (Minneapolis: The University of Minnesota Press, 1985), 162. Henceforth cited in the text as *VE*.

14. *Textures* 6 (Brussels: 1970) 57.

15. Maurice Blanchot, *La Communauté inavouable* (Paris: Minuit, 1983), 54.

of the unforeseeable, wholly inspired by the Nietzschean aphorism: "I love the unknowability of the future." A politics completely opposed to that which is anchored in reality, this mediocre waiting period which calls itself political, is convinced that there is nothing left to do but manage a history bereft of surprise, such as Kojève described it.

The politics of the impossible seems, then, like an answer to the confusion of the thirties: it calls for a revolt against anything that pretends to be completed, full, transparent, and necessary. It calls for a refusal of waiting, a refusal of the patience which endures the randomness of the world. Ultimately, it is underpinned by a double refusal:

—a rejection of the Hegelian-Marxist eschatology which portends the ineluctable end of History.

—and a rejection, as well, of that kind of irrationalism to which the history of Heideggerian Being gives rise, and which welcomes the event as an incomprehensible "miracle."

Is this to say that the politics of the impossible becomes confused with a voluntarist position that holds that history is always the product of conscious beings? One would think so to read, in *Contre-Attaque*, a declaration such as that of Ambrosino and Gilet which predicts a "moral Revolution," under the auspices of Nietzsche: "The world born tomorrow will be the world announced by Nietzsche, a world which will liquidate *all* moral servitude" (*OC*, 1, 391–92). It could also be drawn from a reading of the brilliant text which Bataille entitled "Politique": "It is a strange paradox: if one perceives the profound lack of a way out, the profound absence of an end and of meaning, then—and only then—can one actually, with a liberated spirit, lucidly tackle practical problems" (*OC*, 6, 251).

But voluntarism calls for power and the politics which results from it aspires to political control. The politics of the impossible, on the other hand, avows powerlessness as its controlling motive. As Blanchot writes in *L'Entretien infini*, 308: the impossible is "ce en quoi nous ne pouvons plus pouvoir" [that in which we are no longer able to be able], and that is what the man at the end of History discovers in himself: negativity which discovers itself to be useless.

Hegel made voluntarism and any politics of the control of power inherently vain. That is why Bataille's political thought, at the end of the thirties, turns in tune with Nietzsche's, to thoughts of sovereignty. This is also why the politics of the impossible, breaking with the classic problematic of power, ends up in an unexpected formulation: "It is no longer a question of meeting the failings of authority: it is, more modestly, about REPLACING GOD." Such a declaration leads one to believe that the sovereignty sought by those who shall henceforth exceed mastery and servitude distinguishes itself from political power. It is not, therefore, in conflict with the masses, which are by definition cut off from power. The best that one can ultimately hope to obtain from those who assume this sovereignty is that they form a community, for which secret societies offer the best historical model.[16]

Therein lies the last word for Bataille on the eve of the war. The *Contre-Attaque* movement aborts itself (primarily because, according to Bataille, it exposed its militants to the trap against which they fought) and Bataille gives it, as its posterity, a secret society, *Acéphale*, which "turns its back on politics and foresees only a religious goal" (*OC*, 6, 485n.). To examine the nature of this religious goal would require other developments which lead us to believe that the experience of the impossible—an experience of the limits of power and ultimately of death—necessarily ends in the quest for communication. This communication quickly appears to be yet another way of designating this politics of the impossible, ever torn between the discontinuity which keeps men apart and subjugates them to the possible, on the one hand, and the fundamental continuity which joins them in an anticipation of death, on the other.

Evoking the theme of communication in Bataille's work would be, in any case, another story, bringing us to that part of his work opened by the creation of the College of Sociology, in 1937, and concluded by *La Part maudite*, having reached its apogee in *La Somme athéologique*.

In this essay I have tried to plot out the wanderings of the thirties, where revolt and fatalism, messianism and despair, intentionality and eschatology blended together, and to suggest that these wanderings are articulated in the definition of a politics of the impossible which underpins revolutionary action while it resolutely rejects the goal of a takeover of political power.

Translated by Amy Reid

16. *OC*, 6, 251–52. See also Jean-Michel Besnier, *Politique de l'impossible—Système et communication chez Georges Bataille* (Paris: La Découverte, 1988).

ALLAN STOEKL

Truman's Apotheosis: Bataille, "Planisme," and Headlessness

Was Georges Bataille a fascist? This grossly simplistic question, amazingly enough, is still occasionally asked: most recently, one of Bataille's old editors, Boris Souvarine, stated quite baldly, in the introduction to the reedition of the *Critique Sociale*, that Bataille, in effect, was not only a fascist sympathizer, but a would-be collaborator as well.[1] Clearly, in the simplest, biographical sense, it can be stated that Bataille was neither a fascist sympathizer nor a collaborator. Indeed some of his most important early pieces, such as "The Psychological Structure of Fascism" (1933—which Souvarine himself first published) are among the very first writings by anyone to consider, from a neo-Marxist perspective, the impact and effectiveness of the fascist appeal in the light of recent psychological, anthropological, and sociological work (Freud, Durkheim, Mauss)—thereby providing a much richer analysis of fascism than that provided by a Marxist critique alone. The astuteness of such articles, in fact, at the time made them all the more effective as political critiques of fascism. It seems particularly perverse, then, to accuse Bataille of the very thing he was most effectively combating.

1. *La Critique Sociale* was a pioneering Marxist review—an anti-Stalinist one— published in Paris in the early 1930s. In his preface to the reedition of the review (Paris: La Différence, 1983), Boris Souvarine states in effect that Bataille was in sympathy with the occupier, and would have rallied to his cause if he had had the courage of his convictions. Maurice Blanchot, who knew Bataille well during the period of the Occupation, flatly denies this (see his article "Les Intellectuels en question," in *Le Débat* 29, (March 1984): 20.
　　Michel Surya, Bataille's biographer (*Georges Bataille: La Mort à l'œuvre* [Paris: Séguier, 1987] told me he was surprised to find, when he started work on his book, that quite a few people with whom he discussed his project, including some members of Bataille's generation, assumed that Bataille "was a fascist."

YFS 78, *On Bataille,* ed. Allan Stoekl, © 1990 by Yale University.

Political questions, however, are never so easily resolved, and quite often a person starts to take on the colors of his enemy in the very act of fighting him. Bataille leaves himself open to the charge of fascism because, to use an old cliché, he wants to "appropriate the weapons of his enemy"; specifically, he argues that much of the strength of the fascists comes from their use of devices that the left cannot afford to ignore—myth, the collective exaltation involved in public ceremonies, and so on. Certainly, in the French context in which Bataille was writing, and after Durkheim's celebration of the "fête," this valorization of public gathering and the emotion that follows from it was nothing new. But it is possible to argue that attempting to put what amounts to irrationalism in the service of a good cause only places one in the camp of his enemies. Certainly Bataille's use of "mythical figures" (such as the "acéphale") that work to disrupt the fascist, fully "headed" mythical figures (such as that of the Führer himself) can be seen to lead to an impasse: even though the Bataillean figure might very well be the totem of headlessness, dispersion, and expenditure, it nevertheless still represents those elements through a unitary, coherent image, around which a group, no matter how marginal, can concentrate. While we can see the new sacred figure's "acephality" as liberating, we can just as easily see its inevitable coherence as repressive.

The problem of Bataille's politics is compounded by the fact that his arguments, particularly those in what is probably his single most influential essay, "The Notion of Expenditure," have much in common with those of Robert Aron and Arnaud Dandieu, two contemporaries who pushed some of Bataille's positions in the direction of what we might characterize as a kind of proto-fascism. Their fascism, however, is marked not so much by a cult of the irrational as by the opposite temptation: technocratism, or, as it is often called in French debates of the period, "planisme." This line of thinking was found in the French and Italian fascist movements (and not in the German); it embraced in a pragmatic way certain modernist movements (Le Corbusier was a prominent "planiste")[2] that linked artistic and formal innovation with central economic planning and (to a greater or lesser

2. Le Corbusier contributed to the review *Plans*, a short-lived effort of the early thirties that was linked, for a time, with Aron and Dandieu's "Ordre Nouveau" group. See Jean-Louis Loubet del Bayle's book *Les Non-Conformistes des années 30* (Paris: Seuil, 1969), 79–120 for a history of "Ordre Nouveau," and 93–101 for a history of *Plans*, and its links to "Ordre Nouveau."

degree) authoritarian political control. The Belgian socialist Henri de Man was also a leading "planiste"; though Aron and Dandieu never achieved de Man's influence, their work nevertheless signals an important alternative to the blood and thunder fascism that Bataille was ostensibly fighting. And yet, as we will see, there are certain "planiste" tendencies in Bataille as well, which come to the surface after the war (in *The Accursed Share* [1949]), and after the limitations of the radically negative "Acéphale" gesture become apparent.

Bataille's shifting allegiances and loyalties—toward the always problematic political inscriptions of "expenditure"—can be traced through the changing representations of America in his work, from the late 1920s right up to the late 1940s. I will try very briefly in this essay to trace these always fluid complicities, which often intersect with the figure of America—a shadow America, it almost goes without saying, that conforms more precisely to Bataille's tactical needs of the moment than to any purported "reality"; and that, in the end, may be the image not so much of a real place as of a certain surplus or lack in a larger project devoted to the inevitably systematic presentation of that which eludes all systematicity and presentation.

It is somewhat surprising that up to now nothing has been written on Arnaud Dandieu and Bataille. Dandieu was almost exactly the same age as Bataille—he was born on 29 October 1897—and, like Bataille, he was a librarian at the Bibliothèque Nationale in Paris. His major work, *La Révolution nécessaire*, written with Robert Aron, was published in late 1933, just after Dandieu's untimely death on 6 August 1933. This was the same year as "The Notion of Expenditure" (published in *La Critique Sociale*, January 1933) and "The Psychological Structure of Fascism," (*La Critique Sociale*, November 1933 and March, 1934). Dandieu, moreover, was a contributor to Bataille's review *Documents*,[3] and Bataille's essay "The Critique of the Foundations of the Hegelian Dialectic" appears in the bibliography of *La Révolution nécessaire*.

Dandieu is known as the "leader" of the "Ordre Nouveau" group. Like many others in the period, "Ordre Nouveau" was a study group, a

3. Arnaud Dandieu in fact contributed two short articles to Bataille's review *Documents*: a definition of the word "Espace" in the "Critical Dictionary," a regular feature of the review (his "definition" was accompanied by one of the same word by Bataille) (*Documents* 1, (1930): 41 and 44); a review of an article by Emile Meyerson, "Le Physicien et le primitif," in *Documents* 5, (1930): 312.

team that edited a review of the same name, and one that assigned itself
the quasi-political role of effecting permanent change in French society, culture and politics. "Ordre Nouveau" had much in common with
other "nonconformist" groups animated by young people throughout
the 1930s—other notable groups were Emmanuel Mounier's "person-
alist" "Esprit" group, and the "young right" spinoffs of the Action
Française, among whose members were Thierry Maulnier, Jean-Pierre
Maxence, and Maurice Blanchot.[4] (In fact Bataille was introduced to
Blanchot in 1940 by Pierre Prévost, a mutual friend, disciple of Dandieu, and one of the leaders of "Ordre Nouveau" after Dandieu's
death.)[5]

It is easy to characterize "Ordre Nouveau" as a proto-fascist group,
but one must be careful: there is no hint of racism in their program,
and indeed—perhaps characteristically, given the period—they considered themselves an alternative to established parties of both left
and right. To grasp the political implications of their work, one must
examine their texts more carefully than have the few critics who
mention them. Like Bataille, Dandieu and Aron take much of their
argument on potlatch in *La Révolution nécessaire* (chapter 2 of Part
One, 89–146),[6] from Marcel Mauss's *The Gift*. Mauss himself, at the
end of that book, decried the heartlessness and cold rationality of
contemporary economies, based as they are on a mere "balancing of
accounts." Rather than attempting to eliminate losses totally, and to
maximize purely quantitative profits, Mauss argues, individuals in
modern economies should emulate so-called "savages": they should
engage in philanthropic gift-giving, and indeed political changes
should be made that guarantee the revival of donation as a foundation
of the economy. "Friendly societies" and charities will once again be
integral components, and even the ends of, modern capitalist economies.[7]

Dandieu and Aron, like Bataille in "The Notion of Expenditure,"

4. Among the reviews of the "young right" in this period were *Les Cahiers, Réac-
tion, La Revue française, La Revue du siècle.* See chapter one ("La Jeune droite") of
Loubet del Bayle's *Les Non-conformistes des années 30*, 37–77.
    5. See *Pierre Prévost rencontre Georges Bataille* (Paris: Jean-Michel Place, 1987).
    6. Future page references to *La Révolution nécessaire* (Paris: Grasset, 1933) will be
preceded by *"RN."* Translations are my own.
    7. See the last chapter of Marcel Mauss's *The Gift: Forms and Functions of Ex-
change in Archaic Societies*, trans. I. Cunnison (New York: Norton, 1967), especially
66–68.

stress the misinterpretation of potlatch by modern (including Marxist) economists.[8] Dandieu and Aron argue that "primitive" exchange is not a barter in which the value of one object is abstractly arrived at through comparison with another; instead psychological, moral, and "personal" factors always enter into exchange, and indeed they have always been an inseparable part of it. The primitive "chief," in giving more than he thinks can be returned, stakes his reputation on his gift in order to heighten his prestige. Nonquantifiable elements—personal goals and limitations, contingent psychological quirks, particular physical limitations—always enter into exchange; in fact they determine it. Thus exchange is never a simple matter of a mathematical equation. Dandieu and Aron define exchange as:

> . . . a personal action that institutes, between the one who offers and the one who demands, a particular physical and psychic relation. Between the two persons considered a link is established that is chiefly made perceptible [rendu sensible] by:
> 1) The matter or the obligation that are the object of the exchange;
> 2) The time that the act requires in order to be realized. [RN, 93]

One can see here an early version of the influence of German phenomenology in France: the stress placed on the necessarily limited perspectives of the individuals (or the "persons," a word used by Dandieu and Aron after 1932 to avoid the overtones of "bourgeois individualism") engaged in exchange (and indeed of the observer); and on the lack of the possibility of a fundamental, fully rational knowledge of the exchange-relation—these bear the mark of the early, if not the profound, influence of Heidegger.[9] The finitude of the "person" acts as both a limitation on the rationalization of the process—no "person" can ever fully grasp or "know" it—and at the same time, the physical, social, and psychological concreteness of the "person," makes the exchange process a vibrant experience rather than a "simple play of writing, as instantaneous in its form as pure thought" (RN,

8. The English translation of "The Notion of Expenditure" is contained in the anthology of Bataille's writings *Visions of Excess: Selected Writings, 1927–1939*, ed. and trans. A. Stoekl, with C. Lovitt and D. M. Leslie, Jr. (Minneapolis: The University of Minnesota Press, 1985). All page references to this book will be preceded by "VE." On the misinterpretation of potlatch as a form of barter, see VE, 121.

9. Husserl's *Méditations cartésiennes* and Heidegger's "Qu'est-ce que la métaphysique" (the Corbin translation, in *Bifur*, 1931) are listed in the bibliography of *La Révolution nécessaire* (RN, 284).

95). Exchange, then, "like money escapes from the domain of pure mathematics and of purely rational constructions" (*RN*, 95).[10]

Dandieu and Aron go on to criticize the favoring of exchange value over use value on the part of economists: while exchange value only reflects what is "homogeneous"—what lends itself to equalization through quantitative measurement—use value entails "qualities that are irreducible to measurement and homogenization: odor, color, and taste produce variable effects, depending upon the person and the time. Arithmetic loses its rights there" (*RN*, 109). Finally, Dandieu and Aron go so far as to imply that in potlatch, and hidden in modern exchange economies, there is a kind of will to expend, linked to a very Nietzschean will to power.[11] The Swedish "match king" Kreuger, a notorious speculator of the 1920s, is a good example: his struggle for a glorious prestige was no different from that of the chief engaging in potlatch. The difference lies in the fact that while the chief's power comes from a very real material wealth, Kreuger's was based only on illusory numbers, the empty and fraudulent equations of a rationalized exchange economy—one that purports to make total knowledge possible, but which leads only to self-delusion, bankruptcy, crash, and suicide. Dandieu and Aron write:

> The life and death of Kreuger were, in fact, a beautiful potlatch; but also a false potlatch, in that its foundations were falsified, and that the will to power of its initiator does not find support in real forces, but on chimerical and abstract banking laws or statistical information. [*RN*, 119]

All this would certainly seem to indicate that Dandieu and Aron would be opposed to any planned economy, which could only know economic exchange—the millions of transactions carried out in every country every day—in an abstract manner. But it is not as simple as that. The critique of rationalization does not lead, as one

10. In fact, in Dandieu's definition of "Espace" in *Documents* (see note 3, above) there is a strong affirmation of irrationality: "we note that this purely irrational space [put forward by Dr. Minkowski] is nothing other than individual contact with nature," Dandieu writes. Bataille in the same period precisely avoided associating what he called "heterogeneity" with simple irrationality; instead his goal was a "science of the heterogeneous."

11. Nietzsche of course was a major influence in French intellectual life of the 1930s; Bataille's "Acéphale" group was openly "Nietzschean" (see the article "Nietzsche and the Fascists" [*VE*, 182–96]); Drieu la Rochelle also invoked Nietzsche from a very different political vantage point ("Nietzsche contre Marx" in *Socialisme fasciste* [Paris: Gallimard, 1934], 63–75), etc.

might expect, to an overt celebration of "expenditure" or Nietz-schean force, even though these are at the basis of all productive activity and indeed of all human life. Dandieu and Aron in fact call for a *heightened* rationalization because the exploitation of labor, which takes place within the rationalized productive process, is itself pro-foundly brutal, and must be curbed. The superficial rationality of modern economies leads to the ignorance or falsification of the pro-found underlying irrationality—and in that way it also leads to an exploitation which is not so much irrational as it is mistaken. Thus a higher consciousness (one that does not "falsify" potlatch) will be achieved thanks to a higher planning, the limits of the rationalized economy having been determined: at the point at which the purely abstract and account-balancing order breaks down, that economy will be curtailed. Within the sphere of rationality—the production and distribution of goods—there must be worked out "the most strictly rational plan to maximize not only the economizing of energy in production, but equity in distribution" (*RN*, 144). Beyond this, how-ever, "a new form of decentralized economy" will be created—one which will not put society itself in jeopardy (*RN*, 144).

Ruthless abstraction and the mindless planning associated with "Fordism" and "Taylorism" are to be replaced by a superior planning, one of whose goals is precisely to assign limits to the realm of abstrac-tion—a realm in which human desires and forces are completely neglected. The ultimate goal of the plan is nothing less than the suppression of the proletariat (*RN*, 249–52). A two or three year peri-od of industrial service, which would apparently replace military service and would be obligatory for all, would assure the carrying out of the "servile labor" now assigned to the working class (the last pages of *La Révolution nécessaire* are devoted to an analysis of statistical tables and a demonstration that yes, indeed, the working class can simply be eliminated if everyone is willing to donate to society a few years of labor). Again we see an echo of Mauss's argument in *The Gift*: the giving of a certain (small) amount of time to society, and the quarantine of abstract rationality to a limited field within the domain of the production and distribution of goods, will result in a more reasonable, and just, society. This higher level planning—which, among other things, will assure the "organization of professional corporations whose goal is to regulate and stimulate creative forms of labor" and "the creation of a civil service charged with distributing unskilled labor throughout society [le corps social]" (*RN*, 251)—is thus, in the end, and in spite of its devices, formally subordinated to such nonquantifiable elements as "happiness," "force," and so on.

In Dandieu and Aron's model we can see how a most rigorous "planisme" both accomplishes something the Marxists can only dream about (the dissolution of the proletariat through a kind of *Aufhebung* in which it is both suppressed and raised to a higher level) and ultimately subordinates the organization it accomplishes to a higher "irrationality" (*RN*, 141) and "spirituality" (*RN*, 135) of the "person" and his or her desires and goals. (Dandieu and Aron are quick to point out that this "spirituality," unlike that promoted by other revolutionary groups, is not detached from the real, but is instead grounded in "concrete matter" [*RN*, 135].) The "Ordre Nouveau" leaders could very easily paraphrase Jean Paulhan, and write that they have "pushed rational planning as far as it will go, and have ended in the irrational."[12]

Dandieu and Aron's work is important not least for the demonstration it provides of how a "planisme" not that different from Henri de Man's, or that of the review *Plans*, can also be linked, through the radical experience it affirms, with "avant-garde" writers such as Bataille (who was, at least in the 1930s, quite hostile to "planisme," as we will see). The game of assigning intellectual filiation and relations becomes a very delicate one here. It should nevertheless be noted that Zeev Sternhell has convincingly identified "planisme," at least as it was elaborated between the wars in Europe, as a proto-fascism.[13]

At this point I would like simply to note several of the motifs in the "Ordre Nouveau" writings that lend themselves to interpretation as fascist "idéologèmes." There is, for example, the theme of "Americanism." In their book *Le Cancer américain*,[14] published two years before *La Révolution nécessaire*, Dandieu and Aron specifically identify a characteristic constellation of evils—international credit, con-

12. "We have pushed Terrorism as far as it will go, and have discovered rhetoric" writes Jean Paulhan in his influential *Les Fleurs de Tarbes* (Paris: Gallimard, "Idées" edition of 1973), 151.

13. See Zeev Sternhell, *Ni Droite ni gauche: l'idéologie fasciste en France* (Paris: Seuil, 1983), and in particular the chapters on Henri de Man (136–59) and on "Le Planisme ou le socialisme sans prolétariat," which largely deals with the "Plan de Man" (pp. 206–33). De Man's distrust of the proletariat in fact links his project closely to that of "Ordre Nouveau."

14. All page references to Dandieu and Aron's *Le Cancer américain* (Paris: Rieder, 1931) will be preceded by "*CA*."

sumerism, abstract (rather than land-based) wealth, mass production and the quantification of the labor process, the anomie of modern urban life—with America. The American government is taken to task most notably for managing, so to speak, a kind of government by credit of post-World War I Europe: the exportation, in the form of the "Banque des règlements internationaux" (BRI) of the American Federal Reserve Board System. The BRI, indirectly controlled by the Americans, is the European version of the Federal Reserve, which guarantees American prosperity not through any rational planning of manufacturing, agriculture, or the distribution of labor or wealth, but through the arbitrary manipulation of empty signs—i.e., by expanding or tightening the money supply (CA, 113–21). All of the interwar American plans for the recovery of Europe—the Young Plan, the Hoover Plan—are seen as nothing more than devices by which American capital will tighten its hold on Europe, instituting a kind of reverse colonization in the guise of rationalization (CA, 159): there will be an irreversible drain of wealth to the US, as the latter's tariff and trade policies assure it an ever greater trade surplus (already an alarming trend in the late 1920s), and ever more power as the world's greatest creditor nation.

As was the case in their discussion of potlatch, Dandieu and Aron here counter this American abstraction with the inevitable irruption of the concrete, which in this case is not so much a "personal" Nietzschean force as it is the unforeseeable effect of nature. The crash of '29 was caused by a short sighted policy on the part of the Federal Reserve, which did not recognize that a bad harvest could cause not only a crisis in agriculture, but could topple the entire makeshift system (CA, 174–77). Thus the irrational materiality of nature, like the unknowable energy of psychic drives (Dandieu and Aron write of a "revolutionary psychological explosion" [CA, 162]) cannot be grasped or utilized by a fundamentally directionless rationalization.[15]

It was no doubt true that official American policies of the period contributed to economic instability, but Dandieu and Aron make a kind of logical leap when they identify actual governmental strategies (or nonstrategies, nonplans) with much more ill-defined cultural phenomena. Thus they blame America for all of the ills that Lukács had

15. Bataille was also wary of any attempt to incorporate a fundamentally unknowable nature in a dialectical or rational scheme; see, on this subject, his "Critique of the Foundations of the Hegelian Dialectic" (VE, 105–15).

identified under the term "reification": the quantification of labor, and the invasion of free time by the need to consume; but the "myth of production" (*CA*, 163) and the monstrous "prosthesis" of technical reason (*CA*, 90) for Dandieu and Aron are due not to a worldwide crisis of capitalism, but instead are the consequences of American economic and cultural imperialism alone. It seems that "America" has become, through a metonymic process, the signifier of what is, finally, the uncontrolled and uncontrollable movement of exclusively differential systems of notation and calculation, systems which are both economic and cultural (or antieconomic and anticultural).

The Americans, however, are not so much "responsible for" the chaos and entropy of modern life as they are the sorcerer's apprentices who have constructed a system beyond human control—but one inadvertantly *designed* to be beyond control. As it careens wildly, the Americans can only fine tune it so that it becomes faster, more frantic, and ever more dangerous—until, of course, the final crash. The Americans' culpability, one might nevertheless argue, is a shadowy one: Dandieu and Aron admit that the Americans did not invent rationality, or even its misuse in economic and technical rationalization. Nor can they be said to be purposely plotting the destruction of Europe and the world—since all their "planning" is, when seen from a larger perspective, planless.

We begin to realize that the singling out of "America" here follows the logic of scapegoating: beyond whatever responsibility certain American capitalists or administrations had for the economic crisis, much more important from the perspective of Dandieu and Aron is "America" as metonym for a modernism gone wrong. Americans, on a cultural level, embody the crisis. This of course was a common theme of the period—one thinks of the portrait of Detroit in Céline's *Voyage au bout de la nuit* (published one year after *Le Cancer américain*), and Heidegger's excoriations throughout the 1930s of "Americanism." In fact anti-Americanism here serves exactly the same function that anti-Semitism serves elsewhere (in, for example, Céline's *Bagatelles pour un massacre*, as well as in Nazi propaganda): the Americans, like the Jews, are the promoters and carriers of cosmopolitanism (the neglect of healthy natural and psychological strength), the destruction of spiritual values, the blind hyper-production of useless junk, the speculation that inevitably ends in collapse. It must be stressed, however, that Dandieu and Aron are precisely not anti-

Semitic; my point is that their anti-Americanism can play essentially
the same role that anti-Semitism plays for others, while enabling
Dandieu and Aaron to escape any overt complicity with the racists
and their obviously naive and sinister pseudoscience of biological
determinism.

The strategy is familiar enough: instead of an attempt at a rigorous
analysis of capitalism and its contradictions—the kind of effort
Lukács was engaged in, whether successfully or not, in *History and
Class Consciousness*–Dandieu and Aron are content to identify a
scapegoat. They must find one, in fact, not least because Marxism in
general is one of the targets of their critique: a long section of *La
Révolution nécessaire* identifies Marxian economics with the bourgeois emphasis on the "balancing of accounts." Here too we see the
links between "Ordre Nouveau" and an openly fascist discourse: the
ills identified by the Marxists will be solved by the elimination of the
working class and the establishment of some governing body that will
issue (for the first time) coherent plans.[16] Yet none of this is, it seems,
to be done following any democratic procedures; while Dandieu and
Aron are concerned with the economic feasibility of the elimination of
the proletariat, they never consider the political feasibility of their
scheme. Would the proletariat vote to abolish itself? Democratic (parliamentary) decision-making, in fact, is associated by "Ordre
Nouveau" with the very "Americanism" they wish to terminate. In
combating the "désordre établi," the "Ordre Nouveau" planners
would therefore necessarily be antidemocratic.

At the end of *Le Cancer américain*, Dandieu and Aron note that
fighting Americanism with its own weapons could end in disaster:
"one is Americanized faster when one is against America than when
one is for it" (*CA*, 239). What is needed instead is a "conspiracy," a
"conjuration" that will result in the subversion and fall of "America."
But, in a strange way, "Ordre Nouveau" and "America" can be seen
already to be in complicity: both would put rationality in the service
of a larger irrationality. The difference, from the "Ordre Nouveau"

16. It should be noted that opposition to the idea of class conflict was a standard
"idéologème" of right-wing discourse in France in the period in which Dandieu and
Bataille were writing: Michael Curtis, in *Three Against the Third Republic: Sorel,
Barrès, Maurras* (Princeton: Princeton University Press, 1959) notes that for Maurras
(the founder of "Action Française") "it was in the name of the unfortunate myth of
class struggle that some dreamt of dismembering the vertical organization of nations
for the profit of a horizontal and international alliance of classes" (152).

perspective, is that Americans are irrational about their own irrationality—they are unknowing, and their planning, such as it is, is arbitrary and limited—whereas the "Ordre Nouveau" directors will be supremely rational in their devotion to the now endangered "spiritual" ("the American cancer is a cancer of the spirit" [*CA*, 239]).

The question that Bataille would pose is this: to what extent does the guarantee of heterogeneity through homogeneity—the use of rational means like planning, and the ordering and control of society through the exercise of a higher authority—only *subordinate* the heterogeneous to the homogeneous? Recall that for Bataille[17] the heterogeneous is not so much a pure irrationality—which can easily be made to serve various rational orders in science, politics, or philosophy—as it is an "end in itself" (*VE*, 138, 143–44). It thus can provide a raison d'être for the various homogeneous systems, which can then indulge in their penchant for account balancing, abstract reason, stable representation and knowledge by invoking a "higher" goal or purpose, that of the heterogeneous order (the sacred, Spirit, God, glory, etc.). The heterogeneous thus is the motivation and the structure of the homogeneous. As we learn in "The Psychological Structure of Fascism," the heterogeneous can in this way simply be mistaken for a subordinate form of the homogeneous: God, the fascist leader, and other forms are themselves made to serve merely as guarantors of the functioning of the homogeneous:

> To combat the elements most incompatible with it [i.e., heterogeneous elements], *homogeneous* society uses free-floating imperative forces; and, when it must choose the very object of its activity (the existence *for itself* in the service of which it must necessarily place itself) from the domain that it has excluded, the choice inevitably falls on those forces that have already proved most effective. [*VE*, 146]

On the one hand Bataille's "heterogeneous," unlike that of Dandieu and Aron, is "radically other" (*VE*, 143); it cannot be established, preserved, or even simply recognized by the homogeneous order. Indeed that order will always act to exclude it: that in fact is how it defines itself. It can be put "in the service" of the homogeneous, but that results only in an "imperative" elevation (temporal power in the guise of religious, political or military authority) that is nothing less

17. In my discussion of Bataille I will quote primarily from the articles "The Notion of Expenditure" and "The Psychological Structure of Fascism."

than a betrayal of heterogeneity as the "unknowable" (". . . as a rule, science cannot know *heterogeneous* elements as such" [VE, 141]). On the other hand, though, Bataille's homogeneous is much more intimately connected with the heterogeneous than is Dandieu's and Aron's version of it. Bataille does not use a scapegoat strategy to associate the homogeneous with a single, guilty source (such as America) in order to purge it. Rather the homogeneous is inseparable from survival itself, from any human activity that subordinates consumption—the end in itself—to utility. From a larger (Bataillean) perspective, "abstract wealth," and the rationalization of Fordism, are not different in kind from any labor that puts the conservation (and utilization) of its products ahead of their spontaneous and pointless enjoyment. This homogeneity in its widest sense is inseparable from the heterogeneous; it guarantees the existence of the heterogeneous (there could be no life without labor and the replenishment of exhausted forces), but it is also logically posterior and subordinate to it: "Men assure their own subsistence or avoid suffering not because these functions themselves lead to a sufficient result, but in order to accede to the insubordinate function of free expenditure" (VE, 129). The "American cancer" for Bataille would be nothing more than a perfected homogeneous activity which has been arbitrarily divorced from the heterogeneous—which lacks, in other words, an end, be it a falsely elevated one (God, Truth) or an insubordinate one (expenditure, the base sacred).[18] Ironically enough, from a Bataillean perspective Dandieu and Aron's approach must fall into the same trap as "Americanism," since it too posits a total break, a Manichean duality, separating a "bad" homogeneous (the American) and a "good" heterogeneous (the force of nature, individual psychic drives). The "Ordre Nouveau" thinkers merely reverse the valorization of their enemies' terms. For Dandieu and Aron, the heterogeneous must return in what Bataille would call its "imperative" forms: direction, order, "higher" spiritual values—it will return, in other words, once again as merely a guarantee of the homogeneous. In this sense, perhaps, the Americans criticized by Dandieu and Aron are more honest than are their French critics, since they at least do not seriously attempt to provide any

18. See Bataille's remarks on American capitalism as a recuperation of the very heterogeneous forces it has created (the abject working class) in "The Notion of Expenditure" (VE, 126). It is the American blacks, definitively excluded, who then become the last repository of the abject and the heterogeneous.

"end" for economic and cultural activity. Dandieu and Aron do, and they only end up deluding themselves.

We can see, then, the ways in which Bataille's critique closely parallels that of Dandieu and Aron, and how it differs. Like the two founders of "Ordre Nouveau," Bataille sharply criticizes the pointless "closed economy" that seems to characterize contemporary bourgeois systems, whose goal is only the "development of a servile human species, fit only for the fabrication, rational consumption, and conservation of products" (*VE*, 97). Like them as well he sees behind the utility favored by the bourgeois a "drive to expend" that nevertheless, with a "horrifying hypocrisy" (*VE*, 124–25) refuses to recognize itself for what it is. Unlike them, however, Bataille refuses to identify this tendency with any given scapegoat, and he refuses to argue for its elimination through devices—"higher" values, authoritarian planning and control, a more sophisticated social engineering—that will only present, once again, a heterogeneous "end in itself" presented as, and subordinated to, homogeneous regularization and—precisely—*order*.

The insubordination of heterogeneity to homogeneity is most dramatically demonstrated by Bataille when he goes in exactly the opposite direction from that of Dandieu and Aron: instead of calling for the elimination of the proletariat—its liquidation, in effect, through a higher intelligence—he cites, in "The Notion of Expenditure," the proletariat as the embodiment of expenditure in the modern world (*VE*, 125–26). Contemporary potlatch for Bataille will be the very "great night" so feared by Dandieu and Aron (and the logical end of the Marxist class struggle they so resented), in which "the beautiful phrases [of the bourgeoisie] will be drowned out by death screams in riots" (*VE*, 128). This is the point where Bataille reveals himself to be a disciple of Georges Sorel: like Sorel, he is not interested in a "utopia," an intellectually elaborated plan for the future, but in a myth, which is less a comprehensible model than it is an incitement to action. As Sorel puts it,[19] writing on the "myth of the general strike" in *Réflexions sur la violence:*

19. I quote from a series of excerpts taken from *Réflexions sur la violence* contained in the collection *Anthologie des philosophes français contemporains* (Paris: Sagittaire, 1931) edited by Arnaud Dandieu. Page references are preceded by "*A.*" This anthology is a highly interesting document, containing as it does a representative cross-section of French philosophy immediately prior to the impact in France of German phenomenology (Hegel, Husserl, Heidegger).

Contemporary revolutionary myths are almost pure: they permit one to understand the activity, the feelings and the ideas of the popular masses who are preparing to enter into a decisive struggle; they are not descriptions of things, but expressions of wills. [A, 38]

We see this Sorelian side of Bataille most clearly in the "Contre-Attaque" tracts of 1935, where it is the leaderless proletariat "in the street" that comes to embody the violence of the mythic general strike. Sorel writes: "Today, I do not hesitate to declare that socialism cannot last without an affirmation of violence. It is in strikes that the proletariat affirms its existence" (A, 42–43). In the same vein, Bataille in 1935 writes: ". . . we are sure that strength results less from strategy than from collective exaltation, and exaltation can come only from words that touch not the reason but the passions of the masses" (VE, 167).

This affirmation of myth can be seen to link Bataille's Marxist "phase" of 1932–1935 with his later, more overtly Nietzschean, "Acéphale" writings (1936–1939). The "acéphale," like the proletariat and its general strike, is a mythical figure whose impact is associated with the force of war and violent expenditure. But in the "acéphale," myth is overtly linked to religion: Bataille still foresees a cultural revolution, if not a political one. The image of the headless man is particularly apt, because this is a mythical figure that represents the very death of representation, control, thought—"Man"—and thus the subordination of heterogeneity to homogeneity (in the guise of "imperative" heterogeneity). But in switching to the "acéphale" from the Sorelian proletariat, Bataille has also given up something: the idea of a mass, a great majority, surging forward uncontrollably in its violent destiny. Now we have instead an elite group, the conspirators who recognize the "acéphale" as their totem, and whose actions will somehow trigger an overwhelming change in the world. Bataille writes in "Propositions," a series of aphorisms first published in the review Acéphale in 1937: "The formation of a new structure, of an "order" developing and raging across the entire earth, is the only truly liberating act, and the only one possible, since revolutionary destruction is regularly followed by the reconstitution of the social structure and its head" (VE, 198–99). The belief that a new government, a new revolutionary institution, will solve the problems of the old is illusory; Stalin is living proof that a new "head" will always reappear. Instead, marginal groups, "orders," must "rage" across the earth, transforming everything but instituting and institutionalizing nothing. But we must note here the use of the word "order," which inevitably retains the ambiguity it had when it was used by Dandieu and Aron: not only a select group, a union of conspirators (the founders of "Ordre Nouveau," in fact, had also called for a "conspiracy"), but a command and a principle of organization. It is indeed difficult to use this word without implying, on some level, a well-centered discipline and direction.[20]

Some of the ambivalence of the word "order" can also be found in Bataille's treatments of America in the prewar period. Though in each case the American figure—or figure of America—is presented as being somehow subversive, the political overdetermination of the American representation of expenditure is very much in question. The functional equivalent of the proletariat as mythical figure, when situated in America, starts to take on a particularly sinister appearance.

First there is the Aztec priest presented in the article "L'Amérique disparue" (1928).[21] This very early article, contemporaneous with *Histoire de l'œil* (1928), implicitly criticizes a rationalized and planned America in that it shows the true America to be that of a civilization literally turning not around trade or investment but around an openly affirmed human sacrifice. In doing so, it also circles the priest, a figure marked by a kind of grotesque black humor:

> . . . in certain sacrifices involving the immediate skinning of the victim, the excited priest covered his face with the bloody skin of the face, and his body with that of the body. In this way, wearing this incredible costume, he prayed in a delirium to his god. [*OC* 1, 157]

The priest rises from below into the garment of his victim's skin. His grisly humor, perhaps characteristic not so much of precolumbian America as of post-World War I (surrealist) Paris, dictates that his hold on his own authority be subversive; he rises to subvert the very authority he embodies when sacrificing. The hideous skin he wears calls attention to the fact that even in his highest authority the priest (literally) embodies not eternity or perfection but laceration, parodic doubling, and death. When the whites finally attack, he cannot take

20. One thinks, for example, of the right-wing author Charles Maurras's book *L'Ordre et le désordre* (Paris: Self, 1948).

21. "L'Amérique disparue," in the *Œuvres Complètes* of Georges Bataille (Paris: Gallimard, 1970), vol. 1, 152–58; hereafter "*OC* 1." Translations are my own.

his own position seriously enough to defend it; he goes down laughing, or in a daze ("The victory of Cortez was not the result of force, but rather of a veritable bewitching" [*OC* 1, 158]).

One cannot help but notice, however, that this quintessential American is nevertheless also identified with a geometric form that Bataille would go on later—during the "Acéphale" period—to identify with "condensation," false eternity, and imperative heterogeneity: the pyramid/obelisk (see the essay "The Obelisk" [*VE*, 213–22]). After all, the priest's actions do guarantee the continued functioning of a large and stable society; like the traffic circling around the obelisk in the Place de la Concorde, the Aztec Empire finds its "center" in the great pyramid on the summit of which, every day, victims are slaughtered, and from which their stripped and open bodies "tumble" (*OC* 1, 157). The priest stays comfortably at the top.

A similar ambiguity seems to mark another representative American whom Bataille presents as a disrupter of the "désordre établi" of democratic capitalism: the gangster, who is both killer and victim. In a book review, in *Documents*, of an American tabloid-type album of photographs of gangsters' corpses, *X Marks the Spot* (1930), Bataille speculates on the links between the decline of the very civilization loathed by Dandieu and Aron, and the fundamental human urge to see violent death, or at least the cadavers of victims.

> It seems that the desire to see ends up winning out over disgust and terror. Thus, if this kind of advertising becomes as widespread as possible, American gangster wars could play the same social role as that of circus games in ancient Rome (and bullfights in contemporary Spain). [*OC* 1, 256]

Bataille even goes so far as to link the decline of protestant, capitalist America with the rise of the gangster and his public popularity; the thug, finally, is associated with the skyscraper as the future of America.

> From there [the idea that gangsters are the modern equivalent of gladiators] it is not far to the idea that gangsters will have the same destiny as the barbarians of the Roman period, who, after having delighted civilized people, went on to overthrow and destroy everything. In fact, gang investments in American society seem no less amazing than the height of skyscrapers . . . [*OC* 1, 257]

In both of these cases—the Aztec priest and the gangster—one notes that the figure's violence and subversion is doubled by erection, centrality, and order; the Aztec's pyramid, the skyscraper associated with the gangster, are the organizing principles, the metonyms, of societies that are brutal and deliriously forceful, even if in decline. And one could say exactly the same thing about the "acéphale": "he" is a figure that bears death, but at the same time "he" is a perfectly coherent and traditional "sacred figure" around which a society, albeit one of conspirators, can be established. "He" is not only the figure of an order, but (like the pyramid or skyscraper) a principle of order. One sees the representation of this political ambivalence—for want of a better word—in the famous "Acéphale" drawing of 1936, by André Masson (*VE*, 180): while the head is clearly missing, the stars (nipples), bowels and death's head (genitals) only go to create another face, another "figure humaine." Further, the death's head itself has a miniature face. . . . The "acéphale," in other words, has lost a head, a principle of organization and order, only to mutate and develop another, more hypnotic, doubled and doubling (replicating) face.

It is no coincidence that, after the outbreak of the war, Bataille gave up the "whim" of starting a new religion and a new "order."[22] As we see from the American example, "sacred figures and myths" seem to have a way of reversing themselves and turning into icons of centrality and oppression. Bataille's later fragmentary writings, in the *Somme Athéologique*, bear witness to his recognition of the need to disrupt any coherent movement, doctrine, or representation, no matter how "acephalic" it might be.

But a renunciation of the marginal or elite "order" in Bataille's case returns him, surprisingly enough, in the last chapter of *The Accursed Share* (1949), to a certain affirmation of "planisme," and specifically to a celebration of the very culture that his Aztec priests and Chicago mobsters had seemed in principle to subvert: the planned American economy of the "New Deal."

Does this mean that Bataille was simply jumping from one proto-fascism to another? After all, as Zeev Sternhell has shown, the links between "planisme," Lagardelle (the editor of *Plans*), "Ordre Nouveau," Henri de Man and, finally, collaboration with the Nazis are clear enough. By jettisoning democratic safeguards, and valorizing a conciliatory social "fusion" at the expense of the proletariat and the class struggle, "socialist" thinkers (and political leaders) like Henri de

---

22. See the autobiographical fragment in vol. 6 of Bataille's *Œuvres complètes*, 370, where he discusses the "whim" of starting a religion.

Man inevitably found themselves in the Nazi camp after the occupation of their countries. After all, parliamentary democracy, the "désordre établi" attacked by the young "nonconformists" of the 1930s,
was clearly on its last legs, feeble and senile (the collapse of the
democracies, France and Belgium, only proved this); "liberalism," the
laissez-faire American economics condemned by Dandieu and Aron,
only led to social chaos and misery. A "third way" was needed, and
when the Germans seemed to offer some form of planning backed by
the authority to carry it out, people who were by no means sim-
pletons—de Man among them—allowed themselves to be taken in, at
least for a time. But is the connection between "planisme" and fascism—even Nazism—inevitable? Dandieu and Aron in *La Révolution
nécessaire* condemn fascist brutality and racism (RN, 276), and Henri
de Man had little use for Nazi tactics either—at least before 1940. Even
Sternhell, whose book seems to imply the inevitability of the
"planiste's" collaboration, notes at one point:

> Certainly, "planisme" in itself could nourish [*alimenter*] any political
> ideology that does not take its inspiration specifically from the most
> extreme liberalism [i.e., "free market economics"—A. S.], and, intrin-
> sically, there is no reason for it to lead to fascism. This was to be the
> case notably in the immediate aftermath of the second World War.[23]

Sternhell goes on to note that "planisme" as a version of "non-
Marxist" socialism nevertheless did contribute to the "growth of the
fascist mentality" when it shied away from "democratic socialism"
and tolerance, and veered toward "corporatism and political au-
thoritarianism." But he specifically omits a study of or even a reference to the one kind of 1930s "planisme" that would not so much
have disproven his assertion (the contribution of "planisme" to fascism) as qualified it: the American New Deal. In effect, after March
1933—two years after the publication of *Le Cancer américain*—Roosevelt instituted a series of reforms whose links to "planisme" are
clear enough: direct economic intervention by the government in any
number of social spheres in order to alleviate poverty, putting people
back to work, and keeping the Communists at bay. The Roosevelt
administration realized that economic fine tuning was not enough:
the "alphabet soup" that followed—the NRA, CCC, WPA, FSA, TVA,
etc.—was really a series of "plans," perhaps not as well coordinated or

23. Sternhell, *Ni Droite ni gauche*, 159.

centrally directed as a de Man would have wished, whose net effect
was to involve the government actively on the side of poor workers
and farmers, thereby coopting (as the European "planistes" hoped to
do) "harder core" Socialists and Communists. Thus the New Deal
was much more interested in class cooperation than class conflict:
the directors of the famous FSA photographic project, for example,
sent Walker Evans and many others out into the field—literally—to
record southern poverty, and the photographs they made were then
seen by northern workers, with the resulting (at least hoped-for) bond
of fraternity motivating both groups to vote for Roosevelt. The important thing, here, is that they would *vote:* the New Deal was never as
authoritarian or as centralized as the "Plans" of the de Mans and
Dandieus; some form of representative democracy was retained. Of
course at the time many groups on both the left and the right in
Europe considered post-1933 Washington, D.C. to be just another
fascist, or at least totalitarian, capital.[24] The very haphazardness of
Roosevelt's "try anything" approach, however, and the retention and
even strengthening of democracy by the New Deal and its avatars (the
Voting Rights Act of 1965) disproved that. *Pace* Sternhell, then, a
"planisme" could be, and was, developed in the prewar period that did
not necessarily lead to fascism, that was "centralized" but was not
authoritarian. One can argue that there is nothing intrinsically "fascist" in "planisme"; it can just as easily be "acephalic" as rigidly
hierarchical. Indeed it was Roosevelt's successor, Truman, who, after
the war, came to replace the "acéphale" for Bataille as the figure of
political and economic (dis)organization.

Bataille starts his presentation of the Marshall Plan—in the last
chapter of *The Accursed Share*[25]—with the recognition that in the
aftermath of the war in the non-Soviet countries, "nothing advances
with any vigor" (*AS*, 169). This is but another version of the familiar
"désordre établi" that the prewar groups, including "Acéphale" and
"Ordre Nouveau," wanted to overthrow. "There persists a powerless

24. Thus Drieu la Rochelle can write in *Socialisme fasciste* (53): "The Revolution
that was carried out in Moscow, the first of the twentieth century rather than the last of
the nineteenth, in Rome, in Berlin, in Washington, will also come to Paris and London."
The French Communist Party, at least between 1935 and 1937, also equated Roosevelt
with Mussolini (see James Steele, *Paul Nizan: Un révolutionnaire conformiste?* [Paris:
Presses de la Fondation Nationale des Sciences Politiques, 1987], 265, note 2.)
25. I quote from the Robert Hurley translation of *La Part maudite, The Accursed
Share* (New York: Zone Books, 1988); all page references will be preceded by "*AS*."

dissonance of moans, of things already heard, of bold testimony to irresolute incomprehension."

Bataille nevertheless recognizes that, while Western Europe is tottering on the brink, the US is the most powerful and wealthy country not only in the world but in history. And yet it, and Europe, are threatened by the Soviets, whose culture is devoted to one thing at all costs: the maximizing of production and the reduction of useless expenditure to an absolute minimum (see the preceding chapter of *The Accursed Share*, "Soviet Industrialization"). Personal liberty, the freedom to do more or less whatever one wants—the very cause of the "dissonance" that afflicts capitalist societies—is brushed aside by the Soviet system.

But how is the US to combat the Russians? After Hiroshima, war is unthinkable: some form of peaceful competition is the only imaginable option. And yet the Soviet challenge is a useful one, because it forces the Americans to act and to work out, in fact, a plan. The other problem that the Americans face, and which dovetails with the threat of the Russians in Europe, is the fact that the poverty of the Europeans is caused by the "balance of payments deficit of the European nations vis à vis the United States" (*AS*, 174). The very seductiveness of the Soviet system, and its military might, are heightened by the wretchedness of Europe.

Bataille is confronting in its intensified, postwar form the same crisis about which Dandieu and Aron wrote in 1931–1933. Somehow a *plan* must be evolved through which military confrontation with the Soviets is avoided; the schismatic violence of the Russian system is defused; and the "American cancer"—the blind movement of a fine-tuned system that funnels all wealth into the American economy—is halted.

The answer, as we know, is the Marshall Plan. First of all, it is just that—a plan. For the first time in international affairs, the Americans have a real goal, and not just a gimmick, a short-term fix (like the Dawes Plan). As Bataille puts it, it is "painful to see a dynamic society given over unreservedly and without long-range plans to the movement that propels it . . . [and to see that] it produces without assessing the consequences of the production" (*AS*, 172). Only now, with the Plan assuring both the salutary use of wealth for development (and not for a dangerous overconsumption in America alone, or for the production of still more armaments) and the checking of the Soviet threat, "mankind considered in general [can] use credit for ends *it would decide on* . . . according to a basic law that is the negation of the rule of profit" (*AS*, 178; emphasis added).

This last point is an important one: the decision, the plan, to give away wealth means nothing less than the destruction of the old profit system, centered as it is in *"isolated* calculations" (*AS*, 176). Bataille thus confronts a problem of the so-called "American cancer": the purely arithmetic calculation of debt, while larger concerns are ignored. As in Dandieu and Aron, a plan will solve the problem; but here the "end" is nothing less than potlatch, the "spending without return" championed in "The Notion of Expenditure."

Bataille has discarded his earlier fetishes, such as the proletariat in the street ("The solving of social problems no longer depends on street uprisings" [AS, 186]) and " 'visions,' divinities and myths" (*AS*, 189). Now lucidity will guarantee both economic development, peace, and the end of economic selfishness. Finally, the very necessity of central planning will make America look like the Soviet Union in that the former will accord more importance to state-planned and financed production. "It [the US] defends free enterprise, but it thereby increases the importance of the state. It is only advancing, as slowly as it can, toward a point where the USSR rushed headlong" (*AS*, 186).

Some form of socialism will be developed in the US, then, as the opposing parties come to resemble each other. But, implicitly at least, Bataille is arguing that an American Stalinism will not arise from this situation, because this state control is devoted not to accumulation (as in Russia) but to expenditure. If the Marshall Plan, and the similar plans that will follow, necessarily negate purely individual concerns and enterprises, then socialist state planning will be inseparable from the giving away of massive amounts of wealth, from potlatch. Even though law and directives will determine activity, the Stalinist "head" will be replaced by a "headlessness." Or we can say, following Bataille's logic, that this nonauthoritarian direction, this "acéphalité," is already in place in America, since the Marshall Plan has been set in motion not by a "head," an oppressive command, but by Roosevelt's successor, who is precisely unaware of what he is doing: "Today Truman would appear to be blindly preparing for the final—and secret—apotheosis" (*AS*, 190). Confrontation will continue between the superpowers—it is integral to the model of potlatch, which is now being elaborated on an international scale—but coercive control, at least in America, seems a thing of the past.

This is "planning without a head" in another sense as well: the "end" of planning is planlessness, the "self-consciousness" that has "nothing as its object," that is the "nothing of pure expenditure" (*AS*, 190). Bataille here, at the end of the chapter, reiterates the argument from "The Psychological Structure of Fascism": accumulation is subordination to some future goal. (It is, in the terms of that essay, homogeneous.) But Bataillean self-consciousness is a "becoming conscious of the decisive meaning of an instant in which increase (the acquisition of *something*) will resolve into expenditure" (*AS*, 190). Just as the most elaborately conceived planning is inseparable from potlatch, so too the most integrated, nonindividuated consciousness (the consciousness that arises at the end of history, through an impossible "awareness" of the [non] "object" of the Marshall Plan) is indissociable from the nothingness it "knows." At this point one can see how Bataille's economic project folds back into the secular mystical experience of the *Somme Athéologique*.

We can see also how different this model is from Dandieu and Aron's. Their authoritarian direction may have been meant to lead to a death of hierarchy, but only through a psychic "individuality" and "spirituality." True, their model was based on potlatch, but the inner motivation of potlatch for them was not the "*nothing* of pure expenditure," but rather the energy of the isolated "person." So even while their planning too may be conceived as a "planning to end planning," it is applied from outside—through an authoritarian state—and its end is self-glorification under the protection of that same state. Confrontation, so integral to potlatch, is completely denied (indeed the abolition of the proletariat is presented as the elimination of class conflict), and we realize that for Dandieu and Aron the affirmation of "primitive" expenditure was nothing more than a justification of a Nietzschean "personal" force. For Bataille, on the other hand, the end of planning—in both senses of the word "end," both goal and death— lies in the "lucidity" of the mystical state, a lucidity that opens onto the extinction of society, the individual, and the state.

The question of Bataille's politics, as one can see from this charting of the figure of "America" in his writings of the twenties, thirties, and forties, is a difficult one indeed. Clearly he was not a "fascist" in the conventional sense of the word—or even in the sense of the word as applied to all the prewar "planistes" and reformers of a decadent, impotent democracy. Nevertheless, in both the immediate prewar and postwar periods Bataille appropriates elements, "idéologèmes," of first fascism (the ecstatic crowds, the "order" of the acéphale) and then of "planisme" (the directed economy, the necessity of a centralized model of foreign-aid distribution) and puts them to his own use. By the time one arrives at the second strategy, however—the "statist" championing of the Maussian Marshall Plan—one realizes that Bataille has conjoined what was most promising in his prewar approach—the affirmation of "headlessness," of a lack of authority—to a necessity of coherent economic development that is not inherently "fascist" in any sense.

One might say, then, that the comparative lack of coercive authority, the relative openness of American planning in the New Deal, was the "acéphale" that Bataille needed all along. His peremptory exclusion of the technical and of coherent "homogeneous" thought in the 1930s had limited him, however, to "American" figures—the Aztec priest, the gangster—that were the ruthless defeat of all planning and technocracy. But by the same token they were also the dangerous embodiment of an "imperative" excess of centrality, of order, of ruthless direction; as figures, they were inseparable from the verticality of the pyramid and skyscraper. In this light, the turn to an affirmation of postwar American centralized planning is a turn from a "bad" centrality to a benign, if not a "good" one: Truman is the "acéphale" who was missing from the equation of the thirties, the principle (or "head") of ordering that is nevertheless the ultimate principle of the "nothing," or the loss of all order; he is the "true man" who is the death of Man.

This is not to say, though, that Bataille's prewar positions are necessarily "mistaken," and that they should straightforwardly be replaced by a homage to what amounts to American state imperialism. Despite all the very real dangers of the thirties "Acéphale" position, we should still recognize that Bataille in that period, however mistakenly, was affirming an uncompromising *refusal* of authoritarian concentration. In the postwar period, on the other hand, Bataille affirms an American state socialism that will, it seems, eventually be as ruthless, as all-embracing and single-minded, if not as "monocephalic," as Stalinism. Indeed, even as Bataille wrote, the first purges and witch hunts were getting under way, set into motion not by McCarthy but by Truman himself. (In any case the paradox of the reappearance of the authoritarian through the antiauthoritarian—of the homogeneous through the decay of radical heterogeneity into imperative heterogeneity—may be, as Bataille himself

recognized, inescapable.) There can be no question, then, of establishing a naive teleology in which a more "progressive" Bataille replaces a
"reactionary" one. It goes without saying that there are no easy political filiations or affiliations to be traced in Bataille's work, no easy
social or economic lessons to be learned from him—there are only, as
he himself "recognized" in his "fiction," conundrums, impos-
sibilities, and versions of impotence and betrayal. "America" in
Bataille is, in the end, a figure of supplementarity, always either lacking or in excess: it is either a radical absence of planning (the entropy
and chaos represented by the gangster) or a vibrant excess of it (the
inconceivable "squandering" of wealth that was the Marshall Plan);
either the bloody, emptied skin of the sacrificial victim or the postwar
salvation of Europe and the world, effected through the "nothing" of
an empty godhead.[26]

26. In this spirit of the conjunction of the lack and surplus of planning, it might be
worth noting that, at the Le Corbusier exhibit at the Centre Pompidou in Paris in
Spring, 1988, there was on display a well-thumbed copy of La Part Maudite, which had
been given by Bataille to the architect in 1949. It carried a warm handwritten dedica-
tion to the planner of the "Ville Radieuse."

JEAN-JOSEPH GOUX

General Economics and Postmodern Capitalism

La Part maudite, Bataille's most systematic and long-considered work, provokes in the reader an inescapable feeling of mingled enthusiasm and disappointment. There is something striking and grandiose about Bataille's attempt to subvert existing political economy, caught within the limits of a utilitarian or calculating rationality, in order to replace it with a "general economics" that would make of unproductive expenditure (sacrifice, luxury, war, games, sumptuary monuments) the most determinant phenomenon of social life. At last a critique of political economy which, while remaining on the decisive terrain of the social circulation of wealth, escapes the confined atmosphere of the bourgeois ethic—so often caricatured—, the cramped and grayish world of petty calculation, quantifiable profit and industrious activity! It is the most extravagant waste—gratuitous, careening consumption, where accumulated wealth is set ablaze and disappears in an instant, wreathing in ephemeral glory him who makes the offering of this blaze which becomes the central phenomenon, the one through which a society discovers itself and celebrates the deepest values that animate it: its religion, its metaphysics, its sense of the sacred.

Bataille's "Copernican reversal" of political economy is a remarkable and dazzling operation of ethnological decentering. It is not the store and the workshop, the bank and the factory, that hold the key from which the principles of the economy can be deduced. In the blood that spurts from the open chest of victims sacrificed to the sun in an Aztec ritual, in the sumptuous and ruinous feasts offered to the courtiers of Versailles by the monarch of divine right, in all these mad

YFS 78, *On Bataille,* ed. Allan Stoekl, © 1990 by Yale University.

dissipations is found a secret that our restricted economics has covered up and caused to be forgotten. We must rethink social wealth not from the parsimonious perspective of an ascetic bourgeoisie that only consents to spend when it expects a return, but from the point of view (nearly delirious to our mind) of the erection of the pyramids or the cathedrals, or of the sacrifice of thousands of herd animals in archaic holocausts. It is in this intentionally unproductive use, in this unlimited expenditure, and not in utilitarian consumption that a secret lies hidden, the "general law of the economy": "a society always produces on the whole more than is necessary to its subsistence, it disposes of a surplus. It is precisely the use made of this excess that determines it: the surplus is the cause of disturbances, changes of structure, and of its entire history."[1] A thesis that is radically opposed to the rationalist, productivist and utilitarian vision. It is the *mode of expenditure* of the excess, the consumption of the superfluous, this accursed share, that determines a society's form. The dominant prosaic vision may be only a recently formed prejudice contemporaneous with the reign of the bourgeoisie, ushered in by the Reformation, and unable to account for the real and ineluctable movement of wealth in a society, a movement that sovereignly engages human beings: their relationship to the sacred through religion, mysticism, art, eroticism.

One cannot deny that this "general economics" has a great force of conviction, the strength of a new critique of political economy which instead of accepting the notions of this discipline (market exchange, need, scarcity, work-value) as Marx did, contests the very metaphysical ground of a utilitarian and productivist rationality whose limitation becomes evident in the anthropology of archaic societies. Better still, far from retreating beyond an economic explanation, as do the spiritualist critiques, this vision generalizes the economic approach, directly placing in its conceptual field notions that do not seem to belong there: religion, art, eroticism. At the heart of Bataille's thought lies the troubling postulate that the distinction between the profane and the sacred—a fundamental distinction of all human society—merges in a broad sense from the economic. Whereas the profane is the domain of utilitarian consumption, the sacred is the domain of experience opened by the unproductive consumption of the

---

1. Georges Bataille, *La Part maudite* (Paris: Minuit, 1967), 143. Henceforth cited in the text. This edition contains "La Notion de dépense" which was published fifteen years earlier.

surplus: what is sacrificed. Henceforth the position of religion or art with respect to the "economic base" as formulated by Marx is completely transformed. The religious or artistic domain is not a simple superstructure of vague whims built on the economic infrastructure: it is itself economic, in the sense of a general economics founded on the expenditure of the excess, on the unproductive and ecstatic consumption of the surplus, through which the human being experiences the ultimate meaning of existence. General economics, unlike restricted economics, encompasses obliquely the entire domain of human activities, extending the "economic" intelligence to highly symbolic practices where formidable energies are consumed for the celebration of the gods, the glory of the great or the dionysiac pleasure of the humble. What becomes apparent then is the *genealogy* of our economic thought. A complete desacralization of life (inaugurated by Calvinism and carried to its limit by Marxism) was necessary for the world of production and exchange to become autonomous according to the principle of restricted utility. The profane and prosaic reality thought by contemporary economics can be constituted only by excluding outside the field of human activity—through the total secularization of ethical values—any impulse toward sacrifice, toward consumption as pure loss.

Bataille is thus proposing a veritable anthropology of history whose guiding thread would be the accursed share and which would achieve a unification of the two forces that have been considered individually the motors of human societies (religion and economics). But this history is marked by a break. Until the birth of capitalism every society is one of sacrificial expenditure. Whether in the *potlatch* of primitive tribes described by Mauss in *The Gift*, the bloody sacrifices of the Aztecs, the building of the Egyptian pyramids, or even the opposing paths of peaceful Tibetan lamaism and warlike Islamic conquest, the expenditure of excess is always inscribed within a principle of the sacred. With the birth of the bourgeois world a radical change takes place. Productive expenditure now entirely dominates social life. In a desacralized world, where human labor is guided in the short or long term by the imperative of utility, the surplus has lost its meaning of glorious consumption and becomes capital to be reinvested productively, a constantly multiplying surplus-value.

In my view it is in this historical outcome that the most serious difficulty lies. This is also undoubtedly Bataille's view: he always wanted to continue his first sketch but this continuation exists only in fragments. On the one hand, there is hardly any doubt that Bataille always harbored a will to subvert contemporary society, a will that was heightened by his searing contact with surrealism and politically engaged groups. On the other hand, it is clear that the discussions in *La Part maudite* concerning "the present facts" of the world situation in terms of general economics are more than disappointing. Everything suggests that Bataille was unable to articulate his mysticism of expenditure, of sovereignty, of major communication—expressed so flamboyantly in *La Somme Athéologique, L'Érotisme* or *La Littérature et le mal*—in terms of contemporary general economics.

Where do we situate Bataille's claim? What happens to the demand of the sacred in capitalist society? How do we reconcile the affirmation that capitalism represents an unprecedented break with all archaic (precapitalist) forms of expenditure and the postulate of the necessary universality of spending as pure loss? This is the difficulty. Bataille wants to maintain as a general anthropological principle the necessity of unproductive expenditure while simultaneously upholding the historic singularity of capitalism with regard to this expenditure. Bourgeois society corresponds to a "general atrophy of former sumptuary processes" (41). An anomaly whereby loss is not absent (which would contradict the general principle) but virtually unreadable: "Today, the great and free social forms of unproductive expenditure have disappeared. Nevertheless, we should not conclude from this that the very principle of expenditure is no longer situated at the end of economic activity" (37). So what happens to ostentatious expenditure in capitalism? And can we really believe, furthermore, that the even more radical desacralization effected by communism could become a libertarian affirmation of sovereignty—the feast of self-consciousness, without divinities and myths?

Everything suggests that Bataille was unable to articulate the mystical tension toward sovereign self-consciousness "without form and mode," "pure expenditure" (224) with a utopia of social life that would make it possible, nor to explain in a *developed* capitalist society the consumption of the surplus beyond its reinvestment in production. Now it is quite clear that today's capitalism has come a long way from the Calvinist ethic that presided at its beginning. The values of thrift, sobriety and asceticism no longer have the place that they held when Balzac could caricature the dominant bourgeois mentality with the characters of père Grandet or the usurer Gobseck. It is doubtful that the spirit of capitalism, which according to Weber is expressed with an almost classical purity in Benjamin Franklin's principles ("he who kills a five shilling coin assassinates all that it could have produced: entire stacks of sterling pounds") [cited by Bataille, 163], could today be considered the spirit of the times. Undoubtedly, the pace at which all residual sacred elements inherited from feudalism are eliminated has quickened. But hasn't contemporary society undergone a transformation of the ethic of consumption, desire, and pleasure that renders the classical (Weberian) analyses of the spirit of capitalism (to which Bataille subscribes) inadequate? If the great opposition between the sacred and the profane no longer structures social life, if communal, sacrificial, and glorious expenditure has been replaced by private expenditure, it is no less true that advanced capitalism seems to exceed the principle of restricted economy and utility that presided at its beginning. No society has "wasted" as much as contemporary capitalism. What is the form of this waste, of this excess?

These questions strike directly at the historical situation and philosophical signification of Bataille's thought. Is it not clear that his passion for the "notion of expenditure,"—which, beginning in 1933, is the matrix of all his economic reflections to come—emerge precisely at a turning point in the history of capitalism, in the 1920s and 1930s, which also saw the appearance of Lukàcs and Heidegger?[2] Can we not perceive within the principles of secularization and restricted economics that were the strength of early capitalism an internal conflict that undermines them, and puts capitalism in contradiction with itself?

To treat these problems in detail and with the developments they deserve would require an analysis that I could not think of completing in a few pages. Almost the entirety of postmodern thought would bear upon this problematic. My task will be facilitated however by a recent attempt at a new legitimation of capitalism—that of George Gilder—who situates himself, curiously, on the same terrain as Bataille, if only to arrive of course at opposite conclusions. Confrontation with this work will lead to a discussion of capitalist morality as envisioned by Bataille, and the correlative concept of utility.

George Gilder was one of the most vocal advocates of the economic politics of neoconservative during the early 1980s. In his book,

2. On this parallelism of the problematics and the divergence of solutions cf., Jürgen Habermas, *Le Discours philosophique de la modernité* (Paris: Gallimard, 1988), chapter 8 on Bataille.

Wealth and Poverty (1981), which according to the *Los Angeles Times* made him "the prophet of the new economic order" (and President Reagan's favorite author), Gilder attempts to demonstrate once again the ethical value of capitalism against the "intellectual consensus" that stigmatizes the moral void on which it rests. The great interest of Gilder's endeavor lies in its ambition: "to give capitalism a theology."[3] Although unaware, we can reasonably assume, of Bataille's theories, Gilder seems to respond word for word to the author of the "notion of expenditure," placing himself immediately on the same terrain. Recalling the analyses of Marcel Mauss in *The Gift* and of Lévi-Strauss in *The Savage Mind*, Gilder undertakes to demonstrate that contemporary capitalism is no less animated by the spirit of the gift than the primitive tribes described by ethnographers. "Feasting and potlatching illustrate a capitalist tendency to assemble and distribute wealth" (26). The most elaborated forms of capitalism are simply a more elaborated form of the *potlatch*. The current notion of a self-interested, parsimonious capitalism, motivated only by the interest of material gain, is erroneous. At the origin of "capitalism" is the gift, not self-love and avarice. The conceptual basis of this seemingly paradoxical affirmation is a classical economic principle known as Jean-Baptiste Say's law: *"Supply creates its own demand."* Such is the modern, contemporary form of the *potlatch*. The essence of capitalism consists in supplying first, and in obtaining an eventual profit only later. The capitalist invests (he supplies goods and services), but he is never sure of the return, of the recompense for his supply. This movement, says Gilder, is the same as in the *potlatch*, where the essence of the gift is not the absence of all expectation of a countergift but rather a lack of certainty concerning the return. "Like gifts, capitalist investments are made without a predetermined return" (30).

Thus capitalism would be in essence no less generous than ritual tribal exchange. Let us cite at length the passage where Gilder summarizes his argument.

> Contrary to the notions of Mauss and Levi-Strauss, the giving impulse in modern capitalism is no less prevalent and important—no less central to all creative and productive activity, no less crucial to the mutuality of culture and trust—than in a primitive tribe. The unending offering of entrepreneurs, investing jobs, accumulating in-

3. George Gilder, *Wealth and Poverty* (New York: Bantam Books, 1981), 7. Henceforth cited in text.

ventories—all long before any return is received, all without any as-
surance that the enterprise will not fail—constitute a pattern of giving that dwarfs in extent and in essential generosity any primitive rite
of exchange. Giving is the vital impulse and moral center of capitalism. [30]

Despite the appearance of paradox, it is understandable why it is
within a capitalism of consumption that Say's adage, which underlies
Gilder's argument, becomes particularly apt. Supply precedes and
creates demand: this means that there is no prior definition of need,
no natural and preestablished demand founded on essential and rational exigencies that could be fixed in advance. Such is, according to
Gilder, the heresy of the socialist economy: it begins with the postulate of a demand assigned a priori, corresponding to an identifiable
essence of need and to which a corresponding production could adequately respond. But the capitalist economy is founded on a metaphysical uncertainty regarding the object of human desire. It must
create this desire through the invention of the new, the production of
the unpredictable. It *supplies* in order to create desire, instead of
satisfying a desire that would already be known by the person who
experiences it. The preoccupation with demand leads to stagnation.
The preoccupation with supply—in the gigantic *potlatch* of the capitalist store, which puts the unpredictable on display in order to
seduce the potential buyer without coercion or certainty—is the "genius of capitalism" (34), its frenetic pursuit of the new.

Thus there is no equivalence in fact between supply and demand,
contrary to what Walras's curves of general equilibrium, for example,
might lead us to believe. The mathematical theory of value, which
locates the determination of prices at the intersection of the curves of
supply and demand, is a false abstraction, a deceptive "reification"
(45). Demand registers only the simple reaction of consumers to a
supply that corresponds to efforts and "sacrifices," a veritable gift,
which is not accounted for by this quantitative equivalence.

It is remarkable that Gilder, starting from this conception of capitalism as *potlatch* (loss being measured by the frightening sums and
energies invested "for nothing" in a society where thousands of businesses are created and disappear each week), arrives at an irrationalist
legitimation of the capitalist universe that stands in sharp contrast to
the Weberian theme of the genesis of modern rationality. It must be
emphasized that for Gilder it is because capitalism is irrational (always suspended in uncertainty, the uncalculable, the indeterminate)

that it is superior to all other forms of society. Criticizing "the secular rationalist mentality" (310), he praises the spirit open to the paradoxes of chance and gambling. For in the end, having taken into account the unmasterable nature of the multiple factors that enter into the success of a business (not the least of which is the unpredictable desire of the client), profit resides in chance. Understood in this way, the spirit of capitalism thus participates in the fundamental mystery of any human situation: its opening onto the unpredictable and the undecidable. "Even the most primitive societies invent forms of gambling (dice in many places precede the wheel)" (296). The ultimate metaphysics of capitalism is the theology of chance—our only access to the future and to providence (299). It is only in this way that the opening is preserved. "Because no one knows which venture will succeed, which number will win the lottery, a society ruled by risk and freedom rather than by rational calculus, a society open to the future rather than planning it, can call forth an endless stream of invention, enterprise, and art" (296).

This sustained praise of the irrationality of capitalism strikes me as thoroughly remarkable. Is it not rhetorically satisfying that at the conclusion of a work on wealth and poverty the term "fortune" regains its most proper meaning: *Fortuna*, the Roman divinity of chance—a term which had acquired by metonymy the more restricted meaning of wealth? While a certain philosophical left, since Lukàcs, Horkheimer or Adorno, and in the wake of Weber—or a certain philosophical right with Heidegger—is bent on denouncing calculating reason as a dominant and alienating form of thought, inherent to capitalism (whose market, exchange side obscures its entrepreneurial side), a displacement is occurring (which is not entirely new since "capitalist anarchy" was denounced a long time ago) of which Gilder's book is a frank and unnuanced expression. Capitalism is irrational (in the last analysis it can rely only on a theology of chance—ultimately opening to the divine, to creativity and to the future) and this is why it is superior to all rationalist (hence socialist) pretentions to master the process of production and consumption, and consequently to prejudge human desire, to mortgage seduction. Is this not in 1981 the formulation of the *postmodern legitimation of capitalism?* Irrationality is no longer a denunciation but a justification, a defense.

Let me make it clear that, if there is no question of my subscribing without discrimination to Gilder's apologetic discourse, on the other hand I take it quite seriously as a pointed ideological legitimation strategy of eighties-capitalism. Gilder's theory is exemplary as an attempt to formulate a morality of capitalism at odds with the heritage of the Enlightenment. If his theory is weak as political economy, it is highly significant (although at times disquieting)[4] as economic politics. Any social critic (to go back to a phrase that Bataille would not disavow) who overlooks this type of contemporary justification risks missing the true target and overlooking once more capitalism's resources and metamorphoses.

Furthermore, perhaps Mauss would not have disavowed Gilder's attempt in principle. The anthropologist does not hesitate to see in the skillful operations of *potlatch* on the part of the Iroquois (in whose simple disinterestedness he is careful not to believe) a prefiguration of the operations of capitalism. And it is also his aim, at the end of *The Gift* to search for something in the contemporary world that could prolong the process of gift and countergift of primitive societies. It is not, however, in "the cold reason of the merchant, of the banker and of the capitalist" (*The Gift*, Chapter 4, Conclusion, vol. 2) that he detects that prolongation, but rather in the liberality of the industrialist who creates family insurance funds or, better still, in national health insurance, where the community gives to the workers something other than a simple salary. We are far from the insane squandering fantasized by Bataille, as well as from the innovator's generous risk invoked by Gilder.

There still remains the question of why neither Mauss nor Bataille have pointed out, in some decisive mechanism of capital, a contemporary continuation of *potlatch*, while Gilder, in 1980, does not hesitate to resort to that ethnological reference, and to make it the guarantee of a moral basis. The reason is that a transformation (already at work but still concealed) has become manifest. In the capitalism of abundance the distinction between luxury and nonluxury has become indeterminable. Clearly, it is only in a regime of luxury, where everything is superfluous, that demand cannot be assigned and becomes open to possibilities that are less and less predictable. It is only in a regime of surplus consumption that the subject (the client who chooses) does not know his own desire, and that

4. Gilder in fact still returns to the simplistic notion of "poverty" of the last century, continuing a well-known tradition that makes poverty the result of vice or of divine disfavor.

supply (founded on still unknown, still unimagined technological and aesthetic possibilities) must necessarily precede demand. The distinction is no longer between the necessary and the superfluous, but between several as yet unimagined possibilities. This is why seduction, the aesthetization of merchandise, plays a primordial role. It is vital for this supply economy to deny the naturalness of needs— including the very notion of need and utility (in the trivial sense). In this sense we are witnessing the aesthetization of political economy.

Gilder's postmodern legitimization of capitalism thus resolves the question of the gift in capitalism by postulating a continuity with the rituals of primitive societies. The capitalist cannot count on an assured, calculable profit from his investment. He agrees to spend money and to spend himself in a project that is always aleatory. Gilder sees the noble and glorious side of the entrepreneur; he makes of him a gambler who sacrifices in order to "supply" with an always uncertain result: wealth or bankruptcy. It is in so gambling that he earns his rank. We should emphasize that Bataille did not completely fail to recognize this ludic dimension of capitalism; rather he was unable to integrate it simply within his vision. The fragments show that he reflected on the coexistence of play and the project in capitalism, but only to conclude that despite this coexistence (inherent in all action) capitalism is essentially a project, even if play and risk intervene necessarily between the project and accumulation. "Play in capitalism is somewhat heterogeneous, it is the effect of a relative lack of power. Capitalism would avoid play if it could."[5] Finally, Bataille summarizes, "the project dominates capitalist activity. Play is restricted to the stock exchange" (*OC*, 220). Denouncing "the avaricious practices of big business and industry," Bataille thus remains attached to the romantic image of capitalism as a moral anomaly. If "a current of *glorious activities* naturally animates the economy," "the bourgeois economy alone is exempted" (*OC*, 201).

But whatever the clear divergence between this position and Gilder's may be, one cannot help thinking that the latter's apologetic attempt ultimately endorses Bataille. For what is remarkable is that Gilder is obliged to resort to the notion of gift and sacrifice at the moment when he is giving capitalism a noble and glorious image, an adventurous legitimation that goes beyond "the secular rationalist

5. Georges Bataille, *Oeuvres Complètes*, (Paris: Gallimard, 1970–1988), vol. 7, 219. Henceforth cited in text as *OC*.

mentality" (Gilder, 310). When it is a matter of giving a theology to capitalism, of infusing it with a grandeur that even its most brilliant defenders generally do not recognize, there is no route but the one Bataille has already mapped out, as if the singularity of capitalism could only be upheld by connecting it, despite everything, with an unchanging, anthropological base, most clearly revealed by primitive societies: the gift alone creates the glory and the grandeur. Therefore, from the start, Gilder is obliged to position himself on the terrain that Bataille has cultivated. He is obliged to begin with Marcel Mauss's *The Gift* in order to bring out, in support of capitalism, the moral challenge constituted by the primitive practice of the *potlatch*. That Gilder must resort to this anthropological paradigm does not tell us much about the real mechanisms of capital and the multiple strategies of profit (it is only a legitimation) but it at least shows the force of the demand of which Bataille has made himself the bedazzled echo.

Morover, Gilder's theology rediscovers more than one notion dear to Bataille: the critique of profane rationalism as well as the final appeal to chance, not as a simple, favorable coincidence, useful for its anecdotal value, but as an existential structure that reveals the most profound mystery of being. "Chance is the foundation of change and the vessel of the divine" (Gilder, 312). Or again: "The crux of change and creativity is chance" (Gilder, 308). Gilder draws on the work of Pierce, well-known as a pioneer in the founding of semiotics, and whose work anticipates certain aspects of deconstruction. In his posthumous volume *Chance, Love and Logic*, "Pierce has shown that chance not only is at the very center of human reality but also is the deepest source of reason and morality" (Gilder, 312). Here again Gilder's arguments which oppose the "closed system of secular rationality" to the "prodigality of chance," strangely echo Bataille's notions even if the final argument is not the same.[6] "The most dire and fatal hubris for any leader" writes Gilder, "is to cut off his people from providence, from the miraculous prodigality of chance by substituting a closed system of human planning" (Gilder, 313). This is a remarkable effort to give the risk and chance of economic innovation an ontological dimension which contradicts rather than agrees with the great narrative of the Enlightenment and its secular rationalism.

6. Georges Bataille, cf., the third part of *Somme athéologique: Sur Nietzsche, Volonté de chance*, (1945).

Gilder is admirable in saying openly, something which both clouds the classical Weberian vision of a capitalism of rationalist legitimation, and illuminates the historical bases of the postmodern rupture: "The tale of human life is less the pageant of unfolding rationality and purpose than the saga of desert wandering and brief bounty . . ." (Gilder, 315). No, capitalism is not rational calculation (individual or collective) but indeterminable, undecideable play, and therein lies its grandeur, its profound ontological truth, and its harmony with the mysterious origins of things. There could be no better formulation of what we have called a "postmodern legitimation of capitalism" than these pages of Gilder. That capitalism legitimates itself today in a postmodern version, and could not do otherwise, not only profoundly illuminates its present nature, but also permits us apparently to decipher the sociohistorical meaning of postmodernism's philosophical (and aesthetic) manifestations. Postmodern thought is in accordance with this legitimation, without allowing us to prejudge the modalities of this agreement. This would justify certain suspicions of someone like Habermas (Introduction) but at the same time would invalidate them by virtue of their lack of adequate historicization, and their lack of a sufficiently articulated and profound evaluation of the necessities of this break between rationality and modernity. This is an essential point for not mistaking the era: the Enlightenment is over.

Therefore, one can now point to an "antibourgeois" defense of capitalism, an apposition of terms which resonate disturbingly, like an enigmatic oxymoron. Everything happens as if the traditional values of the bourgeois ethos (sobriety, calculation, foresight, etc.) were no longer those values which corresponded to the demands of contemporary capitalism. And it is in this way that Gilder's legitimation (which lends almost a sense of tragic heroism, of sovereign play to the creation of businesses)[7] can echo so surprisingly Bataille's critiques of the cramped, profane, narrowly utilitarian and calculating bourgeois mentality. The entrepreneur can no longer count on petty calculation, on the expected profit, at a time when supply must create demand (as in artistic activity or any work of genius, stresses Gilder) and not merely

---

7. It is this adventurous dimension (perceived by Balzac, but in essentially critical and sarcastic terms in response to the narrowness of the bourgeois ethos of the 1830s), which gives birth to the *financial novel*. For example, cf., the mass-produced novels of Paul-Loup Sulitzer (*Money, Cash, Fortune, Le Roi vert*) from the beginning of the eighties, which are closely linked by their themes, their ideological universe, to the vision developed at the same time by Gilder in *Wealth and Poverty*.

satisfy it. An overturning of the founding values of political economy is occurring. The vision of Adam Smith himself is deceptive and dangerous: "In fact, a rational calculation of personal gain would impel an individual above all to avoid risk and seek security. In our world of fortuity, committed to a secular vision, the invisible hand of self-interest acclaimed by Adam Smith would lead to an ever-enlarging welfare state—to stasis and sterility. This is the root of our crisis and the crisis of classical economics today" (Gilder, 321). There is no longer, therefore, an "invisible hand." The divinity of capitalism is no longer the social insurer that guarantees the bourgeois harmony of egotisms. The entire ruse of reasoning whose grandiose philosophical expression was furnished by Hegel, is, in fact, only the ruse of socialism—a "welfare state" of the end of history that stops chance's miraculous prodigality. The marriage of the Enlightenment and political economy is over. "The future is forever incalculable" (Gilder, 314).

We must add, of course, that it is precisely at the moment when the entrepreneur must think himself into the model of the most advanced artistic genius, at the moment when the avant-gardist strategy of innovation at any price becomes the paradigm of dominant economic practice, that the artistic avant-garde necessarily loses its difference, its marginality, its deviance-value. The aesthetic avant-gardes have won. That is what paralyzes them so seriously. When the gadget maker, along with Gilder, borrows from them their critique of bourgeois rationality which becomes in his [Gilder's] eyes "the mythology of a secular rationalist world" (309) and which he calls upon "to plunge into the realm of dark transcendance where can be found all true light and creativity" (309), it becomes more difficult for the poet to distinguish himself from the grocer, more difficult for the surrealist to differentiate himself from the disheveled manager.

Along with this "postbourgeois" capitalism that at once contradicts Bataille's *sociological* interpretation and confirms his *ontological* vision, explode the sociocultural contradictions of capitalism. Daniel Bell has convincingly shown that with the development of mass consumption and mass credit (which he situates in the 1930s) the puritan ideology of early capitalism entered into contradiction with an increasingly hedonist mode of consumption favored by capitalism. The entrepreneur's need to revive seduction, to respond to competition with promises of evermore complex pleasures, inscribes him in a consumerist ideology directly at odds with the "bourgeois" virtues of sobriety, thrift, and hard work that had assured the development of production. In this way, the strict moral confines necessary for production enter into contradiction with the ethical liberation (even moral license) necessary to consumption.[8] Bataille does not seem to have foreseen this conflict born of abundance and the extraordinary sophistication of production. The Weberian image of capitalism that he maintains, the slightly obsolete conviction that Franklin's precepts of economy and sobriety represent capitalism's morals in its pure state, seem to indicate that Bataille did not imagine the paradoxical situation of postindustrial capitalism where only the appeal to compete infinitely in unproductive consumption (through comfort, luxury, technical refinement, the superfluous) allows for the development of production.

One must recognize that Gilder skillfully emphasizes the most seductive aspect of capitalism (the capitalism of abundance as seduction) even if it is by overlooking, or feigning ignorance of, that which can intentionally mislead, deceive, manipulate the consumer, whether it is the fiction of perfect competition or the buyer's lack of control over the real nature of the merchandise (harmfulness, fragility, planned obsolescence) to the profit of its appearance, of its pure transient spectacle. If "an American apple is not an apple," as the poet Rilke used to say in an amazing aphorism, it is not only because generations of peasants have not crystallized their sacred efforts in it, but also because the producer and the seller of that apple preferred to give it all the most stereotyped qualities of the "beautiful apple"— (big, red and shiny, like the one the Witch offers to Snow White), even if it is to the detriment of the real apple (tasteless, fiberless, carcinogenic). This substantive, actually consumed apple must remain a simple "noumenon," inexistent and without interest compared to the "phenomenon," the spectacle of the apple, which alone is at stake in the sale. But that does not prevent this very spectacle, this abstract aesthetization of the merchandise, from going hand in hand with an ideology of consumption that seems to transgress utility value.

We are touching here on difficulties which are linked from the start to the terms "utility," "unproductive consumption" etc. . . . There are ambiguities here that Bataille has not dealt with directly, even if the posthumous fragments offer some questions that nuance and complicate the positions of *La Part maudite*. I would like to note

8. Daniel Bell, *The Cultural Contradictions of Capitalism* (New York: Basic Books, 1975).

220 Yale French Studies

several objections which also concern more recent theories inspired largely by Bataille.

It is clear that even the most unproductive seeming consumption (for example: tobacco, alcohol, but also pleasure trips, movies etc.) produces a profit-making industry, and thereby falls into the economic sphere according to the logic of the general equivalent. If one remains on strictly economic ground, it is in truth impossible to separate productive consumption from unproductive squandering. Ethical criteria alone could claim to make this distinction. It is perhaps one of the aspects of our society to have erased at once the opposition between the sacred and the profane, and with the same gesture, the difference between the useful and the useless, the necessary and the superfluous, primary need and secondary satisfaction, etc. Is it useful or superfluous to manufacture microwave ovens, quartz watches, video games, or collectively, to travel to the moon and Mars, to photograph Saturn's rings, etc.? Condillac had already written that "What is luxury for one people is not so for another, and for the same people, what was a luxury can cease to be one."[9] Condillac and many others saw the very principle of the "progress of the arts" in this relativity of luxury, this movement whereby the choicest goods "enter into common use" (191). And it is doubtless this erasure, this blurring, that makes it so desperately difficult for Bataille to find the opposition between the glorious, sacrificial, spectacular consumption of the accursed share (founded upon the principle of a loss that lends grandeur and nobility) and prosaically utilitarian consumption.

But if this line of demarcation cannot be found, it is the very result of democratic life which has weakened and dismantled these oppositions, which has made them lose their meaning of social cleavage and confined them to the realm of insular individual experience. All the examples of consumption societies that fascinate Bataille are extremely unequal, even cruelly hierarchical societies in which spectacular consumption is the tool with which the powerful maintain their position above the dazzled, miserable masses. The counterpart of the erosion of these hierarchical oppositions (and in the first place, the antimony sacred-profane) is certainly the domination of all activity by the categories of political economy. This does not, however,

9. Condillac, "Du Luxe," *Le Commerce et le gouvernement,* (Geneva: Slatkine Reprints, 1980), chapter 27, 190. Henceforth cited in the text.

imply the reign of the "implacable, serene God of the useful," as Baudelaire writes.[10] Unless we understand it as a production marked by complete *axiological indifference*.

Baudrillard is in fact wrong when he contends that the notion of "use-value" and "utility" has a restrictive moral sense in economics, a sense that implies a naturalist metaphysics of need.[11] It is false that when economists speak of the use-value of goods, they suppose that the goods produced must first have had "utilitarian" value in order to have exchange value. In economics, use-value and utility were separated, from the start, from any moral evaluation concerning their legal or illegal "utility," or the very possibility of their having "use" at all in the current sense. If one may reproach classical political economy for something, it is certainly not, as Baudrillard believes (and mistakenly credits Marx with the same limitation) that it presupposes a metaphysics of need and of the utilitarian (in the trivial sense), but on the contrary, that it operates a radical demoralization of these notions (which gives them complete axiological indifference).[12] Keeping this indifference in mind, we see that it is not really a break in historical development, but a continuity that leads to a capitalism of consumption. From the start, even if the common conscienciousness formed by traditional moral values of utility could not perceive it, political economy has effected a denormativation of use, returning "utility" to the most subjective whims of individual choice. Moreover, when Bataille attacks "the principle of classical utility," he first reduces it prudently to "current intellectual representations ("The Notion of Expenditure," *La Part maudite*, 26)," that is, he reduces it to the most conventional notion of utility. In the fragments that he has left on "the limits of the useful" he has perfectly grasped "the moral indifference of capitalism," "The greatest moral indifference reigns from the start, and does not stop reigning in the use of products" (*OC* 7, 218). Does this observation not contradict the "utility principle" that he denounces in "The Notion of Expenditure"?

Let us reiterate that it would be useless to look for any kind of normativity in the notions of "use-value" or "utility" as political

10. *Les Fleurs du Mal*, poem 5.

11. Jean Baudrillard, *Critique de l'économie politique du signe* (Paris: Gallimard, 1972).

12. Cf., my text "Calcul des jouissances" in *Les Iconoclastes* (Paris: Seuil, 1978). American translation forthcoming in *Symbolic economies*, Cornell University Press, 1990.

economy defines them, either to critique political economy as an enslaving metaphysical vestige or to seek in it a basis for authenticity. Very early on, perhaps even from the beginning, political economy declined all responsibility. And it is doubtless this disengagement, this audacious pulling away, this autonomization in relation to all moral ballast (which the current terms "use" and "utility" still convey) that soon gave capitalism this precipitancy, this careening acceleration, this fever for any form of production, this unprecedented multiplication of supply that did not respond a priori to any demand.

Let us consider, for example, Jean-Baptiste Say. For him, men only attach value to something in function of its "uses," and "this ability of certain things to satisfy men's diverse needs" is called "utility." But, he adds, political economy only takes note of a fact, its task is not to judge whether or not this appreciation corresponds to "real utility." Political economy must not judge in the manner of "the science of moral men, men in society"[13]—the science to which he leaves the task of this judgement. Therefore, "the most useless, most inconvenient item, such as a royal robe, possesses what I am here calling utility, if a price can be attached to its use, whatever that might be."[14]

Elaborating on the same idea Auguste Walras, clearly marks this extension of the term "utility" that requires a separation of "moral utility" from "economic utility" (Walras, 83). This explicit dissociation, which is at the base of the conceptualization of political economy and marks its radical break with all normativity (ancient or medieval) of the useful, renders inoperable and naive those critiques of the so-called utilitarian presuppositions of the notion of "use-value." Auguste Walras writes: "There is this difference between moral and political economy: the first terms "useful" only those objects that satisfy those needs explained by reason, while the second grants this name to all objects that man can desire, either in the interest of self-preservation, or by virtue of his passions and whims. Therefore bread is useful because it serves as our food, and the choicest meats are also useful because they appeal to our sensuality. Water and wine are useful because they quench our thirst, and the most dangerous liquors are useful because men have a taste for them. Wool and cotton are useful because one must be clothed; pearls and diamonds are useful as objects of adornment" (Walras, 82).

13. Jean-Baptiste Say, *Traité d'économie politique* (Paris, 1841) 57.
14. Cited by Auguste Walras in *De la nature de la richesse et de l'origine de la valeur* (Paris: Alcan editor,) 82. Henceforth cited in the text.

What has been described as a "society of consumption," the conspicuousness in the 1960s, of a consumerist capitalism, therefore does not at all subvert the status of the extensive concept of "utility" in political economy, even if it undoes the trivial (moral) notion of the useful. It is, on the contrary, the implications of the axiological indifference of economic "utility" and the historical consequences (beyond all reason) of Say's principle, that are exposed and triumph in the light of day.

A lesson, however, emerges from this. It is not the quantity of waste, the amount of squandering or the importance of unproductive consumption (which is impossible to assign in economic terms, but which supposes a moral criterion) that enables us to distinguish between precapitalist societies, supposedly governed by the principle of pure expenditure, and capitalist societies, supposedly governed by "the utilitarian." Undoubtedly, no society has squandered so much, produced and spent so much merely for the sake of producing and spending, as contemporary industrial societies. The difference lies in the mode of waste, its social *mise-en-scène*, its representation, and finally the imaginary of the expenditure. Without arriving at clear conclusions, Bataille looked for the singularity of modern societies in the individualism of their expenditure (*OC*, "The Limits of Utility," 232 ff.) and its allotment (*La Part maudite*, "La Notion de dépense," 37) (which is opposed to communal and spectacular waste, offered by the rich for their own glorification).

Perhaps Bataille's economic theory is explained not by his discovery of *potlach* in primitive societies, but by the presentiment of what capitalism is becoming. That is why Bataille finds himself in such bad company: in troubling consonance (although one cannot reduce Bataille to what compromises him here) with Gilder's postmodern legitimation. What Gilder reveals is the play of capitalism, which without his knowing it overdetermines Bataille's exaltation and which also, at the moment that it becomes even more visible, dazzling, spectacular, sets off Baudrillard's accelerated derangement. Baudrillard and Gilder map out the same configuration of postmodern capitalism. But Gilder is the *truth* of Baudrillard since he *wants* politically and theologically the social play of which Baudrillard is content to be the appalled television viewer (more than the rational critic). At the moment that Gilder forges the ideological instrument of a libertarian (or rather neoconservative) politics and thus determines a reality, even indirectly, Baudrillard endures the spectacle of that politics in turmoil and unreality. Gilder theorizes postmodern capitalism from the point of view of the active entrepreneur, while Baudrillard raves brilliantly about postmodern capitalism in the televisual armchair of the stupefied consumer. But Gilder's entrepreneurial morality proves that there is indeed in our era an economic political project, a locatable metamorphosis of capital, where Baudrillard sees only a desintegrative and paradoxical poetry.[15]

But if Bataille was unable to think through consumerist capitalism (which took on a more readable form only after the upheavals of the 1960s), if he was unable to think the dissolution of all foundation in the unconvertibility of the general equivalent (which could serve as a definition of the postmodern conjuncture)[16], if he could not think the subsequent legitimations of a "postbourgeois" capitalism which dismisses the Enlightenment and the great rationalist narrative, Bataille did offer a new grid which also facilitates this thought. Moreover, with his fragmented and fissured work, he testified to an unconditional demand that has the volcanic center of the most powerful contradictions, a demand before which his existentialist contemporaries appear—with the passage of time—as mere "men of letters." We know that his work in "general economics" had a major place among Bataille's preoccupations, and that it was undoubtedly the connecting strand of his theoretical efforts. Even the mystical essays of *La Somme athéologique* are indebted to this persistant endeavor, even if only as a moment of distancing, of overwhelming liberation, from the burden of his argumentation. The preceding pages attempt only to mark several guideposts: both the difficulties of the "notion of expenditure" when one tries to link it with contemporary conditions, and the still unexhausted richness of an opening in which we seek the bases of a morality for which the two modes of communication could be articulated. One of these is daily, prosaic exchange, and the other is the stronger mode of love, the festival, and art—communicational unreason.

Translated by Kathryn Ascheim and Rhonda Garelick

15. Especially in *Les Stratégies fatales*, where the reference to Bataille is most direct (Paris: Garnier, 1983), 119.

16. Cf., my analysis in *Les Monnayeurs du langage* (Paris: édition Galilée, 1984). American translation forthcoming at Oklahoma University Press.

III. The "Impossible"
Esthetic

JEAN-MICHEL HEIMONET

Recoil in Order to Leap Forward: Two Values of Sade in Bataille's Text

It is a question here of envisaging the relation between writing, or, in a larger sense, the relation between what Bataille calls "the function of representation,"[1] and, in an empirical sense, action. But discussing Sade in view of Bataille is no small task: for the very simple reason that, historically speaking, Sade escapes from positivism—he is not exactly an agent of history—and that, from what we may call a "literary" point of view, he leads beyond poetry to silence. And, to speak of the secret motor animating history (of Negativity *itself*) or to speak of silence is simply impossible. Impossible at least without betrayal. Evaluating the stakes of this "betrayal" is precisely what Bataille invites us to do through the lucid fascination he felt for Sade.

I believed it possible to entitle the present article "Recoil in Order to Leap Forward," which is a Bataille quotation to which I shall return in closing, but also, "Two Values of Sade in Bataille's Text." Beginning with these values or meanings—which are actually one, double or dual, at once antithetical and complementary—I will show that they correspond to two moments in the experience and thought of Bataille. The first of these I will call the political moment, or activist moment, from 1930 to 1935 when Bataille was active within extremist groups (and it is known that, at that same time, the extremes of the right or left had a tendency to join each other). As to the second, which I will call the theoretical moment—in the sense that Barthes gave to the word: as re-flection, a return of the subject to himself through his

1. (1:307); unless otherwise indicated, all of the quotations of Georges Bataille are from the Gallimard edition of *Oeuvres complètes* in its present state of publication (twelve volumes 1970–1988). All references to this edition are indicated thus: *OC* 1: 307, the first number indicating the volume and the second numeral the pages.

YFS 78, *On Bataille*, ed. Allan Stoekl, © 1990 by Yale University.

language—it corresponds, during and after the war, to the period when Bataille wrote large parts of *La Somme athéologique,* all the while lecturing, an activity which made clearer his ideas on the relations between "heterology" (or the science of the sacred) and literary creation. Against all appearances, there is no break between these two moments, but on the contrary a wholly dialectical complementarity of an implacable profundity and rigor.

At the time of his first break with André Breton, and following the excommunication proclaimed by the "Second Manifesto", Bataille addresses an "open letter" destined to his "current comrades" under the title "La Valeur d'usage de D. A. F. de Sade" [The Use Value of D. A. F. de Sade]. Without entering into the detail of this text— voluntarily not discursive—I will be content to emphasize:

1) that Bataille violently takes exception to those who dared to make Sade the object of commentary, philosophic or literary;

2) and that, in contrast, he suggests becoming silent and putting into practice the excesses represented by the divine marquis.

Indeed, the enthusiasm that Sade's commentators manifest for him remains purely verbal. For even if they praise his stories to the heavens, they refuse concurrently to integrate them into a *practice,* be it private or social. In doing this, they deport Sade (or his text) into a literary ghetto where they neutralize him by excluding him from the political and social realities that constitute the field of the Revolution.

> The behavior of Sade's admirers resembles that of primitive subjects in relation to their king, whom they adore and loathe, and whom they cover with honors and narrowly confine. In the most favorable cases, the author of *Justine* is in fact thus treated as any given *foreign body;* in other words, he is only an object of transports of exaltation to the extent that these transports facilitate his excretion (his peremptory expulsion).[2]

In complete opposition, for Bataille, the only way to be faithful to Sade is to take him from the page to the street, to make of him not the object of a hypocritical contemplation (a bourgeois transgression without risk, appropriate to this "society of the spectacle" which the Third Republic had already become), but the catalyst of a spon-

2. All page references preceded by *VE* are taken from the anthology *Visions of Excess, Selected Writings of Georges Bataille, 1927–1939,* ed. and trans. Allan Stoekl (Minneapolis: The University of Minnesota Press, 1985), 92.

taneous social revolution. To this end, the excremental dimension of Sadian texts must no longer be evacuated (the literary consumption of these texts having had, literally, a function of "flushing"), but on the contrary incorporated by the social organism for which these texts will serve as revolutionary ferment (or fertilizer).

> I am thus led to indicate how, in a way completely different from this usage, the sadism which is not *completely different* from that which existed before Sade appears positively . . . as an irruption of excremental forces (the excessive violence of modesty, positive algolagnia, the violent excretion of the sexual object coinciding with a powerful or tortured ejaculation, the libidinal interest in cadavers, vomiting, defecation . . .). [VE, 92]

Following this, Bataille defines the Revolution—not a premeditated and organized revolution, in the service of a program, and therefore of a language, but the Revolution in an absolute sense, making negativity the stake in a raw state: this is why he writes the word with a capital letter—like a process of *excretion* in two phases. The first is the phase of *separation*, between "two groups of forces, each of which is characterized by the necessity . . . of excluding the other." As for the second, it has to do with the phase of *expulsion:* "The second phase is the violent *expulsion* of the group that has possessed power by the revolutionary group" (VE, 100).

However, since any revolutionary group, once it has the power, is likely to entrench itself in order to become in its turn a conservative group, Bataille envisages a third phase in the Revolutionary process. This third phase does not take the form of an *Aufhebung* [neutralization], that of a reconciliatory third period during which the unleashing of violence would be integrated by the positive economy. Its function is, on the contrary, to assure the continuous excitation of the social base. *Permanent* Revolution, however, is not guided by Trotskyist rigor, but is inspired rather by the irrecoverable losses of Sadian excesses. This third phase, Bataille writes, "implies the necessity of a division between the economic and political organization of society on one hand, and on the other, an antireligious and asocial organization having as its goal orgiastic participation in different forms of destruction, in other words, the collective satisfaction of needs that correspond to the necessity of provoking the violent excitation that results from the expulsion of heterogeneous elements."

Such an organization can have no other conception of morality than the one scandalously affirmed for the first time by the Marquis of Sade." (*VE*, 101)

Dating from 1929, "The Use Value of D. A. F. de Sade" immediately precedes Bataille's participation in groups of the extreme left, the "Democratic Communist Circle," then "Counter-Attack." During the course of this intense political activity, Bataille is led to mistrust the outcome of the Revolution. The "great night" which was to see the triumph of the Sadian ethos through the destruction of the bourgeois state, seems to have led to a funereal though implacable dialectic, one which drives him to violent totalitarianism, whether Stalinism of fascism:

> The term of the tearing apart provoked by capitalism and class struggle . . . could simply be the archaic presence, barely believable, of the chief-gods: Lenin dead, Mussolini, Hitler, Stalin . . . [*OC 2*: 210]

Nevertheless, this dead-end, whose risks he lucidly measured, does not compel Bataille to a banal turnabout. He will never hereafter deny his passion for "leftist heterogeneity," or "from the bottom," for the black face of the sacred that he had discovered in the materialism of gnosticism. Twenty years later, against all expectations, he returns to Sade in order to become in turn his commentator.

In the text of *Literature and Evil* which he devotes to Sade, Bataille begins by insisting on what separates, in general, the periods of historical upheaval from literature and, in particular, the work of Sade from the French revolution. He recalls that in favoring the fall of the Bastille by the harangues he spewed from the height of his prison, Sade contributed to the annihilation of his work, since the manuscript of *The One Hundred and Twenty Days of Sodom* was lost in the combat that prolonged the riot: when the mob penetrated the fortress, Sade had already been taken away. This ironic conflict between historical reality and literary activity leads Bataille to conclude in paradoxical form, in contradiction to what he might have written twenty years earlier: "The sense of the revolution is not given in Sade's ideas; in no way are these ideas reducible to the revolution" (*OC 9*:240). If therefore the Sadian text remains heterogeneous to the reality of social struggle, what can be this "practical value" that Bataille dreamed of attributing to him twenty years earlier? We are now invited to seek this literariness in "the poetry of Sade's destiny." A poetry that for all its actual literariness corresponds in no way to what Hegel defined the exile of "the beautiful soul": ethereal, idealistic poetry, situating itself from the start above or beyond the historical real.

Seeing his manuscript destroyed, a loss which, by his own admission, caused him to shed "tears of blood" (*OC* 9:244), Sade worked out the destiny he had demanded, not only for the victims represented in his books, but for his work and for himself. On this question Bataille recalls the instructions given by the Marquis in his will: that "the traces of [his] tomb disappear from the surface of the earth" so that "[his] memory may disappear from the memory of man," and he concludes:

> The meaning of an infinitely profound work is in the desire that the author had to *disappear* (to resolve himself without leaving any human trace); for he was nothing more in his estimation. [*OC* 9:244]

Sade, who wanted to stir up history while transcending it, sees himself, on the contrary, as dispossessed by it. Wanting absolute power over the world and his peers, he only achieves it through the text, through a derisory power, a power of paper reduced to nothingness by a blind force. However, this literary power is not historically ineffectual, since through a series of relations as complex as they are ironic, it worked in favor of the taking of the Bastille, an event which, Bataille emphasizes, "was going to shake [and], even to some extent deliver the world" (9,241). We are thus led to explore the dialectic that associates history and literature, or more precisely, effectual action and the "function of representation."

Here the part of the text to which I just alluded is entitled: "La Volonté de destruction de soi" [The Impulse to Self-Destruction]. Such an impulse, if one excludes suicide, is clearly paired with sacrifice. In 1930, in the article "Sacrificial Mutilation and the Severed Ear of Vincent Van Gogh," sacrifice is defined as: "the necessity of throwing oneself or something of oneself *out of oneself*" (*VE*, 67) or yet again: "the rupture of personal homogeneity and the projection *outside the self* of a part of oneself" (*VE*, 68).

Here in the text on Sade, Bataille gives a similar definition. "In the awed apprehension, full of horror, of the sacred," sacrifice would be the movement by which "the spirit [becomes] equal to *that which is* (to the indefinite totality that we cannot know")" [*OC* 9:255]. But Bataille also notes that, conceived as such, sacrifice remains "passive," for it is founded on an elementary fear, [it is] the operation by which the world of lucid activity (the profane world) liberates itself from a violence that would risk destroying it. [*OC* 9:255]

In Sade, the sacrificial opening is at once more subtle and more demanding; it operates by a sort of dissociation. Bataille notes indeed that "Sade was very different from his heros in that he displayed human feelings" (9,253). Thus he recognizes that there are *two* Sades, or at least what feeds the work is not what feeds the life of its author. In putting this dissociation into practice, Bataille continues, Sade places us on the path of a "difficult liberty" (9,250). He succeeds in revealing a violence inherent in all men, upon which the social edifice is based, but which is the very thing censured by society—and this amounts to the same thing—society recuperates it in the name of an alleged literary gratuitousness. If the human spirit has not ceased to "answer to the need that leads to sadism" Bataille states, it has always been done hypocritically,

furtively, during the night that results from the incompatibility between violence, which is blind, and the lucidity of consciousness. Frenzy distances consciousness. For its part, consciousness, in its anguished condemnation, denied and ignored the sense of frenzy. [*OC* 9:253]

In order that violence be perceived as the basis of humanity and of history, it was necessary to wait for Sade, who was the first to endure the tension created by the conflict between violence's blindness and the lucidity of conscience, and to permit this revelation. The experience of dissociation requires at the very least this condition: that Sade live enclosed "in the solitude of his prison":

Without seclusion, the disorganized life that he led would not have left him the chance to maintain an interminable desire which presented itself to his reflection without his being able to satisfy it. [9,257]

Desire is essentially allergic to consciousness, but even more than the desire is its *satisfaction*, for it is always accompanied, Bataille emphasizes, by a "great disorder of the senses." In this disorder, where the subject and object merge, conscience is excluded, supplanted by what passes it by; it slumbers in "the animal night." Doubling requires therefore that the subject be at once ardent desire and the consciousness of this desire, desire primed but frustrated since it cannot be satisfied, and consciousness alerted, but also humiliated to sense itself on the verge of its excess. Let us note that it is not at all a question of sublimation; desire is not made into metaphor, transformed into images whose elevated character would be substituted for its material baseness. It is, on the contrary, experienced with full force; but it is pulled in by the object, it concurrently resists this pulling in. In order to speak of doubling, consciousness must remain separated from desire, sufficiently lucid so as not to censure it, but sufficiently strong so as not to give in to it. To put it in Hegelian terms: the consciousness must remain the spectator of a negative which is also its negation. This is a dialectic which requires, in Sade in particular and in general for any man, seclusion, "reflection wed to the momentary impossibility of satisfying the desire, then the inclination to satisfy it more "consciously" (OC 9:256).

Sadian doubling represents, then, more than and something other than a simple sacrifice, and finally, for Bataille, the only authentic sacrifice. Not an impulsive opening—all in all too easy—in a subject "beside himself," beyond his consciousness, but rather a lucid view of this opening, a rending apart, quartering of a subject tensed for the leap but nevertheless held back on the verge of the abyss of total alterity. Bataille had already evoked in 1933 in the famous article "The Notion of Expenditure" this second, more demanding form of sacrifice—that one could call *auto-sacrifice*, providing that the prefix "auto" be stripped of any egocentric or proprietary will:

> The term poetry, applied to the least degraded and least intellectualized forms of the expression of a state of loss, can be considered synonymous with expenditure; it in fact signifies, in the most precise way, creation by means of loss. Its meaning is therefore close to that of sacrifice. [VE, 120]

If poetry is alone capable of accomplishing such a sacrifice, it is because in poetry the need of a passage to the limit—of an exit leading out of what Derrida calls "the closure of representation"[3]—remains inseparable from the inverse exigency, which is that of forcing a passage into *consciousness*. "Production by means of loss," poetry is the manifestation of violence of negativity, to the detriment of the empirical power of the subject. That is why it is not reducible to the exile of a "beautiful soul," but remains attached to history by the most fragile

3. See Jacques Derrida, *L'Ecriture et la différence* (Paris: Seuil, 1967).

but also profound ties that exist. Certainly not to current or punctual history, recognized by the shell of facts, but to the substructures of a *crypto-history,* and more profoundly to the negative "self" which is its substratum. As Bataille wrote in 1937 to the Hegelian Master Kojève: in a world where the end of history has already occured, in which there is *nothing more to be done,* nothing to which man may henceforth devote his life, limit-poetry, that of Sade, but also that of the authors whose work is explored in *Literature and Evil,* represents the most faithful expression of a "negativity out of work." And it is as such, as revelation and spontaneous combustion of violence, that this poetry *communicates,* that it addresses all men. "Without 'the poetic scandal'," Bataille writes, "Sade's truth would not humanly have its human reach" (9,257).

Doubling, as a putting into action of an "auto"-sacrifice by which the subject expresses its negativity while renouncing his expulsion into the world, is thus what permits us to pass from Sade's *historical value* to his *poetic value,* without falling into the trap of the "beautiful soul."

But Sade's poetry cannot have an exemplary meaning: it would rather have the status of an exception since his use of it is tied, as we have seen, to the particular conditions represented by his incarceration. Of course, one cannot incarcerate all men, place them in a simultaneous state of intensification and frustration of desire. As soon as it is not dictated by such a constraint, what can be the value of poetic usage, what can be its function in terms of sacred sociology? How can poetry simultaneously express violence while preventing it from happening? Bataille asks this question in a 1947 lecture entitled "Le Mal dans le platonisme et le sadisme" [Evil in Platonism and Sadism], which I will summarize briefly.

In a world where God is dead because he was a "reasoning being," dead for having become profane, man is driven to seek the good, toward which he aspires and for which he lives, in *excess,* in all the forms of transgression that accompany what Bataille calls the "empassioned unleashing." Faced with this exigency, man remains torn apart, wracked between his desire to spend and the necessity of his conservation. Before leaping, faced with the unbounded, he is frightened and recoils. However, Bataille continues:

At man's core there is a voice that wants him never to give in to fear.
But if it is true that in general man cannot give in to fear, at the

very least he postpones indefinitely the moment when he will have to confront himself with the object of his fear, at the very least he postpones indefinitely the moment when he will find himself naked before himself, when he will no longer have the assistance of reason as guaranteed by God, or when he will no longer have the assistance of God such as reason guaranteed.

It is necessary to recoil, but it is necessary to leap, and perhaps one only recoils in order to leap better. [*OC* 7: 372]

For Bataille, Sade is the only one who carried out this perilous leap without losing his humanity, who achieved it while maintaining his oscillation; in other words, *while watching himself do it:* "Sade's cruel representations can be considered exactly as the definition of the leap" (*OC* 7:372).

But Sade aside, considered as an example invalidating the rule, how can poetry, inasmuch as it is a "function of *re*presentation," *present* itself as what it should be: the very tension of doubling? That is the ultimate question against which Bataille seems to stumble, but to which he in fact makes us return. If poetry that recognized the necessity of the leap still allows itself the time to defer its urgency in order to let it flow into a pleasing form, it works thereby at its own alienation. Here is the last sentence of the lecture:

The leap can be poetry, but when poetry pretends to leap at the moment it evaluates itself, when it perceives the leap that must be made, and when it has not yet destroyed everything, then poetry is also the powerlessness of poetry. [*OC* 7: 374]

Beyond poetry—or in order that poetry realize itself in the purest authenticity—the only possible outcome comes down to *silence.* Bataille recognizes this explicitly in the written version for publication:

Discourse is only elevated to poetry by abandoning a lucid gait. Further, it is subject to heaviness: the demands of which it is the object, continue to show, emphasizing in every way, the difficulty I am speaking of, and which silence alone has the power to resolve. [*OC* 7:452].

But this silence does not have the dullness of failure. It vibrates, prompted by conflict, or more precisely, by conflictual complementarity, maintained by literature and evil, Spirit and History, the creation of forms and the creation of forces. In this silence we must strive to understand what makes the work the *pure* (nonempirical) negative of power and of violence. The impossible site where the subject, having tried to attain a sacred character, opens up toward others: his next of kin and his fellow beings, his doubles in language.

Translated by Joaniko Kohchi

MARIE-CHRISTINE LALA

The Conversions of Writing in Georges Bataille's *L'Impossible*

The text entitled *L'Impossible*, first published in 1947 under the title *La Haine de la poésie* later reissued in 1962 under the definitive title, does not cease to astonish the reader.[1] Since the earlier title was not understood, Bataille preferred to substitute the notion of the "impossible," although the latter is itself not much clearer. From the first reading on, the composition of the text is disconcerting; it is hard to grasp the reason for the juxtaposition of two stories—"A Story of Rats" and "Dianus"—followed by poems accompanied by a commentary, "The Oresteia." Every interpretive effort finds itself on terrain as slippery as "shifting sands": on the terrain of language itself.

Endlessly escaping explanation, Bataille's practice of writing can be seen to deploy itself in an extreme tension between sense and nonsense, at the limit of the endurable. Amid violence and excess, the writer must indeed sustain in his own person the "truth of the impossible and of death." This involves extracting and explicating the effects of the sense contained by the word, but without thereby eluding the impact of the truth of language measurable by the weight and the gravity of silence. What renders access to Bataille's text difficult is that the reader is challenged to renounce traditional attitudes towards the literary text. Meaning slips away, and consequently, "we have to respond to something that, not being God, is stronger than all rights: that impossibility to which we accede only when we forget the truth of all rights, and only when we accept disappearance. Bataille replaces the metaphysical alternative between sense and non-sense with a rhythm alternating between appearance and disappearance.

1. Georges Bataille, *Oeuvres complètes*, (Paris: Gallimard, 1971), vol. 3.

YFS 78, *On Bataille,* ed. Allan Stoekl, © 1990 by Yale University.

We are then compelled, not to tear sense out of non-sense, but rather to understand, finally, the extent of the movement that departs from the "disappearance of death" to release the "meaning of the disappearance."

In the preface and notes, Bataille himself brings up at several points the elements that will justify what he wanted his book to show. Thus, for instance, we read: "I myself find it hard to explain publishing, in one book, poetry and a contestation of poetry, a dead man's journal and the notes of a prelate friend of mine. Still, these sorts of whims are not without precedent, and here I would like to say that, judging by my experience, they, too, can translate the inevitable." With its strangely diverse writings, *L'Impossible* presents itself as a text apart in Georges Bataille's *oeuvre*, as an original text that responds practically to the question of how to "translate the inevitable"? How to render the "impossible" accessible by and through writing, without betraying its own singularity?

I propose to examine the textual configuration by which Bataille stages this impossible, at the limit of reference and of representation. At the same time, I will show that this text functions like an exploratory model in which a mechanism of transformation is put to work, intervening, in a series of conversions, at the level of the story, of the enunciation, of the figures of discourse, of poetic language. *L'Impossible* offers an exemplary site: a strategic device in language to put the resources of poetics into play.

I. STORY AND CONVERSION

Bataille at times links his thought to a narrative form, in order to take the way traced by fiction as far as possible, the only way to outline the "category of the impossible." An analysis of the events of the story and its discourse[2] opens up an initial approach to this "something"— impossible, yet inevitable—that congeals and crystallizes at one point, only to displace itself and finally to escape. The apparent ease with which Bataille's writing slips away leaves the reader with an impression of astonishment and non-sense, in a moment of silence. Each utterance of thought content finds itself destroyed from within: this emptying of meaning completes itself through repetition through displacement.

2. Emile Benveniste, *Problems of General Linguistics*, trans. Mary Elizabeth Meek (Coral Gables: University of Miami Press, 1971).

In following the regulated play of relations between story and discourse, we glimpse the outlines of an alternation in which the story has no corollary but the death of the story, that is, its own blackout. This tragic alternative sustains the mobility of the discourse, gives it life, all the while mounting and undoing the drama of the object's disappearance. Thence a double threat: the vanishing of the story presents a risk for the discourse, whereas the loss of the loved object presents a risk for the subject of the enunciation. The discourse sustains the story that nourishes it, and if the story vanishes, the discourse breaks off. Similarly, the place of the vanished object a lack carves out a space where absence is marked.

Starting from the staging of the separation from the object in the story, Bataille reveals subjectivity as a problematic part of the man who confronts and looks directly at his own death:

> How not to be tempted, seized with vertigo, feeling in myself an *intolerable* movement, to rear up, to curse, to want at all costs to limit that which can have no limit? How not to break down telling myself that everything demands of me an end to this movement that is killing me?

If the story comes to an end, the threat that weighed on the subject of the enunciation becomes reality, for the *nothing* which the retelling of the story masked evidently presents itself to consciousness as a *void:* "What have I done, I thought, thus to be in all ways thrown back into the impossible? . . . "

The undertaking of the story is endlessly frustrated, despite redoubled efforts. In "A Story of Rats," after the separation from B (the female partner), the narrator wanders in search of the object of his love. Journeying through illness, snow, and cold he is led towards the "castle" of B's father. Having fainted in the snow and been brought inside the castle, he awakens to discover a dead body in the next room: the corpse of B's father. As if the castle were no more than an empty form, prefiguring the presence of the "dead brother" in "Dianus," the next story: D's body is laid out "in a deathly silence."

From the first story to the second, there is the revelation, at the level of the structure of the story, of a void point. The story unveils its impossible, linked to the impossible of love, in a suspension of sense inseparable from incest. At the limit of representation, the symbol of the sword between Tristan and Isolde rejoins the myth of Oedipus wandering with his eyes torn out. This moment of excess, accessible by way of "sovereign conducts" such as intoxication or eroticism, is exhibited by the story as its impossible limit. The void point thus exposed can be interpreted in various ways. Separation from the object and absence of sense (madness) or absence of God (despair), the empty form laid bare by the impossible story redresses the logical structure of a lack. In this moment of excess, at this limit of the impossible, "being is given us in an intolerable going beyond of being" . . . . From its overt interrogation by the poetics of the text, the nothing of non-sense takes on all its impact, in its existential bearing and with its ontological value.

It is always the same move that is replayed, and this repetition sustains, from "A Story of Rats" to "Dianus," the coherence of the text, which otherwise would dislocate itself and dissolve in the flight of the referent. In this eternal return of parody, what is truly accomplished is the movement of a return to the same point; but this point endlessly decenters itself in order to mark itself anew as a void. This movement proceeds in "a world of ruins and the gnashing of teeth," for its origin and outcome is the fact that man measures himself against death. The problem of death posed in language and in enunciation, starting from the story, sets off a distance that cannot be overcome. The tension of this divergence is hard to sustain, but it must be maintained, for it leads towards the reversal of the impossible into new possibility:

> What do we know of the fact that we are living if the death of the beloved does not let horror (the void) enter to the very point where we cannot endure its entrance: but then we know what door the key opens.

The distance set off by the object of lack installs a break that separates fiction from commentary. The place of the "putting into question" is thematized in the "torture," along with "sacrifice" of "the guilty one" [*le coupable*]. This space of absolute silence must be preserved as a sacred or "cursed share" ("The Temple's Roof" in *Inner Experience*) and, at the same time, coherence must be reestablished on another basis, since the story concludes with the exhaustion of the referential function of language. Narrative theory stumbles over this problem, which it cannot resolve on its own: how to theorize the moment of excess and of the truth of the impossible and of death? So the narrative function of language, deployed in the first two stories, coverts the rest of itself into what is left over: O/RESTE. The referential function checked in "A Story of Rats" and "Dianus" gives way to the poetic function of language in *The Oresteia*. The passage to the third panel of the text, juxtaposed with the preceding ones, finishes unfolding the explication that narrative theory cannot give. A new disposition of the text takes up the task by converting narrative into poetic fiction doubled by a commentary on the poetry.

II. THE WORK OF DEATH AND THE THEORY OF THE SUBJECT

The void point exposed is occupied by death. Like the key to a paradox or a "lewd key" opening the possible: "Like a marvelous madwoman, death endlessly opened or closed the doors of the possible. In this labyrinth I could lose myself at will, giving myself over to rapture, but at will I could discern ways, managing a precise passage to intellectual procedures." At points "rife with the impossible," death is close to bliss. It gives itself as a power that *operates* effectively to reveal the sovereign enunciation.

Through the evocation of the "dead" (woman or man), the presence of death is functional. It serves to free up the place where the subject of the enunciation will die and be (re)born:

> The wreckage that I am at this table, when I have lost everything and the silence of eternity reigns in the house, is there, like a piece of light that may be ruined, but shines. . . .

The subject of this practice is the subject of writing or the *sovereign subject* (Dianus or "The king of the woods"). He can know himself and recapture himself in the flash of his failing, for this moment of fainting is constitutive of symbolic effectuation: "Thus I can say of my unhappy reflection, which would have been burdensome without the extreme anguish, that, at the moment where I am about to succumb, it yields sway to me . . ."

In the process of its feigned putting-to-death, the instance of the sovereign subject renews itself infinitely to the extent that its disappearance becomes the sign of its Dionysian resurgence. But this rebirth is not an assumption since it is still marked by the experience of loss and the fall, by extreme anguish. Impossible and thematizable at once, the "sovereign subject," following from the layering of the enunciation is marked out on the level of the text's writing and finds its formula in the theme of *Sovereignty*. This development constitutes the third volume of *La Part Maudite* (The *Accursed Share*), a chapter which will remain unfinished and published only posthumously.[3]

The utterance of a similar proposition—"I know my wound cannot be healed"—does not imply a morose and plaintive complacency on Bataille's part. On the contrary, it calls for a transformation: "Using fictions, I dramatize being, I tear up its solitude, and in the tearing, I communicate." Death at work, in language and enunciation, favors the shattering of the sovereign subject. From the unhappy consciousness to the position of sovereignty, the trajectory traversed yields a moment of transfiguration where suffering is converted into the exuberance of desire.

III. POETRY AND CONVERSION

Starting from the tropes and figures of rhetoric and recalling Freud's work on dreams and Jakobson's on the functions of language, an analysis of the mechanism of writing in *L'Impossible* will confirm our first conclusion from another direction.[4] The theory of literature is linked to the problem of death.

For metaphor, combines with the rhetorical figure of antithesis to contribute to the progressive bringing to light—by displacement and condensation—of the problematic of enunciation indissociable from the work of death. In *L'Impossible*, the numerous antitheses form a network in which contrary notions are confronted, the richest of them being the one that opposes day to night. At the crucial point of the separation, the point that threatens to break the horizontal axis of contiguity, the trope by resemblance (metaphor) favors the turn by which contrary and opposing terms meet—for a moment—at the extremes, before:

> Night is the same thing as light . . . but no.
> The truth is that, in the state I am in, nothing can be said but that the turn has been taken.

The trope by resemblance (death=night) and the trope by correspondence (sun's ray=light) combine in the antithesis (night≠day and death≠life) to authorize the reversal into the contrary. From the initial image resting on the identity of contraries—"Night is the

3. Georges Bataille, *Oeuvres complètes*, (Paris: Gallimard, 1976), vol. 8.
4. See Roman Jakobson, *Essais de linguistique genérale* (Paris: de Minuit, 1963).

same thing as light" (night=day), one passes through transformation ("the turn has been taken") to another image, one of the creation of the text: "the sweetness of death shone from me" (death=life).

In this tightly woven network of antitheses, the mechanisms of metaphor, metonymy, and synecdoche (tropes of resemblance, connection, contiguity), combining with the rhetorical figure of antithesis, transgress the order of the categories of logic so as to set off another logic: one of movement. Arriving at the end of the process that achieves them, the tropes become the freedom of the movement that carries them. Associated terms oppose or resemble each other, but their combined confrontation authorizes reversals and inversions into their contraries. Reversing through reversals, this movement captures the move of writing.

The stopping-point is no more than the *pivot* of a transformation. The void is not a nothingness; it is an unmarked term (nothing): blinding light, charm, ecstasy, presence and transparence of death, lightness of a bird on a branch, the coolness of nudity. . . . An instant of suspense that allows the reversal of contraries. In the "Epilogue" to "Dianus," the commentary explicitly poses the question of the identity of contraries in relation to the theory of the subject. Where contiguity is broken (the sinkhole of sleep, a fall), in the place where the subject is torn from itself (the leap), contrary terms pass from one to another: life/death; high/low; joy/sorrow; impossible/possible. . . .

In no sense is there resolution of the contradiction, but rather passage from one term to another, and conversion.

At the point of juncture there is disjunction, for the point of fusion is likewise the point of dissolution. . . . The sovereign subject emerges as "an impossible human instance" seized in this movement of incessant and unexpected reversals. The rhetorical figure cannot be sublimating: it serves as a pivot for the reversal of values, for the discovery of what Nietzsche calls "the other side of things."

This analysis enables a further outline of the point where sovereignty presents itself as impossible: it can be designated as a point of fusion *and* of dissolution, of juncture *and* of disjunction, so as "to take to their extremes contraries that cannot be eliminated." Thus contrary terms, confronted and held together, only reveal themselves as identical in a flash, flaring up for an instant. While the signified slips away, always impossible to formulate, the poetic function of language ends by exposing itself through the random play of signifiers: "Dying logic was delivered of mad riches" . . .

Having faced the void, the subject of writing turns up like the rolled die of chance, randomness seized in the move of writing: "The game board is this starry night where I fall thrown like a die on a field of ephemeral possibilities" . . .

All of the possibilities are authorized by substitution, but none refers to the final reference. It is an endless sliding in which no last term comes to close the chain. The signifiers play out their constellations in the infinity of the poem:

A ma mort	At my death
les dents de chevaux des étoiles	horses teeth of stars
hennissent de rire je mort	neigh laughing I death

From the first to the third panel of *L'Impossible,* the test of the impossible and the "work of death" authorize the emergence of a subject that divides itself. The signifier risks itself as the subject of fiction, and simultaneously it recaptures itself in the immediate afterwards so as to recompose itself in another way in the symbolic and communicate the range of the experience from which it results. The subject of criticism, from then on it can utter "the contestation of poetry."

Bataille thus recovers the meaning of poetry reversing itself into its contrary: in "the hatred of poetry." The move of "contestation" refutes pretty poetry so as to rediscover the meaning of authentic poetry: the meaning of poetry reversed into *hatred* of poetry. The hatred of poetry is the hatred that makes poetry authentic by maintaining the force of hatred at work in language as a force of renewal and a source of infinite resurgence: "Can we without interior violence assume a negation that takes us to the limit of all possibility" . . .

This is the significance of "adding to poetry the glory of its defeat," since "poetry that does not rise to the non-sense of poetry" is no more than the emptiness of "pretty poetry." To preserve the glory of a defeat is to refuse the fusion and conciliation of irreconcilables "in a brilliant and blind interior" (Breton). In the move of contestation, the decision is made to express and uphold, without evasions, the force of the truth of hatred. This "affirmation of sovereignty" defuses the effects of deadly destruction contained in hatred. The effect of truth that the impossible then produces is not mortal: in a flash it frees life in its brilliance, it frees the spark in which life is renewed, in an instant of conversion.

Starting from the significance of "the work of death," the reader can grasp the import of the "category of the impossible." It involves maintaining the *void* as an effective force, a negative but affirming force. By his specific practice of writing, Bataille proceeds to expose the powers of the negative in the seizure of the movement of transformation and the moment of passage. A reference to Hegelian negativity is outlined here, albeit against the background of Bataille's critique of it, via a reading of Nietzsche. Hegel receives sovereignty "as a weight he drops," whereas, on the contrary, the negation at work in affirmative synthesis must be maintained so as to strengthen the move of sovereignty. Negative and destructive effects are neither repressed nor eliminated, but taken to the extremes of tension in the dynamics of movement. Decomposing every form, every synthesis, they permit its recomposition and its renewal.

Two equal forces are, however, confronted: attraction and repulsion. Neither defeats the other; whence the ambivalence that renders latent violence ambiguous. At the point where meaning is ruptured and suspended, something irreducible is given. This is undoubtedly the moment of greatest contradiction between life and death. Negativity is endlessly reactivated by the effects of the death-drive working its inversion into the life-drive. In a flaring-up that radiates (a burst of beauty) a blinding flash articulates a point where life and death cease to be perceived as contradictory, at the timeless moment where they reveal themselves as nothing other than contradiction. The impossible is an empty theme, at first taken for non-sense, but one that keeps alive the moment of vital contradiction (the node of energy) forever endangered by its passage to the limit. The impossible and "the work of death," in fact, function like the logical operator of a transforming mechanism, by playing in Georges Bataille's writing and thought the role of a conversion-sign [*opérateur de conversion*].[5]

Translated by Robert Livingston

5. Marie-Christine Lala, "L'Oeuvre de la mort et la pensée de Georges Bataille," *Littérature* no. 58 (May 1985).

STEVEN UNGAR

Phantom Lascaux:
Origin of the Work of Art

What is the origin of art? Where does it come from? What is at stake in this determination? In raising these questions, I propose to study how a concern with origin and difference in Georges Bataille's 1955 *Lascaux or the Birth of Art* illustrates a prime function of art in his general economy. Despite a growing readership in the years since his death in 1962, Bataille is still cast as a difficult writer whose essays are esoteric and whose fiction borders on the obsessive and the pornographic. Difficulty in this context can be understood in at least three ways. It designates above all a conceptual breadth whose textual density places exceptional demands on the reader. Secondly, it points to a predilection for accounts of violence and sexuality that many readers find offensive. Finally, difficulty refers to the frustration of readers who find themselves unable to locate Bataille within conventional categories of literary practices.

Because casual approaches invariably fail to do justice to Bataille's writings, difficulty breeds ambivalence in response to a demand for greater attention to which not all readers are willing to respond. The perplexity that results in this final instance is often a prelude to rejection. Roland Barthes provided an apt account of "difficulty" when he described the problems of organizing Bataille's disparate writings around a central authorial identity: "Is this writer a novelist, a poet, an essayist, an economist, a philosopher, a mystic? The answer is so uncertain that handbooks of literature generally prefer to leave Bataille out."[1] The bias also extends to art historians and critics

1. "From Work to Text," in *The Rustle of Language,* trans. Richard Howard (New York: Hill and Wang, 1986), 58.

YFS 78, *On Bataille,* ed. Allan Stoekl, © 1990 by Yale University.

among whom Bataille's writings tend to be seen as marginal and nonconformist.[2] A comprehensive survey of Bataille's writings on art would range from his articles on architecture and numismatics ("Architecture" and "Les Monnaies des grands Mogols au Cabinet des Médailles") of the late 1920s to the 1955 monograph on Edouard Manet and *Les Larmes d'Eros* published shortly before his death.[3] I have chosen instead to focus on the Lascaux essay because it raises questions of writing, discipline, and authority which remain today the objects of inquiry and debate among critics, philosophers and historians alike.

The problematic status of Bataille's writings goes beyond the difficulties they pose to classification by genre or discipline. It is not simply a matter of validating an ongoing and open-ended inquiry into violence and its social representations. Nor is the marginal status often conferred on Bataille and on texts such as *Lascaux* simply a territorial reaction against a nonspecialist's incursion into matters reserved for more technical or specialized inquiry. It is, however, just as inappropriate to attribute Bataille's notoriety solely to convention or to the mediocrity of others when the depictions of violence and sexuality in narratives such as *Histoire de l'oeil, Madame Edwarda,* and *Le Bleu du ciel* openly provoke strong reactions on the part of the reader. In Bataille's nonfiction, this provocation is displaced from representation to method. *Lascaux* recasts the assumptions that inscribe questions of origin as belonging to—that is, somehow limited to or associated by tradition with—the practice of philosophy into terms and methods more suited to studying the institutions and practices of social existence. What begins as a meditation on the origin of art soon engages questions involving specific forms of cultural expression that increasingly fall under the aegis of the social sciences. The resulting inquiry oversteps the conventional limits of discipline separating philosophy from the hybrid of linguistics, sociology, and anthropology known in France as the human sciences, falling somewhere between critical ethnography and philosophy . . . . with a difference.[4]

2. Mario Ruspoli, for one, expresses a prevailing view when he dismisses Bataille's essay on Lascaux as abundantly illustrated but "of debatable interest in the eyes of the prehistorian." *The Cave of Lascaux: The Final Photographs,* trans. Sebastien Wormell (New York: Abrams, 1987), 205.

3. The first two are reprinted in volume 1 of Bataille's *Oeuvres complètes* (Paris: Gallimard, 1970) and the latter two in volumes 9 (Paris: Gallimard, 1979) and 10 (Paris: Gallimard, 1987), respectively.

4. I use this expression in preference to what George E. Marcus and Michael M. J.

The displacement of method and elision of disciplinary limits transpose the gestures of transgression that fascinate Bataille into textual effects whose intensity is unsettling. These, in turn, occur both in the representation of violence and sexuality as well as in the liberties of method and style noted above. If I distinguish momentarily between representation and writing, it is only to draw attention to their combined impact in the form of textual effects commonly taken to be tendentious and transgressive in the sense that they operate at the limit of what convention allows. In so doing, they force an explicit recognition of limits formerly understood only by implication. Alternatively, they extend those limits. Because I take this transgressive dimension as integral to understanding *Lascaux or the Birth of Art,* I want to preface my own remarks with an opening excursus (*sortie*) in the form of a caveat included by Bataille's friend and colleague, Michel Leiris, in his introduction to the 1951 reedition of *L'Afrique fantôme:*

> Passing from an almost exclusively literary activity to the practice of ethnography, I meant to break with the intellectual habits that had been mine until then and—in contact with men of a culture other than my own and of another race—to break down the partitions between which I was suffocating, so as to widen my horizon to a truly human dimension. Conceived in this way, ethnography could only disappoint me: a human science remains a science and detached observation could never on its own lead to contact; perhaps, by definition, it even implies the opposite, the mental attitude suitable to the observer being an impartial objectivity hostile to all effusiveness.[5]

Fischer describe in similar terms as interpretive anthropology (*Anthropology as Cultural Critique* (Chicago: University of Chicago Press, 1986), 17–44. See also James Clifford's essays collected in *The Predicament of Culture: Twentieth-Century Ethnography, Literature, and Art* (Cambridge: Harvard University Press, 1988) as well as those contained in Dominique Lecoq and Jean-Luc Lory, ed., *Ecrits d'ailleurs: Georges Bataille et les ethnologues* (Paris: Maison des Sciences de l'Homme, 1987). With a theoretical understatement that is admirable, John Van Maanan's *Tales of the Field: On Writing Ethnography* (Chicago: University of Chicago Press, 1988) surveys the factors of style and rhetoric that bear on what Clifford and others refer to as the problematic of ethnographic authority. It is thus a straightforward companion to the loftier discussion in Clifford Geertz's *Works and Lives: The Anthropologist as Author* (Stanford: Stanford University Press, 1988).

5. Michel Leiris, "Introduction," *L'Afrique fantôme* (Paris: Gallimard "Collection Tel," 1988), 12–13. The book was first published in 1934. Unless otherwise noted, all translations are mine.

Leiris's early misgivings about the status of ethnography as a human science were strong. They also served him as a pretext to write and to replace detached observation with passion ("effusiveness"). I had long wanted to study Bataille's 1955 essay on the cave paintings at Lascaux when it occurred to me that the questions and issues he raised surrounding the origin of art shared an affinity with Leiris's narrative of his participation as secretary-archivist on the 1931–1933 Dakar-to-Djibouti expedition led by Marcel Griaule. For Leiris, the objectivity and dispassion associated with scientific inquiry soon yielded to an openly subjective account and to an involvement whose initial tone was harsh and negative: "Bitterness. Resentment toward ethnography that imposes such an inhuman position of observer in circumstances where one should abandon oneself" (Leiris, 433). The expression of such emotion is rare among ethnographic accounts of the period. It suggests that the strong confessional element in *L'Afrique fantôme* derives as much from the assumptions and predilections of the would-be ethnographer as from what he takes for the ostensible object of his study.

Viewed in conjunction with *L'Afrique fantôme*, *Lascaux* reads like an experiment in ethnography in which Bataille matches Leiris in participant involvement and in a recognition of the elusiveness of his object of inquiry. But whereas Leiris writes *L'Afrique fantôme* in reaction to his initial disappointment, Bataille is motivated from the start by a fascination that removes his inquiry from any claims to practical knowledge. As a result, *Lascaux* is an openly involved account whose engagement with the creative process straddles philosophical inquiry and the self-conscious participant observation I have referred to above as critical ethnography. In the pages that follow, I propose to examine Bataille's encounter with the question of art's origin in terms of an engagement with philosophy and the human sciences conveyed by the allusion to Leiris under the title of *Phantom Lascaux*.

Where (when? how?) does the beginning begin? Bataille's *Lascaux or the Birth of Art* begins by transposing the question of art's origin to a second degree in order to consider the origin of origin. The initial sense of Lascaux as the site or birth*place* of art denoted by the essay's title extends toward a figurative origin that Bataille expresses as a blossoming or passage from the stagnation of winter toward rapid springtime efflorescence. This metaphor of natural (botanical) animation is, in turn, set against others of ceremony and ritual that convey the difference between man and beast as the spectacular form of a miraculous art. Out of the mixed botanical and spectacular metaphors comes a definitive formulation of the origin of art as a consequence of movement and excess: "As if, the life in him quickened, man were suddenly seized by an acceleration of movements, an unexpected overstepping [*dépassement*] that intoxicates and, like a strong alcohol, gives a feeling of power. A new life begins, a life which has retained the material harshness that is its essence; it is always a risky fight, but the fresh possibilities that it raises have the savor of an enchantment."[6]

The metaphor of drunkenness removes Bataille's reflections on origin from conventional attempts to determine the liminal point between nature and culture in precise historical terms. Lascaux thus becomes the site of a passage whose occurrence is evoked in essence and function rather than reconstructed in moment and detail. This figurative determination also departs from an anthropocentric vision. The images of violence and change in the passage quoted above recall Alexandre Kojève's reading of dialectic movement in Hegel's *Phenomenology of Mind* (see Kojève's *Introduction à la lecture de Hegel* [Paris: Gallimard, 1947]), but supplement its concern for development toward an ideal social condition with a sense of ritual and ceremony more in line with the importance Bataille confers on prohibition and transgression. Finally, a distinct Baudelairian ring evokes the dualities of odor and being in "Correspondances": a natural order of odors is set against a second order whose potential for infinite expansion foreshadows Bataille's belief in the creative process as an inaugural moment of excessive expenditure. As in his monograph on Manet published in the same year as *Lascaux*, Bataille violates the historical nature of his project. The gesture is intentional rather than accidental. Taken as a set or series of two, the essays on Lascaux and

---

6. *Lascaux or the Birth of Art*, trans. Austryn Wainhouse (Geneva: Skira, 1955), 23. I have modified this translation in a number of places. Future references will cite this translation as *Lascaux*. They will also cite as *OC* 9 the corresponding page in the French version: "Lascaux ou la naissance de l'art," in Georges Bataille, *Oeuvres complètes*, 9 (Paris: Gallimard, 1979). The latter includes a dossier (317–76) of related articles, fragments, lectures, and notes for a screenplay. Bataille's seasonal metaphor makes for an inadvertent contrast with "The Winter Wind" ["Le Vent d'hiver"], a talk that Roger Caillois presented to the Collège de Sociologie in March 1937. See "The Winter Wind," in Denis Hollier, ed. *The Collège of Sociology* trans. Betsy Wing (Minneapolis: University of Minnesota Press, 1988), 32–42.

Manet are inscribed as moments in a history of art for which Bataille makes no claims to rigorous linearity. The resulting inquiry addresses a major problematic of the human sciences by setting temporal determination—Lascaux as the birth of art, Manet's painting as the birth of a modernist painting—within more systematic and abstract considerations.

Bataille first addresses the questions of art's origin in a 1930 review of G. H. Luquet's *L'Art primitif* (Paris: G. Doin, 1930) that appeared in *Documents, 7*. What draws Bataille to Luquet's study is its attempt to approach primitive art by addressing both its genesis and its essential features. Luquet starts by considering primitive representation as a mimetic practice. He then argues that despite variable factors of heredity and environment, each child seemingly invents drawing (*le dessin figuré*) as though for the first time. Alongside this model of mimetic competence, Luquet notes a material immersion in which many children—and some adults, too—stick their fingers into paint so as to leave traces of their passage on the surfaces of walls and doors. Bataille agrees with Luquet that such signatures serve a psychological function of affirmation: "And in this sense, M. Luquet connects them to one of the rare means by which children assert their personality: the destruction of objects, the doings of 'children who break everything', a comparison which warrants further comment" ("L'art primitif," *OC 1*, 248). It is when Luquet tries to support his theory of primitive figuration with empirical and historical data that Bataille notes an oversight which, in turn, leads him to sketch a notion of primitive figuration that he will develop in the 1955 essay on Lascaux. Luquet describes one kind of figuration at work in images that reproduce what the eye of the adult sees ["ce que son oeil en voit"] and another in images that reproduce what the mind of the child knows ["ce que son esprit en sait"]. The former he terms *visual realism* and the latter he calls *intellectual realism*. In intellectual realism, the drawing contains elements "that are not seen but that the artist takes to be indispensable; inversely, it neglects elements of the model that are visually prominent ["qui sautent aux yeux"] but that the artist sees as devoid of interest" (*OC 1*, 250).

Bataille writes that while Luquet's notion of intellectual realism can serve to classify various graphic artifacts, it is essentially inapplicable to the three-dimensional nature of sculpture. Moreover, the distinction between visual and intellectual realism that Luquet proposes fails to account in full for what Bataille sees as the phenomenon of alteration that primitive art reserves for representing the human form:

> To tell the truth, I am astonished that those who seek to define a kind of art opposed to that which is traditional in Europe have not immediately referred to an evident and even shocking duality at the origin of figurative representation. The reindeer, buffalo, and horses are represented with such a perfect precision of detail that if we could also see such scrupulous images of men themselves, the strangest period of human avatars would immediately stop being the most inaccessible. But the designs and the sculptures that have been seen as representing the Aurignacians are almost all without form and much less human than than those representing animals; others, like the Hottentot Venus are undignified caricatures of the human body. [*OC 1*, 25][7]

Luquet limits alteration to a stage of intellectual realism that he associates with a childlike practice and a developmental model leading to successful imitation. Bataille, however, sees willful alteration as an essential feature of figuration in both varieties of realism proposed by Luquet. In the first phase, any surface—a wall, a sheet of paper, a toy—suffices. At a later point, the restriction of this graphomania to certain objects suggests a more complex function in which alteration sets the drawing subject against a chosen object. (Bataille cites Marcel Griaule's discovery of graffiti that the Godjam children used to draw on church doors and columns while services were being held inside.) Repetition also results in a second degree of alteration: "Finally, in the course of the repetition, the new object is, in turn, altered by a series of deformations. Art, since that is unquestionably what it is, proceeds in this sense by successive destructions. In such a case and to the extent that they are libidinal, these instincts are sadistic" (*OC 1*, 253).

Bataille concludes his review by raising two issues that he will readdress at length some twenty-five years later in *Lascaux or the Birth of Art*. The first concerns the fact that the second degree or mimetic alteration occurs in the representation of animals, but not in that of humans. It is a discrepancy that Bataille observes in the Aurignacian drawings as well as in the drawings of most children and (so-called)

7. Bataille qualifies this first reference to the concept of alteration as follows: "The term alteration has the double advantage of designating a partial decomposition analogous to that of corpses and at the same time the passage toward a perfectly heterogeneous condition corresponding to what Professor Otto calls the totally other. See Rudolf Otto, *The Idea of the Sacred*, (*OC 1*, 251n).

primitive peoples of the present. Second, an apparent regression is visible in a contemporary art of decomposition and destruction whose effect Bataille describes as hardly less painful to many people than the sight of a decomposing corpse. Bataille's review of Luquet allows him to formulate preliminary conceptions of figuration and the primitive. The inadequacy of Luquet's analysis stems from its failure to account for the elements of violence and alteration that Bataille sees as essential to all figuration, from prehistoric and so-called primitive practices to the neoprimitive art of the twentieth-century.

Bataille affirms the specific nature of his inquiry into the origin of art when he writes at the start of *Lascaux* that what he sees in the cave paintings is less of an absolute historical determination than a point of passage at which the light of day is born within the night. Significantly, Bataille characterizes this passage in terms of a miracle. In so doing, he removes the "birth" of art from anthropocentric conceptions associated with the sovereignty of reason over passion and the objects that constitute material existence: "'Lascaux Man' created—created *out of nothing*—this world of art in which communication between individual minds begins" (*Lascaux*, 11; *OC 9*, 12). For Bataille, Lascaux represents a phantom origin of art to the extent that the variety and condition of its cave paintings provide him with the elements out of which he, in turn, projects an excess of meaning that overwhelms him: "What is one to say of this cavern in which are accumulated a multitude of insignificant details, almost indecipherable engravings, and the patterns of interlocking motifs?" (*Lascaux*, 15; *OC 9*, 15)? The artifice of this projection is apparent in the terms that Bataille uses to frame his description in conjunction with a cultural modernity that he evokes as follows: "The cavern whose description we will give below opens today slightly above the ground, at the edge of the industrial world, several hours from Paris. We are necessarily struck—struck with utmost force—by the extreme contrast that it represents with the world we know" (*Lascaux*, 17; *OC 9*, 17).

Bataille's reference to the "Lascaux man" who creates the world of art out of nothing converts the Biblical account of genesis as the divine creation of order out of chaos into one of distinctly human origin. Moreover, Bataille confers on the passage toward art at Lascaux a sense of power and euphoria that is more often associated with ancient Greece. The reasons for this displacement are not merely historical, even though Bataille ties them via analogy to the invention of tools. For as work devolves from the invention ("birth") of tools, so art devolves from the invention of play: "Art was first of all and remains primarily a game. While toolmaking is primarily work. To determine the meaning of Lascaux (by which I mean the epoch of which Lascaux is the culmination) is to perceive the shift from the world of work to the world of play" (*Lascaux*, 27; *OC 9*, 28). For Bataille, Luquet's approach to prehistoric figuration derives in large part from positivist ambitions. The paintings in question are studied as documents to be described, analyzed, and classified within an archive to which subsequent data is added according to what he describes as the reigning practices of logic and scientific observation. The conception of prehistoric art growing out of this accumulation neglects the fact that the difference between the animal and the human results not simply from intellectual and physical traits, but from the prohibitions [*interdits*] to which men consider themselves subject. And among these, the prohibitions growing out of an awareness of death and sexuality are particularly apt to the "birth of art" Bataille sees illustrated at Lascaux.

Prohibition is the differential factor that separates animal and human representation in Bataille's account of art's origin: "The world of Lascaux of which we are trying to catch a glimpse is above all a world ordered by a notion [*sentiment*] of prohibition: we will not succeed in entering it if we do not see it in this light from the very start" (*Lascaux*, 32; *OC 9*, 34). Where prohibitions uphold the social practices related to work and its distribution by gender and collectivity, art is a prime expression of play as nonwork: that is, an area where the restrictions that bear on conventional social existence are consciously broken and set aside in the name of a new value. Because this new value—known variously as the sacred or the religious—departs from the specific goal of maintaining physical existence, Bataille sees it as truly human. Art expresses the transgressive moment as a destruction of the principles that uphold a social cohesion based on the economy of work that is restricted rather than unlimited and festive: "In the strongest sense, transgression exists only from the moment when art reveals itself; the birth of art in the Reindeer Age coincided fairly closely with the outbreak of tumultuous play and festivity [*fête*] announced deep in the caverns by these figures from which life bursts forth in excess and to its fullest in a game of death and birth played on stone" (*Lascaux*, 38; *OC 9*, 41).

The "birth" of art that Bataille seeks should not be misconstrued as a vision of progressive phases. Lascaux represents less the negation of social practices and institutions associated with the restricted economy of work than an illustration of conflict between them. It is the passage from acceptance to transgression that marks the origin projected onto Lascaux as the site of art's birth. In such terms, Bataille readily admits that his project is less of a true genealogy than a reconstitution of the conditions governing the passage from prohibition to transgression:

> The share of hypothesis that I introduce, limited to situating the passage from prohibition to transgression, is understood at the moment that transgression, given free flow in a movement of festivity, is finally granted in activity the eminent place that religion has conferred on it. Such a principle could not be opposed to precise determinations which each work would allow for on its own. A work of art and a sacrifice participate, if I make myself clear, in a notion of festivity going beyond the world of work and—if not the letter—then the spirit of prohibitions necessary for the protection of this world. On its own, each work of art has a meaning independent of the desire of wonder that it has in common with all the others. But we can say in advance that a work of art in which this desire is not intelligible—one in which it is weak and hardly comes into play—is a mediocre work. Likewise, every sacrifice has a precise meaning, such as the abundance of harvests, expiation, or all other logical goals; it nevertheless responds somewhat to the search for a sacred instant going beyond profane time, where prohibitions guarantee the possibility of life. [*Lascaux*, 38; *OC 9*, 42]

The inclusion of the artwork along with sacrifice under the category of the sacred is neither arbitrary nor coincidental. The separation between animal and human orders follows a logic of difference and self-effacement that Bataille considers a distinctive mark of the human. The description also serves as a narrative that imposes order and continuity onto so-called "unintelligible signs" that nonetheless contain the emanation of a primitive and graceful meaning. The fact that the animal is primarily portrayed as the prey in hunting scenes is less important than the value of the sacred that Bataille sees in the phenomenon of man "clad [*paré*] in the prestige of the animal." The prevalence of animal figures does not simply negate the human. Instead, Bataille notes a more complex and ambivalent attitude that inscribes the animal within the realm of the sacred. This inscription is a mark of the human: "If he admitted to having human form, he hid it in the same instant by giving himself the head of an animal. As if he were ashamed of his face so that while wanting to point himself out, he also had to don the mask of another" (*Lascaux*, 115; *OC 9*, 63).

Bataille explains the paradox of "l'homme paré du prestige de l'animal" as a necessary stage in which the animal elements subsist as objects of horror, promoting reactions on a par with those imposed by prohibition. The representation of animals is a sacred activity to the extent that they embody the forces of life and death which can be dominated more readily within the cave than outside it. The depiction of animals stages a violence that is openly at odds with the reality of the hunt. Because this depiction engages superior forces which are not understood, the passage toward human existence occurs as an encounter with difference and otherness in the form of the nonhuman. This encounter, in turn, induces an initial sensation of shame whose force inverts the negation of the animal to that of the human. It is as if men turned onto themselves a shame that they more often directed toward the animal. What figuration negates is the self-representation associated with the profane time of work. The birth of art coincides with an overstepping of existence understood purely in terms of life and death, an overstepping that Bataille sees symbolized in the figuration of animals at Lascaux. Because work and profane time persist after the birth of art, the passage from animal to human existence is neither clearcut nor complete. Nonetheless, negation—in this case, a suppression of human representation—is necessary for the passage toward the human and the social to occur: "It was a matter of negating man to the extent that he worked and calculated by working the effectiveness of his material actions; it was a matter of negating man to benefit a divine and impersonal element linked to the animal that neither reasons nor works" (*Lascaux*, 121; *OC 9*, 69–70).

Bataille's interpretation of the cave paintings at Lascaux extends his account of the ambiguous status of animal figuration. Clearly, the emphasis he places on the opposition between work and animal figuration sets Bataille's views apart from those for whom the origin of art springs directly from the practical functions that he locates within the profane world of work. The differences in question are both of order and degree. Elie Faure, writing some thirty years before the discovery of the Lascaux paintings, associates the birth of art with immediate usage: "Art cannot yet be an instrument of philosophic generalization, since man could not know how to utilize it. But he

STEVEN UNGAR 257

forges that instrument, for he already abstracts from his surroundings
some rudimentary laws which he applies to his own advantage."[8]
Faure allows for only a minimal abstraction beyond immediate usage;
for him, art is primarily instrumental. Bataille, on the other hand,
associates the origin of art with phenomena of ritual that emphasize a
symbolic function placing men and women at odds with overwhelming forces. The result transposes the activity of the hunt into a life-
and-death struggle played out against animal adversaries whose exceptional powers border on the divine: "In my view, the animal ranks
at Lascaux on the level of gods and kings. This is the place to recall
that, in history's most ancient days, sovereignty (the condition describing he alone who is an end unto himself) belonged to the king,
that the king and the god were not readily distinguishable from each
other, nor they, in turn, from the beast" (*Lascaux*, 126; *OC 9*, 76).

This equation of gods and kings with the phenomenon of sovereignty refers back to Bataille's earlier view on the coincidence of
art's origin and the overstepping of the profane world of work. It
suggests a further distinction between the utility of objects such as
rocks and pieces of wood that can be refashioned by work into tools or
weapons, and animals whose usefulness one might appropriate instead by acts [*opérations*] of worship, prayer, and sacrifice. Once
again, the suprahuman powers that Bataille sees conferred on animals
at Lascaux imply that "Lascaux Man" contends with his environment through symbolic as well as physical acts. When these symbolic
acts are repeated with regularity, they fulfill the ritual function that
Bataille sees as a mark of the sacred that supplements the profane
economy of work: "The majesty of the cavern appeared afterward as
though it were a fortuitous gift or the sign of a god-given world"
(*Lascaux*, 129; *OC 9*, 79). It is this presence of the sacred within the
profane—and the social practices and institutions resulting from it—
that Bataille sees staged *for the first time* in full detail and variety at
Lascaux. "Gazing at these pictures, we sense that *something is stirring, something is moving. . . .* It was the first step, it was the beginning" (*Lascaux*, 129; *OC 9*, 81).

Early in *Lascaux*, Bataille uses the term "miracle" to describe the
state of the cave paintings at the time of their discovery in 1940—

---

8. "Before History," in *History of Art* trans. Walter Pach (New York: Harper, 1921),
vol. 1 ("Ancient Art"), 6. The first French edition was published in 1909.

reportedly by children at play. Throughout the essay, a sense of the miraculous pervades the symbolic function he attributes to the paintings, extending the myth of origin known as cosmogony toward a founding fiction of human order. This extension is a consequence of effect and total meaning rather than detail. For Bataille, Lascaux provides a master narrative of life and death forces that is staged rather than simply illustrated or drawn. This staging—rather than any temporal determination of origin—inaugurates a human order set apart from the profane world of work. What sets Bataille's account of Lascaux apart from those by specialists in art and prehistory is his view that the work of art is distinguished from the products of other work by a destructive force associated with transgression and the sacred.

Despite the differences with Bataille noted above, Elie Faure concurs that the origin of the work of art occurs as a collective phenomenon: "The real childhood of humanity has left us nothing, because it was incapable, like the childhood of a man, of continuity of effort. The art of the troglodytes of Périgord is not this impossible art of human childhood, but the necessary art of human youth, the first synthesis which the world, naïvely interrogated, imposes on the sensibility of a man, and which he gives back to the community" (Faure, 16). What Faure refers to as the first synthesis appears in Bataille's *Lascaux* as the coincidence of the origin of the work of art and the transgression of prohibitions. Lascaux stages this transgression in scenes devoted almost exclusively to animals as the objects of prohibition related to death and sexuality on which social orders are based. Faure and Bataille both posit origin as a symbolic function whose occurrence as synthesis (Faure) and miracle (Bataille) projects meaning onto a certain past. The symbolic origin that Lascaux represents never coincides with strict temporal determination because it occurs fully in the present: "No trace whatsoever of origin can be read there . . . but only an excess (*surcroît*) of divergent signs, an overimposed figuration, the unprecedented use of natural space."[9]

A final element of Bataille's *Lascaux* study is evoked by the echo in my subtitle of Martin Heidegger's 1935–36 essay, "The Origin of the Work of Art." As with my earlier comments on *L'Afrique fantôme*, comparison is not intended to elide obvious and irreducible differences. Nonetheless, what Bataille refers to in *Lascaux* as the

9. Jean-Michel Rey, "Le Signe aveugle," *L'Arc*, no. 44 (1971), 54.

birth of art extends Heidegger's account of art's origin in the truth of disclosure or unconcealedness (*aletheia*) that results from an ongoing conflict between world and earth: "The world is the self-disclosing openness of the broad paths of the simple and essential decisions in the destiny of a historical people. The earth is the spontaneous forthcoming of that which is continually self-secluding and to that extent sheltering and concealing."[10] For Heidegger, the opposition between world and earth establishes the essential ambivalence that the work of art objectifies as a simultaneous clearing and concealing. *Lascaux* recasts as transgression the element of alteration Bataille had elaborated in his 1930 *Documents* article on Luquet. In both texts, the work of art supplements those actions needed to sustain physical existence. Because he sees that supplement in opposition to the profane order of work, Bataille confers on art a transgressive function that marks a passage toward the distinctly human category of the sacred.

The conjuncture of Bataille and Heidegger also points to a semantic instability involving the term and concept of work. While it is clear that the term refers primarily to a noun (*oeuvre* in French and *Werk* in German), the expressions *oeuvre d'art* and *Kunstwerk* both convey a secondary sense of process carried over into English from the German noun as "artwork." (This is so despite the differences in both languages between nominal and verbal forms: *oeuvre* and *travailler*, *Werk* and *arbeiten*, respectively.) How then, are we to understand the relation of the process of artwork to the work of art that results from it? To rephrase the question somewhat differently, we might ask what constitutes the work of the artwork. For Heidegger, the essence of the object that the work of art discloses occurs as an elusive truth that simultaneously reveals and covers. Referring to Van Gogh's painting of peasant shoes, Heidegger asks what is at work in the work ["was im Werk am Werk ist"] before characterizing the nature of disclosure as follows: "If there occurs in the work a disclosure of a particular being, disclosing what and how it is, then there is here an occurring, a happening of truth at work" (Heidegger, 36). This disclosure is the sense of the work of art as truth at work—what I have described

10. Martin Heidegger, "The Origin of the Work of Art," in *Poetry, Language, Thought* trans. Albert Hofstadter (New York: Harper and Row, 1971), 48–49. Disclosure and unconcealedness are the usual English equivalents of the German noun *Eröffnung* and its variants in Heidegger's usage. In the sentence quoted above, for example, Hofstadter translates *öffnende Offenheit* as "self-disclosing openness."

earlier in the function of staging. Unlike Heidegger, Bataille does not locate the origin of the work of art in a Greek antiquity whose experience he approximates via etymology. The birth of art at Lascaux occurs as a passage into history via excess and transgression. It is a passage whose recurrence does not refute the mystery of origin that Bataille affirms openly as a miracle and thus in opposition to claims to scientific understanding: "Gazing at these pictures, we sense that *something is stirring, something is moving.* . . . It was the first step, it was the beginning" (*Lascaux*, 129; *OC 9*, 81).

The Bataille-Heidegger conjuncture inscribes a concern with origin within an assertion of the difference between animal and man that also serves as the limit between inhuman and human orders. As with Bataille's description of Lascaux "at the edge of the industrial world, several hours from Paris," the assertion of difference ("its extreme contrast") is relative rather than absolute. This also means that the difference between the animal and the human can be understood spatially in terms of proximity. It is in the proximate relations to living things—to the animal as animal and yet other than human— that the human emerges as human. By effacing himself as man and by representing himself as animal in the paintings at Lascaux, Bataille understands the birth of art as consubstantial with man's first philosophical understanding of himself as that which exists in relation to—*in proximity to*—living things.

The spatial metaphor of proximity has strong associations with the dialectical model of thesis, antithesis, and synthesis that illustrates the coming into being of Mind or Spirit (*Geist*) in Hegel's 1806 *Phenomenology of Mind*. In particular, the complexity of cancellation (*Aufhenung*) as both negation and affirmation implies that the animal/human relation is both a relation *to* and *against*. It also evokes the distinction between stone, animal, and human worlds— the expressions used are without world [*weltloss*], poor in world [*weltarm*], and world-forming [*weld-bildend*], respectively—around which Heidegger organizes his 1929–30 Freiburg lectures.[11] Ironically, Lascaux can be seen as a privileged site where the three ele-

11. The animal *has* and *does not have* a world. Its privation is a mode of proximity and of potential [*"Armut—Entbehren—als Nichthaben im Habenkönnen"*] whose negativity is distinct from that of the worldlessness associated with stone (Jacques Derrida, *Of Spirit: Heidegger and the Question*, trans. Geoffrey Bennington and Rachel Bowlby [Chicago: University of Chicago Press, 1989], 50). Proximity also aligns Bataille and Heidegger with—or against—Nietzsche, especially in terms on the pages on Zarathustra's animals in Heidegger's postwar *Nietzsche*.

ments converge. From a Heideggerian perspective, Bataille's account of the emergence of man through art at Lascaux is not metaphysical. It occurs as a product of the difference between the human and the animal taken in a strict sense as the assertion of difference between the human and the not-human. Significantly, the human derives from and supplements the not-human.[12]

Finally, Bataille's remarks on the animal and the human in *Lascaux* also recall Alexandre Kojève's distinction between animal and human desires. Along with Raymond Queneau, Jacques Lacan, and Maurice Merleau-Ponty, Bataille is listed as a participant (*auditeur assidu*) for three (1934–36 and 1937–38) of the six years (1933–39) during which Kojève gave a seminar on Hegel's *Phenomenology of Mind* at the Ecole Pratique des Hautes Etudes in Paris.[13] In the written version of the lectures edited by Queneau under the title *Introduction à la lecture de Hegel* (Paris: Gallimard, 1947), Kojève described the initial stage or moment of self-consciousness as a struggle (a "bloody battle") for recognition between desiring humans in conflict with each other. This struggle in the cause of human desires—as much symbolic as physical—culminates in the threat of imminent death rather than in death itself. Human desires thus derive from—and in contradistinction to—animal desires that are necessary to prolong physical existence. Where Kojève posits the distinction between human and animal desires in terms of violence directed toward different objects, Bataille transposes physical violence into its symbolic representation. Bataille's account of the initial trace of the human at Lascaux is fully compatible with the origin of community that Kojève sees as coextensive with the human (Roth, 104).

12. Debate surrounding Victor Farias's *Heidegger et le nazisme* (Paris: Verdier, 1987) makes it difficult to overlook the implications of the thematics of animality for the ongoing inquiry into Heidegger's links to National Socialism. In particular, Heidegger's reputed 1949 remarks—cited by Emmanuel Levinas in "As If Consenting to Horror," *Critical Inquiry* 15: (1989), 487—on agriculture as a mechanized food industry whose essence is comparable to the manufacture of corpses in the gas chambers and death camps suggests that the Jew is nonhuman: that is, closer to technology's product than to the emergence of the nihilistic Nietzschean "man" associated with National Socialism. The Jew is seemingly equated with the animal—"poor in world" rather than "world-forming"—and thus excluded from the human. I thank Herman Rapaport for alerting me to Heidegger's treatment of animality and its consequences.

13. See the EPHE's *Annuaire* and *Registre des Inscriptions* listed in the appendix to Michael S. Roth's *Knowing and History: Appropriations of Hegel in Twentieth-Century France* (Ithaca: Cornell University Press, 1988), 225–27.

Exactly what is born at Lascaux? Bataille's meditation on the origin of art posits a vision of culture as a field of interaction between contested codes and representations. These, in turn, entail the problems of description, analysis, and authority that James Clifford calls the historical predicament of ethnography.[14] That *Lascaux or the Birth of Art* inadvertently does this in the form of a passionate ("involved") account suggests that—like Leiris before him in *L'Afrique fantôme*—Bataille wrote in awareness that culture is continually invented and reinvented not merely by an accretion of understanding, but because the very claim to knowledge from which such understanding derives is itself the product of systems of meaning and representation. The elusive nature of a phantom Lascaux results less from the dubious epistemological status of a founding fiction than from Bataille's demonstration that the knowledge of cultures—both past and present—to which we make claim relies on systems of description and interpretation that are, in turn, continually reinvented. Heidegger's remarks on "The Origin of the Work of Art" suggest likewise that the truth disclosed by the artwork is fleeting and that any claims to knowledge one might base on it must by necessity contend with the openness that makes it definitely elusive. *Lascaux* illustrates that for Bataille, the origin of art—wherever we locate it in space, time, and history—is always sought and invented in a present that remains open to ongoing supplement and disclosure.

14. "Introduction: Partial Truths," In James Clifford and George E. Marcus, ed., *Writing Culture: The Poetics and Politics of Ethnography* (Berkeley: University of California Press, 1986), 2.

Contributors

Hilari Allred teaches in the French Department at Yale University.

Kathryn Ascheim is a lecturer in the Department of French at Yale University.

Jean-Michel Besnier, Professor of Philosophy at the Université de Compiègne, is the author of *Chronique des idées d'aujourd'hui: éloge de la volonté* (Paris: PUF, 1987) and *La Politique de l'impossible: L'Intellectuel entre révolte et engagement* (Paris: La Découverte, 1988). He is on the editorial board of *Esprit*.

Rebecca Comay is Assistant Professor of Philosophy and Literary Studies at the University of Toronto. She is the author of *Underlining the Difference: The Question of Limits in Hegel and Heidegger* (forthcoming, SUNY Press) and is currently working on a book on art and politics in the 1930s, with specific reference to Heidegger and the Frankfurt School.

Christopher Carsten is a student in the Department of French at Yale University. He is working on René Char.

Rhonda Garelick is a student in the Department of French at Yale University. She is working on the notion of the Dandy and the Dancing Girl in *Fin de Siècle* Literature.

Jean-Joseph Goux, Professor of French Studies at Brown University and program director at the "Collège international de philosophie," is the author of *Economie et symbolique* (Seuil, Paris, 1973) and *Les Iconoclastes* (Seuil, Paris, 1978) forthcoming in one volume at Columbia University Press (1990). A translation of *Les Monnayeurs du langage* (Galilée, Paris, 1984) will be published by Oklahoma University Press.

YFS 78, *On Bataille*, ed. Allan Stoekl, © 1990 by Yale University.

SUZANNE GUERLAC is Associate Professor of French at Johns Hopkins University. She is the author of *The Impersonal Sublime: Hugo, Baudelaire, Lautréamont* (forthcoming, Stanford University Press). Her essays have appeared in *MLN, Diacritics,* and *New Literary History.*

JEAN-MICHEL HEIMONET is Professor of French at the Catholic University, Washington, D.C. He is the author of *Le Mal à l'oeuvre: Georges Bataille et l'écriture du sacrifice* (Paris: Parenthèses, 1987), and *Politiques de l'écriture, Bataille/Derrida: le sens du sacré dans la pensée française du surréalisme à nos jours* (Chapel Hill: The University of North Carolina Press, 1987).

DENIS HOLLIER is Professor of French at Yale University. He has recently edited *A New History of French Literature* (Cambridge: Harvard University Press, 1989); a translation of his essay on *Georges Bataille, La Prise de la Concorde,* has just appeared as: *Against Architecture* (Cambridge, MIT Press, 1990).

MARIE-CHRISTINE LALA has organized a number of seminars, including several on Georges Bataille, at the Collège International de Philosophie, in Paris. She has published a number of articles on Bataille.

ROBERT LIVINGSTON is a student in the Department of Comparative Literature at Yale University.

JOANIKO KOHCHI, a graduate student in French at Yale University, is currently working on the occurrence of male narrators in search of stories from women in Balzac, Barbey D'Aurevilly, and Marguerite Duras. She is currently teaching at Tulane University.

KATHERINE LYDON is a graduate student in the Department of French at Yale University. She is working on Montaigne.

JEAN-LUC NANCY is Professor at the Université de Strasbourg. His book on Bataille, *La Communauté désoeuvrée,* in translation is forthcoming at the University of Minnesota Press.

AMY REID is a graduate student in the Department of French at Yale University.

MICHÈLE RICHMAN is the author of *Reading Georges Bataille: Beyond the Gift* (Johns Hopkins University Press, 1982), articles dealing with relations between anthropology and literature, she is currently completing a study on *Anthropology and Modernism: From Durkheim to the Collège de sociologie.*

ALLAN STOEKL is Associate Professor of French at Yale University. He has recently completed a book, *Agonies of the Secular Cleric:*

Subjectivity, "Commitment," and the Performative in Durkheim, Nizan, Drieu la Rochelle, Sartre, Paulhan, Foucault, Derrida, de Man, and Bataille.

JONATHAN STRAUSS is a doctoral candidate in French at Yale University. He is completing a dissertation on fragmentations in nineteenth- and twentieth-century literature.

STEVEN UNGAR, Professor of French and Comparative Literature at the University of Iowa, is the author of *Roland Barthes: The Professor of Desire* (1983) and coeditor of *Signs in Culture*. He is completing studies on Maurice Blanchot and the culture of the Popular Front.

The following issues are available through **Yale University Press,** Customer Service Department, 92A Yale Station, New Haven, CT 06520.

63 The Pedagogical Imperative:
     Teaching as a Literary Genre
     (1982) $14.95
64 Montaigne: Essays in Reading
     (1983) $14.95
65 The Language of Difference:
     Writing in QUEBEC(ois)
     (1983) $14.95
66 The Anxiety of Anticipation
     (1984) $14.95
67 Concepts of Closure
     (1984) $14.95
68 Sartre after Sartre
     (1985) $14.95

69 The Lesson of Paul de Man
     (1985) $14.95
70 Images of Power:
     Medieval History/Discourse/
     Literature
     (1986) $14.95
71 Men/Women of Letters:
     Correspondence
     (1986) $14.95
72 Simone de Beauvoir:
     Witness to a Century
     (1987) $14.95
73 Everyday Life
     (1987) $14.95

74 Phantom Proxies
     (1988) $14.95
75 The Politics of Tradition:
     Placing Women in French
     Literature
     (1988) $14.95
     Special Issue: After the
     Age of Suspicion: The
     French Novel Today
     (1989) $14.95
76 Autour de Racine:
     Studies in Intertextuality
     (1989) $14.95
77 Reading the Archive: On
     Texts and Institutions
     (1990) $14.95

Special subscription rates are available on a calendar year basis (2 issues per year):

Individual subscriptions $22.00   Institutional subscriptions $25.90

- -

ORDER FORM   **Yale University Press,** 92A Yale Station, New Haven, CT 06520

Please enter my subscription for the calendar year
☐ **1990 (Nos. 77 and 78)**   ☐ **Special Issue**   ☐ **1991 (Nos. 79 and 80)**

I would like to purchase the following individual issues:

_____

_____

For individual issues, please add postage and handling:
Single issue, United States $2.00   Single issue, foreign countries $3.00
Each additional issue $.50   Each additional issue $1.00
Connecticut residents please add sales tax of 8%.

Payment of $ _____ is enclosed (including sales tax if applicable).

Mastercard no. _____

4-digit bank no. _____ Expiration date _____

VISA no. _____ Expiration date _____

Signature _____

SHIP TO: _____

_____

_____

- -

See the next page for ordering issues 1–59 and 61–62. **Yale French Studies** is also available through Xerox University Microfilms, 300 North Zeeb Road, Ann Arbor, MI 48106.

The following issues are still available through the **Yale French Studies** Office, 2504A Yale Station, New Haven, CT 06520.

19/20 Contemporary Art $3.50	43 The Child's Part $5.00	57 Locus: Space, Landscape,
23 Humor $3.50	44 Paul Valéry $5.00	Decor $6.00
33 Shakespeare $3.50	45 Language as Action $5.00	58 In Memory of Jacques
35 Sade $3.50	46 From Stage to Street $3.50	Ehrmann $6.00
38 The Classical Line $3.50	47 Image & Symbol in the	59 Rethinking History $6.00
39 Literature and	Renaissance $3.50	60 Cinema/Sound $6.00
Revolution $3.50	49 Science, Language, & the	61 Toward a Theory of
40 Literature and Society:	Perspective Mind $3.50	Description $6.00
18th Century $3.50	50 Intoxication and	62 Feminist Readings: French Texts/
41 Game, Play, Literature	Literature $3.50	American Contexts $6.00
$5.00	53 African Literature $3.50	
42 Zola $5.00	54 Mallarmé $5.00	

Add for postage & handling

Single issue, United States $1.50   Single issue, foreign countries $2.00
Each additional issue $.50   Each additional issue $.75

- -

YALE FRENCH STUDIES, 2504A Yale Station, New Haven, Connecticut 06520

A check made payable to YFS is enclosed. Please send me the following issue(s):

Issue no.   Title   Price

_____   _____   _____

_____   _____   _____

_____   _____   _____

                                                   Postage & handling   _____

                                                              Total   _____

Name _____

Number/Street _____

City _____ State _____ Zip _____

The following issues are now available through Kraus Reprint Company, Route 100, Millwood, N.Y. 10546.

1 Critical Bibliography of	11 Eros, Variations...	25 Albert Camus
Existentialism	12 God & the Writer	26 The Myth of Napoleon
2 Modern Poets	13 Romanticism Revisited	27 Women Writers
3 Criticism & Creation	14 Motley: Today's French Theater	28 Rousseau
4 Literature & Ideas	15 Social & Political France	29 The New Dramatists
5 The Modern Theatre	16 Foray through Existentialism	30 Sartre
6 France and World Literature	17 The Art of the Cinema	31 Surrealism
7 André Gide	18 Passion & the Intellect, or	32 Paris in Literature
8 What's Novel in the Novel	Malraux	34 Proust
9 Symbolism	21 Poetry Since the Liberation	48 French Freud
10 French-American Literature	22 French Education	51 Approaches to Medieval
Relationships	24 Midnight Novelists	Romance
		52 Graphesis

36/37 Structuralism has been reprinted by Doubleday as an Anchor Book.
55/56 Literature and Psychoanalysis has been reprinted by Johns Hopkins University Press, and can be ordered through Customer Service, Johns Hopkins University Press, Baltimore, MD 21218.